Seven Names for the *Bellbird*

Seven Names for the *Bellbird*

Conservation Geography in Honduras

Mark Bonta

Texas A&M University Press
College Station

The paper used in this book meets the minimum
requirements of the American National Standard for
Permanence of Paper for Printed Library Materials,
Z39.48D1984.
Binding materials have been chosen for durability.

∞

Library of Congress
Cataloging-in-Publication Data
Bonta, Mark, 1969–
  Seven names for the bellbird : conservation geography
in Honduras. — 1st ed.
      p. cm.
Includes bibliographical references and index (p.   ).
  ISBN 1-58544-249-6 (cloth : alk. paper)
    1. Birds—Honduras. 2. Birds—Honduras—Folklore.
3. Birds, Protection of—Honduras. 4. Birds—Effect
of human beings on—Honduras. 5. Human ecology—
Honduras. I. Title: 7 names for the bellbird. II. Title.
  QL687.H8 B66 2003
  333.95'816'097283—dc21

                                        2002154063

To Mom

Contents

Illustrations

Acknowledgments

Burt Monroe, Jr., was the single most important authority on bird distribution in Honduras. His work is the bible of all serious ornithogeographical study of the country. I have also been greatly influenced by the writing of Jesús Aguilar Paz, an outstanding Honduran geographer, and Archie Carr, the naturalist.

For my lifelong obsession with birds I owe thanks to my upbringing in rural Pennsylvania, especially the influence of my mother, Marcia Bonta, and my brother Steve. For encouraging my becoming a geographer I want to thank my father Bruce Bonta as well as Peter Gould and Amelia Harding.

I am grateful to the two outside readers, Gay Gomez and Carrol Henderson, for their insightful comments and suggestions. I thank also my father and mother, and my brother Dave, who read and offered suggestions on an early draft of this work. The book started as my master's thesis at the University of Texas, where I owe a special debt of gratitude to Robin Doughty, who kept me on course. Indeed, it was his support more than anything that got this project off the ground. At UT, I also want to recognize the support of thesis readers and mentors Ian Manners and Greg Knapp. At Louisiana State University, I owe special thanks to my dissertation chair Miles Richardson, who offered comments on a draft; to Bill Davidson, untiring supporter of all things Honduran; and to Mary Lee Eggart, who prepared the excellent maps. At Texas A&M University Press I want to thank all the staff, who have been wonderful.

My foremost informant and an expert on her native Olancho is my wife Luz, without whom *Seven Names* would have very little substance. My most vocal partisan is my daughter, Eva Luz, who will soon be old enough to trek to La Picucha. In Olancho, I owe special thanks to the following people—*mil gracias para la ayuda de las siguientes personas*: Dolores Mayorquin and Alfonso Bardales; Olivia García, Tomás Guillén, and Nicolás Mayorquin; Berta Muñoz; Oscar Flores Pinot; Beto and Lesbia Madrid; Elmer Maradiaga; José and Margarita Mendoza and family; Clara Luz Rojas; Eliberto Torres; Esteban and Edita Urbina and family; and Francisco and Fausta Urbina. I also want to recognize three informants who died before the publication — *quisiera reconocer tres personas quienes murieron antes de publicación*: Juana Gutierrez, Emilia Cardona, and Victor Rubí.

My gratitude goes to Jorge Betancourt, Ana María Erazo, and Manuel Rey, who were influential in my Peace Corps years when I was learning about conservation in Honduras. A good number of *gringos* also shared birding expertise and other thoughts: David Anderson, Robert Gallardo, Dan Grimm, Lisa Lemke, Jeffrey Mellmann, Vince Murphy, Peter Nebel, Anthony Novak, Ray Sabella, Daniel Thompson, and Pilar Thorn. Pilar has done more than anyone to further bird education in Honduras. Dave is the best Honduran ornithologist I know.

Finally, numerous people from the following communities offered the primary inspiration for this book: Juticalpa, Catacamas, El Murmullo, El Boquerón, La Avispa, Gualaco *pueblo,* Las Lomas, La Venta, Pie del Cerro, El Ocotal. *Que siga la lucha de Babilonia!*

Seven Names for the *Bellbird*

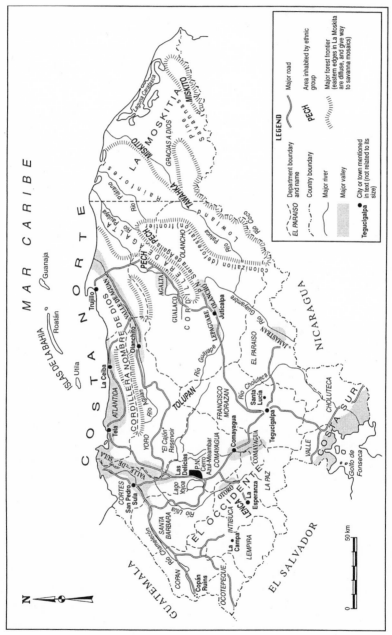

1. Map of Honduras. Drawn by Mary Lee Eggart.

Introduction to Conservation Geography

In eastern Honduras, the Three-wattled Bellbird is a wanderer of many names and inspirations. In one village it is *pájaro cafetero,* the coffee bird that heralds a ripening crop. In another it is *pimentero,* bellwether of the allspice harvest. Olanchanos call it bell ringer, bell tuner, bellbird, *calandria,* a lark in the rural imagination. This loudest of birds competes with the jet-plane roars of mantled howlers along the cloud forest spine of the Cordillera de Agalta, drowning out the calls and cries of intrepid human visitors. Well below Agalta's jagged ridge crests, young male bellbirds practice their calls in the canopy of Hurricane Mitch–scarred coffee farms, straying occasionally to the highland pine woods and even to tropical dry forest near human dwellings in the densely settled lowland plains.

Bellbird refrains infiltrate the soundscapes of rural culture on the eastern Honduran frontier, conveying multiform meanings to farmers and hunters, scientists and conservationists. In Vermont-sized Olancho (the largest of eighteen Honduran provinces), bellbirds are among the most flamboyant of an avifauna numbering close to six hundred species. Their evocative names signal connections between people and birds that characterize Olancho and many other parts of Latin America. These connections can be highly productive relationships in which species, habitats, and ecosystems flourish in the presence of people.

This book is a paean to sharing, a geographical tale of intimate but immensely significant ways in which people and birds coexist in a Neotropical world. I show that "conservation geography" should be a geographical approach to conservation that cuts across artificial boundaries separating what is "natural" from what is "cultural" in the landscape. In the chapters that follow, I suggest by example that we analyze and appreciate local conservation knowledge and practice before attempting to impose new beliefs and new techniques. I show that outsiders need not condemn local relationships between people and birds as somehow inherently harmful or "anti-nature."

My ethnographical approach to understanding and writing about relationships between local people and birds focuses on stories of individuals and families, their traditional knowledge of the avifauna, and in some cases their participation in avian conservation efforts that may or may not follow "official" bird protection guidelines and projects. However, I do not attempt to prove that birds have secure futures in Neotropical landscapes that I recognize to be ravaged by human pressures and unpredictable natural events such as hurricanes. I am trying to tell a story that in some ways gives the lie to assumptions about people in the Neotropics destroying birds and habitats because they want to do so. Indeed, in many instances, birds are safe and even thrive in the immediate presence of local people, some of whom celebrate the birds as often as others persecute them. There is little support in Honduran culture for dislike and destruction of biodiversity beyond needs for sustenance and sport.

During a decade in the field in Honduras, I became convinced that outside experts who focus only on habitat destruction and bird persecution can easily amass data "proving" that rural Hondurans are anti-bird, anti-tree, anti-forest, anti-nature. I followed another path, searching instead for what I thought at first were rare cases of bird-friendly people who could inform and aid conservation projects. I found such people with little effort, and it may surprise and please people elsewhere to know not only that certain types of ornithocentric behavior exist in Honduras but also that many Hondurans observe and appreciate birds, weaving them into folklore and protecting them as far as possible.

As I searched, I found that many—perhaps most—Hondurans do not celebrate habitat destruction and consequent loss of biodiversity. Indeed, they are horrified by it; but they understand that the true culprit is not the slash-and-burn farmer. Rather, it is a complex web of worsening economic and political conditions at the national and international level. Honduran peasants often tell me, for example, that they don't cut down the forest because they hate it; they destroy their resource base because their only other option is to emigrate to the cities or abroad. Nevertheless, readers may doubt that Hondurans favor birds and conservation, because this flies in the face of conventional wisdom about Neotropical biodiversity loss. I therefore offer numerous examples and intricate details in this book, in the hope that each example can be understood as a victory. Each quetzal or bellbird or owl unharmed on a coffee farm or cattle ranch or in a town plaza is evidence that the destruction of biodiversity is not as generalized and purposeful as it is sometimes portrayed to be.

I am an expert on neither birds nor biology. As a cultural geographer, I am trained to document the relationships between people and nature. I study the entangling of human and nonhuman elements in the landscape. One way to do this is through ethnography, a method that combines practices of research and documentation in the field with retrospection and writing "back home." Ethnography can be realized only by close observation and especially participation in events within the society being studied. My research informants are my friends, confidants, and confidantes, from whose experiences I have built my case for conservation geography.

Ethnography serves in this book as a bridge between academic geography and on-the-ground conservation — between documentation and action. I hope conservationists will recognize that human geography complements biology and that knowledge of both is necessary to protect biodiversity. In essence, I am attempting to show that conservation strategies informed by knowledge of how cultural landscapes function will be far more effective than strategies predicated on a view of humans simply as agents of disturbance, destruction, and fragmentation.

To help the stories flow more smoothly, I try not to clutter the body of this text with too many suggestions, reflections, and prescriptions relating anecdotes to conservation. Most of my substantial suggestions are summarized in chapter 9, where I depart from what is in essence an ethnography of birds and enter the realm of conservation geography through a laundry list of prescriptions.

Conservation geography, I submit, is the preaching and practice of geography with conservation in mind, and in this book the term applies specifically to the problems of Neotropical biodiversity protection and the contributions of knowledgeable local people. Conservation geographers should attempt to understand the intertwining worlds of birds and people before trying to alter them, and to that end we are aided by a preexisting Honduran and perhaps Neotropical tendency to respect, to shelter, and to cherish birds. Chapter 1, "Ornithophilia," contains vignettes of a Honduran and of a birder when they were still children in the Olancho landscape. They, like others portrayed later, are indicative of a cultural reality present probably in all places and in many people. My neologism hearkens to "topophilia," the love of places, coined by philosopher Gaston Bachelard and popularized by geographer Yi-Fu Tuan, as well as "biophilia," Stephen Kellert and E. O. Wilson's famous hypothesis. Ornithophilia is within us all, to a greater or lesser extent. It is manifest in individuals, families, social groups, and entire societies in some cases. Bird lovers, because they are such rich mines of ethnographic information, are keys to unlocking many secrets of human-bird relationships. Some of the secrets that proliferate in later chapters are deceptively simple, like this one: "I love birds because they are pretty."

Chapter 2 sketches a background history and geography of birds and people in Middle America, Honduras, and Olancho. Later I aim to convey the vastness and complexity of Olancho itself, as felt by its 420,000 inhabitants. As a preliminary, though, it is necessary to establish without a doubt that certain types of relationships with birds are generalized in the region and that birds have been a preoccupation of people in Middle America, and Latin America in general, since remote times. This is a result not only of indigenous beliefs but also of African and Iberian mores.

In chapter 3 I look at what rural women and children know and do about birds in a society dominated by men. Two families introduce everyday Olancho and some of its ornithophilic inhabitants. Women and children have a lot to say that is highly distinct from the perspectives held by men. The rhythms of their lives are different, and the places women and children frequent—home, river, and the undersides of hedgerows, for example—are subject to patient observation and painstaking discovery.

A Latin American provincial urban center, Juticalpa (Olancho's capital), is the subject of chapter 4. The *zopilote,* or Black Vulture, and the *zorzal,* or Clay-colored Robin, are two of Honduras's most popular birds. In urban areas, they represent, respectively, the boisterous, contaminated public sphere and the quiet, introspective private sphere. The words of townspeople in this chapter make evident not only the microgeographic intimacy of people and birds in cramped spaces but also the increasing disconnection between city and country that is occurring across Honduras.

Can large private landowners be conservationists? The answer given in chapter 5 may be surprising, given that Honduran society at large and many outsiders vilify large landowners (in many cases justly) for their tactics of land-grabbing and oppression of the rural poor. They often seem, as a group, to be concerned solely with profit, social status, high-yield export agriculture, and above all cattle. However, several *terratenientes* in Olancho profess ornithophilia, in some cases making their lands de facto reserves for waterfowl and terrestrial species. The Black-bellied Whistling-Duck or *pichiche* is especially cherished. Another species, the Honduran Emerald (*Amazilia luciae,* a hummingbird), depends for its survival as a species on the thorn scrub of large ranches. It is Honduras's only endemic bird, and ranchers who for a variety of reasons preserve thorn forest on their properties in the Valle de Agalta should be the recipients of substantial conservation attention.

Chapter 6 describes the *pajaral* or "place of many birds," the rural domestic landscape mosaic of kitchen gardens, orchards, and woods in and around villages. This is a landscape worthy of intense scrutiny by conservation geographers because the situation of its biodiversity is highly distinct from the extensive monocultures of the large landholders or the ongoing drastic transformation of woods to field occurring on the rain forest frontier. Olanchanos entertain their most intimate and frequent contacts with avifauna in their lush home villages, and it is in these *pajarales* that biodiversity conservation may be most successful.

Anyone unfamiliar with the landscapes of Honduras may be surprised to learn that rain forests are the natural vegetative cover only of certain regions — the majority of the country is given over to drier pine-oak woodlands and broadleaf deciduous ("tropical dry") forests and savannas. This is not a result of recent "degradation" caused by human beings; rather it is a natural consequence of the region's complex geology and mountainous terrain, where rain shadows that favor intense dry seasons are common except in the far eastern Moskitia, the North Coast, and the cloud forest tops of the higher interior ranges. Though pine forests and dry forests are biotically impoverished in comparison to rain forests, they nevertheless hold unique avifauna that cannot be found in wetter regions. Too often, non–rain forest habitats are ignored by biologists and conservationists because they appear neither "virgin" nor in possession of a great number of important species. The result is that certain avifauna are marginalized or ignored, even when they may need protection as desperately as rain forest species do. Chapter 7 looks at a few of these situations in Olancho, where remote and inaccessible non–rain forest areas contain a plethora of intriguing species. Birds of another type of margin, the night, are also important in this context because they include some of the species most endangered by local cultural practices.

The Montaña de Babilonia, one of the largest and most rugged montane rain forests in Central America, is the subject of chapter 8. I describe its birds within the context of local lifeways such as the coffee harvest, which brings thousands of pickers from the low-lying plains (*valles*) up into the outer fringes of the forest — the buffer zone of the Parque Nacional Sierra de Agalta — for several months of the year. Here, as everywhere, raptors are the group of birds most affected by direct human persecution, while Three-wattled Bellbirds and Resplendent Quetzals are mostly left alone. The landscape at the edge of the great forest is a meeting ground for birds that thrive in human landscapes of the plains — Groove-billed Anis, Melodious Blackbirds, and Clay-colored Robins, for example — and birds such as Great Curassows and Great Tinamous that come out of the deep *pura montaña*. Meanwhile, subsistence hunters penetrate the old-growth forest in search of avian and mammalian prey. Rather than condemn all human practices affecting the zone of highest avian diversity in Honduras, I suggest that there is common ground between farmers and park managers (as long as frontier expansion is halted), because local conceptions of the deep forest's enchanted qualities coincide with outsiders' near-religious obsession with tropical rain forest biodiversity.

Chapter 9, "Landscape Dialogues," returns to the theme of conservation geography. I propose various general approaches to avian conservation geography that are both low-cost and effective. One such project is the bird count workshop.

All translations of texts and conversations in Spanish are mine unless otherwise indicated. I have utilized the American Ornithologists' Union *Check-list of North American Birds,* seventh edition, in its online version as my authoritative source for common and scientific names. The AOU *Check-list* online (http://www.aou.org/aou/birdlist.html) is kept current as the "List of the 2,030 bird species (with scientific and English names) known from the A.O.U. Check-list area" and incorporates changes made in supplements 42 and 43 to the *Check-list,* as published in the *Auk* 117:847–58 (2000) and 119:897–906 (2002). Some readers will note that AOU varies slightly in taxonomic sequence and nomenclature from the two most useful field guides for the eastern Honduran region (Howell and Webb 1995, Ridgely and Gwynne 1989). Because neither guide alone contains plates of all possible species in eastern Honduras, avid birdwatchers may want to carry both guides into the field in Olancho; a North American guide is also useful for plates of Neotropical migrants. For plants, I have relied on Cyril Hardy Nelson's wonderful two-volume *Plantas comunes de Honduras* (1986). Fiona Reid's 1997 *A Field Guide to the Mammals of Central America and Southeast Mexico* is my authority on mammalian names.

Throughout, at the suggestions of several reviewers, I have insisted on the use of local Spanish names for birds wherever possible. At the beginning of chapter 1, I have placed the Spanish name in parentheses after the English name; in later chapters I generally employ the Spanish name first, with the English name in parentheses. To a limited extent I do the same with plant names, mammal names, and landscape terms, aiming to give the work a certain Olancho flavor without unduly taxing readers who do not speak Spanish. Spanish terms are also translated and explained in the glossary.

Finally, I have included as an appendix a list of 476 bird species known to occur in central Olancho, with names in English, Spanish, and Latin. This is a summary of a long-running bird inventory containing far more detailed data, produced by Francisco Urbina and me in 1994 and updated three times since then.

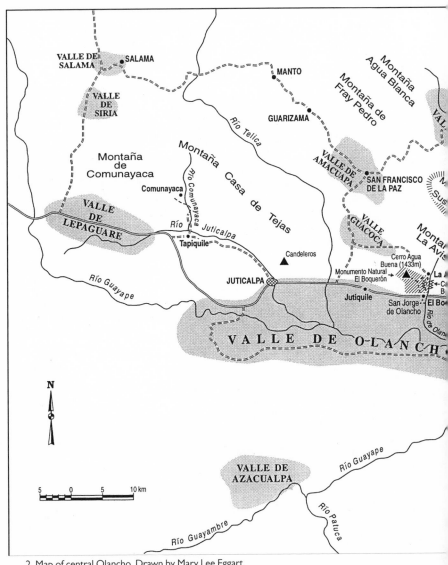

2. Map of central Olancho. Drawn by Mary Lee Eggart.

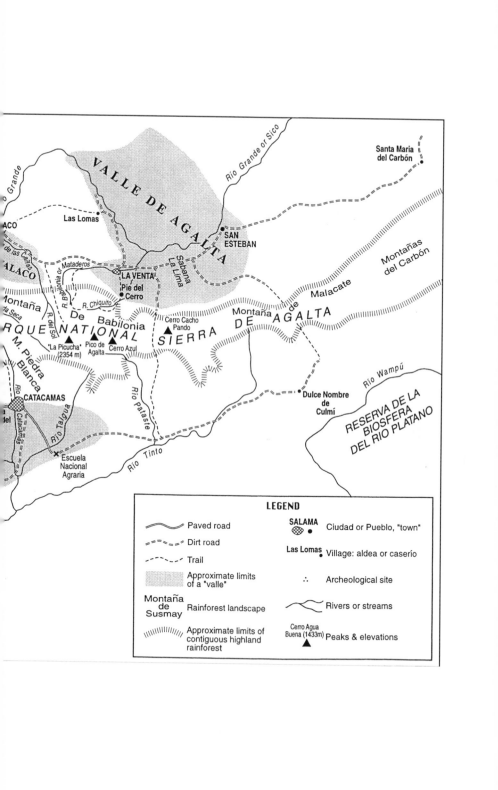

VALLE DE AGALTA

Río Grande or Sico

Santa Maria
del Carbón

ACO

Las Lomas

SAN
ESTEBAN

ALACO

Montañas
del Carbón

de las Cañas

Mataderos

LA VENTA

Pie del
Cerro

R. Babilonia or Mataderos

R. del Sol

R. Chiquito

Montaña

Sabana
La Lima

Cerro Cacho
Pando

de Malacate

Montaña

De   Babilonia

Montaña   de   AGALTA

la Seca

PARQUE

NATIONAL

SIERRA

DE

Cerro Azul

"La Picucha"
(2354 m)

Pico de
Agalta

M. Piedra

Blanca

Río Pataste

Río Wampú

CATACAMAS

RESERVA DE LA
BIOSFERA
DEL RIO PLATANO

del

Río Talgua

Dulce Nombre
de
Culmí

Río Catacamas

Escuela
Nacional
Agraria

Río Tinto

LEGEND

Paved road

Dirt road

Trail

Approximate limits
of a "valle"

Montaña
de
Susmay

Rainforest landscape

Approximate limits of
contiguous highland
rainforest

SALAMA   •   Ciudad or Pueblo, "town"

Las Lomas   Village: aldea or caserío
          •

∴   Archeological site

Rivers or streams

Cerro Agua
Buena (1433m)   Peaks & elevations
▲

Ornithophilia

A Clay-colored Robin's dawn song flutes from its nocturnal roost in the backyard avocado tree while the first Black Vultures skim the rooftops of Juticalpa. Lucita, her mother Clara, and grandmother Eva are washing down crumbly rolls with coffee to fortify them for the excursion. Before sunup, *doña* Clara sends her mother and little daughter on their way to catch the rattletrap bus to Tapiquile. Lucita is fidgeting in anticipation of a weekend on her Uncle Elmer's ranch in the backcountry.

The decrepit road through pastured mountains accompanies the Juticalpa River upstream along emerald floodplains and copses of gallery forest whence flocks of doves and parrots erupt and scatter across the dawn sky. The bus driver pauses frequently at villages and hamlets along the route: Casas Viejas, El Ojustal, La Vega, Sincuyapa, El Caliche, Panuaya. More than once, he brakes for cattle blocking the road and waits patiently for stick-wielding boys to clear the way. As his ancient machine leaps and plunges through the hilly landscape, Lucita and her grandmother spot a Lesser Roadrunner (*alma de perro*) fleeing from the berm into a hedgerow. Three Inca Doves (*turquitas*) whir up from their morning feeding spot in the road ahead, narrowly escaping the wheels. Perched precipitously on barbed-wire fences, pairs of glistening black Groove-billed Anis (*tijules*) spread their wings in the moist sun, then flap awkwardly out across the meadows, calling *ti-jul, ti-jul, ti-jul.* Despite the noise of the engine and the obscuring effect of grime-streaked window panes on the panorama, Lucita and her grandmother revel in the marvelous flights, hues, and calls of birds that herald the morning's birth in the Olancho countryside.

They alight at *don* Cornelio Matute's house in the riverside village of Tapiquile. *Doña* Eva gossips with Cornelio and his family; Lucita fidgets impatiently on her three-legged stool as a horse is saddled for the half-hour ride to her uncle's house. She drinks in the stories of local happenings that Cornelio tells so well over coffee and a bit of breakfast. Lucita admires Cornelio because although he lacks a formal education, he has an impressive knowledge of his own world, its people, forests, birds, and animals. She cherishes the wisdom he shares with her and remembers it when she sets off on her own explorations of hedgerow and orchard.

Clinging tightly to her equestrian grandmother, the little girl is entranced by the pastoral landscape and the surrounding peaks cloaked in pine, and by the local farmers going about their daily labors in corn and beans. After four splashing fords of the Comunayaca River, a league at a trot delivers them to the gate of her uncle's ranch. Elmer Maradiaga's modest hacienda is embraced by the fragrant pine forest, what Olanchanos call *serranía*. In Lucita's mind, she has arrived at the very edge of the *montaña,* though local farmers know that the true *montaña* (montane rain forest) begins farther back in the hills, where pines give way to humid broadleaf forest planted in coffee. Nevertheless, for a town girl with a powerful imagination, the wilderness claws at her uncle's doorstep. For one subjected to treeless, crowded streets and tiny, walled backyards, these tick-filled pastures, labyrinthine *buruscos* (vine tangles) and *guamiles* (fallow fields grown into brush), humid, stagnant streamside woods, and airy slopes of pine and brambles compose a landscape of mystery and excitement.

Something is always going on in Lucita's *montaña.* There is the coffee harvest, the sowing and reaping of corn and beans, the births and deaths of cattle. Hours are different than in town: women get up at three to make tortillas; men at four, and by five they are on their way to the fields. Things start to slow down before midday when the workers return home, and many afternoons are spent on porches, discussing and resolving the problems of the world. Viscous coffee flows through every kitchen, lubricating the endless conversations. But silences also abound, and the quiet expectation of visits. Every family knows its importance to society in the hamlet of Comunayaca, wedged in a gully where the sun hits for not too many hours. Quick dusk comes on at five, and by seven most are asleep.

Lucita, like everyone else, does her rounds. She frequents the cottage of China, an ancient woman who enthralls her with endless tales. One story that appeals particularly to Lucita's imagination is of the *Estiquirín,* a ghastly nocturnal spirit who carries away naughty children. China describes a yellow-eyed wraith on silent wings, its call — "Es-ti-qui-*rín*" — chilling potential victims on certain moonlit nights. Lucita's eyes grow round with excited terror, for she has heard the call, if not seen the thing itself. Uncle Elmer later tells Lucita that the *Estiquirín* is a type of owl (*búho*) that the old-timers claim it is bad luck to kill. It is, however, mere flesh and blood, the Great Horned Owl, death to house cats mesmerized by its stare.

A somewhat spoiled "special guest" from town, Lucita has but a few light chores to do. Mostly, her wise uncle and grandmother allow her to get out and explore. They figure that *doña* Clara will take care of removing the dozens of seed ticks clinging to her daughter's skin. Back in Juticalpa, Lucita loves to show off her ticks to kids in school, making them jealous of her weekend in the country.

Lucita's Fascination with Nests

For several years, Lucita's favorite hobby has been the single-minded pursuit of birds' nests (*niditos*) to add to her collection. She finds something especially attractive and comforting about their woven homes of sticks and mud and spider silk. Her incessant curiosity often draws her into those deep recesses of prickly hedgerows where abandoned *niditos* are most abundant. Lucita adores the intricately woven nests of small birds like the *cucarachero* (wren) — these are veritable prizes to hoard back in Juticalpa. Another treasure is one she found by the creek, blown down from a tree: the sac nest of a *chorcha* (oriole), one of her favorite birds.

Lucita believes that birds live in their nests all year round. Mother and father birds fashion perfect little round shelters for life, homes that make the brush tangle a child's miniature facsimile of the greater world of adult people roundabout. A few times, Lucita has found an irresistible nest still occupied by eggs or young and has stolen it anyway. For such a crime, her grandmother and uncle scold her. They ask whether she would like someone coming and taking her own home away. Fighting her powerful will to collect, she returns the nests to their rightful and frantic owners.

Not all Lucita's encounters with nests and their occupants have been restricted to the innocuous little birds of briar patch and field. Once, she clambered recklessly up a tree to reach a massive, ugly stick nest lodged in a fork of the trunk, and retreated rapidly on encountering a grunting *zopilote* (Black Vulture) chick with fluffy white down and beady, bulging eyes. That unpleasant meeting left her with a strong distaste for vultures, but it did little to curb her curiosity.

Among the local children, living their lives close to wild plants and animals, birds and nests do not occupy such a privileged place within their imaginative geographies. But eager to embark on exciting new outings, they lead Lucita to the good nest places. Their preferred routes zigzag from fruiting tree to fruiting tree, where they gorge on mangos, guavas, *nances,* or whatever other fruits happen to be in season.

Since a marauding flock of *loras de montaña* (White-crowned Parrots), *huachires* (Melodious Blackbirds), or *torditos* (Bronzed Cowbirds) can quickly wipe out a family's corn crop, local boys, under orders from their parents to rid the fields of these pests, usually carry slingshots wherever they go. Some find great sport in stoning harmless as well as destructive birds. Lucita, even if she were so inclined, knows her own family would never allow such carnage.

Among the birds of glittering plumage, the *guardabarrancos* (Turquoise-browed Motmot, "cliff guardian") is Lucita's favorite. One does not have much chance of finding these in Juticalpa, but in the countryside they are common and easy to see on fence posts along roadsides, displaying their green, black, blue, and orange feathers while switching their long tails back and forth like pendulums. These creatures are highly mysterious to Lucita. Where do they keep their nests, she wonders? Longing to have one, she persuades a local girl to indulge her. The town girl's exotic and mysterious bird is familiar and commonplace to the rural child. Everyone knows that the *guardabarrancos* lays its eggs in cavities it excavates from roadcuts and stream banks.

Lucita couldn't collect a motmot nest, but her mother doesn't mind, because she thinks the child has enough dusty nests already, arrayed on a shelf in Juticalpa. With the years, Lucita's nests fade and disintegrate, and she grows into other collections and interests. But she never loses her love of nests, and even as an adult she is still known to take the occasional plunge into the briar patch.

🐝 *Lessons for a Birder*

I had glimpsed a motmot many years before in the Peruvian Amazon, but it didn't really count. Motmots, like all "glamour" birds, do not seem worthy of being added to my lifelist until I have a nice view of them. "Lifelisting" such birds as the Resplendent Quetzal, Purple-throated Fruitcrow, or Turquoise-browed Motmot after the tour guide has identified one for me from a distant call or flash of plumage seems dishonest. So I recall my first *real* motmot with clarity because it came to perch in plain view, letting me observe without binoculars for several minutes. It was June, 1991, and I was in Santa Lucía, a hill town in central Honduras, undergoing several months of intensive training for the Peace Corps. I was preparing for a two-year assignment to a remote and wild cloud forest, the Sierra de Agalta National Park, on the eastern frontier in the department of Olancho. There, experienced Peace Corps volunteers had assured me, I would find such exotics as quetzals, cotingas, and toucans (not to mention jaguars and tapirs). In contrast, the tame domestic landscapes of central Honduras — house and field and orchard set among the endless pine forests — frustrated me as I noted down impatiently the common, ordinary Great-tailed Grackles, Melodious Blackbirds, and Groove-billed Anis in preparation for future expeditions among the Harpy Eagles and Resplendent Quetzals of Olancho.

The woodpeckers and jays of the highland pine forests around Santa Lucía evoked the Colorado Rockies more than the Neotropics.[1] Red Crossbills, Steller's Jays, and Chipping Sparrows plied the cool and fragrant woods in roving flocks, while Greater Pewees, Eastern Bluebirds, and American Kestrels called and hunted from perches. Only the occasional flock of White-throated Magpie-Jays or Green Parakeets reminded me that I was in the Neotropics and not somewhere much farther north.

Imagine my surprise one day when a motmot flashed out of the undergrowth to land on a branch some ten meters away, next to a house a few blocks down from where I was staying. At first, I thought the bird must be a vagrant, out of its normal rain forest habitat; I had not read the bird literature too carefully. So immersed was I in this sublime encounter that I forgot to note the field marks that would allow me to identify it as

either a Turquoise-browed or a Blue-crowned motmot (by the elevation — 1,400 meters above sea level — I assume it was the latter).[2]

From that point on, I looked more carefully at people's backyards and
other "unnatural" habitats. I began to understand that Hondurans and
birds live in the same places. Birders, I learned, can be satisfied elsewhere
than the ancient forest; indeed, most of us have but scant opportunity to
visit the remote haunts of the Harpy Eagle. Most of the time, we spend
our everyday lives in everyday places, making do with the birds we
glimpse through our windows or on a ramble down the local hike-and-
bike trail, often forgetting that these birds are themselves spectacular. It's
difficult to describe logically just why we are attracted to birds to the
point of wanting to identify them all. When birds absorb us, we enjoy a
pronounced case of what I call "ornithophilia," a condition common to
humankind.

In 1995, many years after Lucita was stymied by motmots, she and I
married. The Peace Corps, which occupied me from 1991 to 1993, had
been both extremely frustrating and deeply rewarding. At first, I equated
reward with field trips to the virgin rain forest, sightings of rare birds on
a regular basis, tracking jaguars, and being defecated on by furious spider monkeys. Assigned to work on the conservation of the Parque Nacional Sierra de Agalta, a national park established by law in 1987, I often
had opportunities to get out into the rain forest as well as up to the cloud
forest and elfin heath that had not been explored by scientists. I was living out my own childhood fantasy of exploring the unexplored and
charting the uncharted.

When I slogged up the frigid crystalline rivers into the Sierra, leaving behind the last and latest agricultural clearings, toponyms became
scarcer. There is a point where streams and peaks no longer have names.
The rugged montane forest diminishes in height with altitude, and its
biodiversity becomes more mysterious. Many were the expeditions in
which I participated when researchers found plants and animals new to
science. Though the heady atmosphere of discovery tended to make the
human landscapes of the lower slopes and *valle* plains seem second best
to an explorer, I was finding out that humanized places had their appeal
as well. Indeed, the entire province of Olancho — rain forest, pine forest,
dry forest — is still a wild frontier region in many ways and contains a fair
share of fabulous and sometimes dangerous creatures. Even human
landscapes and their avifauna are far from tame; Ornate Hawk-Eagles are

known to spend time near villages. I became so entranced by the mysteries of Olancho that after finishing with the Peace Corps, I found reasons to return again and again for extended periods.

In 1991, my co-workers and I began a bird inventory that grew rapidly until the list for the Sierra de Agalta and surrounding plains topped 450 species. I heeded the messages of the motmot that Luz and I had learned independently. This meant, on one hand, *look for birds everywhere,* not only in the rain forest. No landscape should be viewed as second best or "trashed," because each is different and unique. On the other hand, it meant *question local people,* because they are the ones most likely to know which birds are found where. Even when we combined interviews with bird guides and a fair notion of what could be expected, we were still likely to be surprised. The biogeography of eastern Honduras is imperfectly understood, which helps explain why it is common to encounter birds that are not supposed to be where one finds them. Ornithologists are familiar with this phenomenon: it is one of the reasons Neotropical landscapes are so fascinating.

From what I had studied in college and learned while working in environmental jobs, I had half-expected to be hit by birds dropping out of the skies from shotgun blasts and to see every child armed with a slingshot. These turned out to be exaggerations, though both practices are serious problems throughout Honduras. In much of Olancho, the Scarlet Macaw has disappeared (see chapter 6), and many other birds are fading, within the experience of local residents not even fifty years old. But I found other more positive relationships between people and birds in Olancho, giving me cause for hope. The dooryard kitchen gardens and orchards so characteristic of Central America abound with birds, and usually the gardeners appreciate and protect rather than persecute their avifauna. Riverside gallery forests teem with Neotropical migrants, while some ranchers are protecting whatever birds can share the fields, copses, and ponds with cattle. Pine forests and their avifauna are resilient, recovering after logging, burning, and hurricanes. Shaded coffee farms, ersatz rain forests, are rich in biodiversity. Even the old-growth rain forest, which is fast being converted to human use, holds traditional importance and value, especially where it protects coveted water sources.

Olanchanos and other Hondurans have rich traditions of caring for birds. People tell stories about birds, attracting them to yards and eaves, caging them, talking to them, and setting them free. Birds appear in folklore and place names, novels and short stories, and wisdom in many forms.[3] In the chapters that follow, I write not only of destruction and extinction but also of appreciation and conservation. Ornithophilia is at work wherever and whenever a *zorzal* (Clay-colored Robin) builds a nest in someone's avocado tree and is not harmed, enriching the lives of curious children. It may be at work when a quetzal family is left un-molested on a shaded coffee farm, and where *pichiches* (whistling-ducks) and *cigüeñas* (Wood Storks) find shelter at a cattle rancher's pond. Orni-thophilic farmers who hang bark houses for doves under their eaves in rural Olancho and urban dwellers who delight in the hummingbirds and *viuditas* (Blue-gray Tanagers) that visit their gardens are all engaged in environmental protection.

Historical and Geographical Background

The variety of birds with which the supernatural author has populated the land, wind, and water in these Americas is so great that many books would not be enough to tell of them all, so I will only talk of the most common and well-known ones, which are few, because every day new types are discovered in every Province.

Fray Francisco Ximénez, introductory words to *Título III, De las aves,* in *Historia natural del Reino de Guatemala,* written around 1722

Birds and people share a long history in what is today Honduras. For close to ten thousand years, humans have dwelt in or near pine woods, rain forests, prairies, savannas, and thorn forests and have witnessed these landscapes yield to each other in complex sequences caused by continental placation, climate change, geologic events, and human agency. Archaeological evidence indicates that in pre-Hispanic Middle America, sacred traditions anchored birds to the cosmos as incarnations of the gods, as divine messengers, tricksters, or fortune-tellers. Such beliefs were not unique to this part of the world: peoples everywhere, in all times, have revered birds. Their flights have inspired angels while their gazes speak of wisdom, and their songs and bones foretell what might come to pass. For many peoples, birds have been personalities with whom to reckon, endless founts of inspiration, of symbol, image, and metaphor, connecting earth with sky and day with night. They have called the cycles of the year into being, singing winter's hope that spring is near and summer close behind. To many peoples, including the ancient Americans, birds have been kindred souls in the riotous life that teems in the air, trees, ground, and water.[1]

Inseparable from the spiritual meanings of birds were their material offerings of meat and plume that sustained diets, lifeways, and trade networks. From the journals of Christopher Columbus to the eve of the nineteenth-century penetration of Latin America by scientific ornithology, there is a substantial literature on birds compiled by Catholic bishops, Franciscan friars, Spanish royal chroniclers, and biographers of conquistadors. While chroniclers Peter Martyr (1524) and Gonzalo Fernández de Oviedo (1526–1540s) are among the best known for their vast syntheses (both report frequently on birds), many others made significant contributions as well, especially in Peru and Mexico. From these accounts, we learn not only about indigenous practices but also how the Iberians encountered local traditions and how the American and the European were woven together into new traditions.

Featherworking in Middle America

Francisco López de Gómara, Hernán Cortés's biographer, wrote some oft-repeated accounts of the roles of birds in the Aztec Empire.[2] Before the Spanish destroyed Tenochtitlán, Moctezuma kept aviaries containing eagles and other birds of prey, feeding them on fish and domestic turkeys. The scale and splendor of the Aztec emperor's zoological collections was also detailed by other chroniclers. But featherworking was perhaps the Mexicans' most famous use of birds, and this art form endured well into the Spanish era. As late as 1656, Antonio León de Pinelo recounts the existence of an Aztec feather tapestry in an Amazonian mission.[3] These magnificent works were on demand in the courts and monasteries of the Old World, and it was said that they were finer than any European tapestries. The Aztec feather tapestries contained intricate, iridescent detail, and their elaboration was supported by a long-distance trade network between central Mexico and Central America. During the reigns of the last Aztec emperors, birds supported a network of feather traders, sellers, and workers. Scarlet Macaw and Resplendent Quetzal plumes were probably among the items brought from as far away as Honduras.

We know substantial details about the significance of feathers from the accounts in Franciscan friar Bernardino de Sahagún's 1579 *Historia general de las cosas de la Nueva España* (translated as the *Florentine Codex*), the most detailed ethnography of Middle America ever produced.[4]

Sahagún not only compiled accounts of everyday life among the 1570s Nahua in the words of local informants but also obtained oral histories and drawings of older practices that had already disappeared or were fading. Sahagún's section on local birds (*Codex,* book 11: *Earthly Things,* pp. 19–56), mostly about waterfowl, is extraordinary for its symbolic complexity and also shows that local people appreciated the rhythms of migration and breeding. To the Nahua on the shores of the Lake of Mexico, the Brown Pelican was their most sacred bird. They called it the "heart of the water": "These water folk consider [the pelican] as their mirror. For in it they see what each is to merit in their profession as water folk" (Sahagún, *Codex* 11:29; translation by editors).

Book 9, *The Merchants,* details the history of the feather industry. This, more than any other early colonial account, shows the importance of birds in Middle America. In central Mexico and throughout the Americas, the working of feathers into ornamental and everyday garments was a common artisanal practice. But with the growth of the Aztec Empire, what had been a "humble" craft involving plumes of common local birds such as egrets became an imperially sanctioned practice that supported the procuring of certain iridescent feathers from the tropical lowlands of both coasts. One amusing incident, recounted Sahagún's informants, was the introduction and strict imperial protection of the *teuzanatl,* or Great-tailed Grackle, valued for the male's iridescent tail plumes. Later, as grackle populations exploded in the Valley of Mexico, it became a pest, its former exotic status a joke.

The armies of the Mexica, when coming into contact with tropical lowland kingdoms, were awestruck by the elaborate quetzal and macaw plumes in their banners, headdresses, and other accoutrements, because such birds did not live in the Valley of Mexico. As Aztec feather art developed in the late 1400s, traders would sneak into enemy territories to procure the plumes of certain highly coveted and valuable birds. This passage is to my knowledge the first written account of the altitudinal migration of Resplendent Quetzals:

Because this very place was where all the quetzal birds descended. They came down when spring set in and here ate the acorns of the oak trees. And the lovely cotingas and the blue honeycreepers came to eat the fruit of the black fig tree. And when they caught the lovely cotinga, they could not seize it with their hand. They only swiftly plucked, they grasped, a handful of green grass, with it they seized the bird. For if only with the hands one were to take it, then the lovely cotinga's feathers were blemished; the blue became as if soiled. (Sahagún, *Codex* 9:21; translation by editors)

After arriving at Tenochtitlán, the finest plumes made their way into the hands of the royal featherworkers for fashioning into the elaborate tapestries and other works over which the emperor had strict control. More ordinary feathers, made into articles of everyday use among the populace and used for bases of tapestries, were sold in the street markets:

The feather seller
The feather seller is a feather worker, a merchant — the man [with] the basket. The good feather seller [is] a gentle worker — one who esteems [his wares], who is dedicated. He sells various feathers — precious feathers; he sells fine green feathers, chili-green feathers, those curved at the tip, the feathers of young birds. He sells [feathers] of the trogonorus, the troupial, the blue cotinga. The bad feather worker [is] a [fraudulent] embellisher of feathers, a treater of feathers with glue. He sells old, worn feathers, damaged feathers. He dyes feathers; he dyes those which are faded, dirty, yellow, darkened, smoked. (Sahagún, *Codex* 10: 61; brackets in original; translation by editors)[5]

Sahagún's informants also give elaborate descriptions of the exact processes by which the tapestries were made and used. The woven detail that so impressed the Europeans resulted from the use of thousands of hummingbird feathers.

Evidence of featherworking in indigenous Honduras is slight, largely due to the fact that unlike in Mexico, a body of early colonial chronicles and codices does not exist. Colonial Honduras was an imperial backwater and did not attract the likes of Sahagún. But in later documents, the evidence for indigenous featherworking in Olancho is intriguing. In 1854, the explorer William Wells came close to finding out how Indians, presumably Pech, wove garments from feathers. He describes attendees at Juticalpa's 1854 celebration of its patron saint:

Among them moved the . . . Indians . . . from La Conquista, San Estevan, and Dulcenombre. . . . Among them might be seen specimens of the beautiful art apparently confined to the American Indian races, feather-robe making. Some of these were made with rare skill, evincing a taste in the disposal and contrasting of colors which might have been in vain attempted by more cultivated artists.

The gaudiest plumed denizens of the tropical forest are laid under contribution for these robes. One of the Indians . . . promised me a description of the method of making them. (Wells 1857, 326)[6]

Unfortunately, Wells gave no further details. More recent writings on the Pech do not mention the practice.

Encounters with Birds in Early Colonial Honduras

From historical accounts and archaeology, we know that birds dwelt in significantly humanized landscapes in Honduras around the time of contact. Local human population densities had often been high, and fire-fallow agriculture, hunting, and gathering, as well as chiefdom-level polities, dominated over large areas. Archaeological evidence indicates that most of Honduras was settled on the eve of Conquest, even areas that today are blanketed by old-growth forest. In 1492, the total population of what is today Honduras was probably between 500,000 and 1,000,000, a size not reached again until the twentieth century.[7] Sixteenth-century accounts of birds from Honduras are few but include the chronicler Gonzalo Fernández de Oviedo's 1540s description of the province as especially notable for eagles.[8]

There is a bird [Black Hawk-Eagle or dark phase of Crested Eagle] that is larger or about the size of a peacock, with yellow bill, yellow talons, and on the upper breast its plumage is very black, like velvet, and on the lower breast striped, one white and one black, in such beautiful harmony that it is the most beautiful plumage that can ever be seen; and the legs down to the talons are feathered, and the eyes very beautiful, and on the head a crest as long as a finger, and straight, of feathers, black and very shiny; and if it looks at the ground, it declines the crest toward the ground, and raising its head, it flattens it back behind. The tail is short, of the same black color, and slightly longer than a dove's, and the wings are tucked back. It is a bird of prey, and if it can't find any other thing to eat, it feeds on some long-tailed monkey, since there are many of those. There are other birds of very beautiful plumage, and each has two crests pointing upward, like an owl, but larger; and they move those plumes or crests very easily, and often hold them flattened behind, and when they gaze at the ground, they point them toward the ground as well, and it is something to see; and they are also birds of prey with fierce talons [Harpy Eagle]. There are black eagles [Solitary Eagles, Great Black-Hawks, or Common Black-Hawks], like very fine and highly polished jet, large and with large talons, and they eat many of those *guabiquinajes* [meaning unknown: possibly crabs] of which there are many in that land. (Oviedo 1541, p. 394; brackets mine)

Another account is by Cristóbal de Pedraza (1898), a Church official sent to the province of Honduras e Higueras, about which he wrote a *Relación* to the Crown in 1544.[9] His is perhaps the best of the few relatively detailed landscape descriptions of sixteenth-century Honduras. The following extract is about the birds around the Spanish north coast settlement of Trujillo and the nearby island of Guanaja.

There are many *gallinas de la tierra* [domestic turkeys] that they [the Spaniards] call *pavos* here, and many *de Castilla* [chickens] which breed in great quantities; as well as *palomas de las torcazas y de las zoritas* [two types of doves]. Many *codornices* [quail] and *tortolas* [ground-doves] in very great numbers and many *faisanes* ["pheasants"] like those of here [Spain] and *patos* [ducks]. *Perdices* [partridges] have not been seen. There are many birds of prey of diverse types: *águilas* [eagles], *azores* ["goshawks"] and *halcones* [falcons] and many other beautiful birds of this type, that swoop down to take hares and rabbits and *palomas* and *codornices,* much more beautiful than all the other birds that are hunted here [meaning the raptors], and many other birds that are eaten, tiny ones of diverse colors and habits, red, blue and yellow, black with red collars, in size almost like the finger and even some like the little finger [hummingbirds] and many others painted in diverse colors. There are many beautiful *papagayos* [parrots] of the green type, with one [colored] like an egg yolk with yellow amber on the head [presumably the yellow-naped parrot], the best there are in all the Indies and that most easily talk without being taught. And the best of this province are those of an island that is almost eight or ten leagues distant from this city of Trujillo that is called island of the *guanaja* [domestic turkey] that measures up to two leagues around, such that from many parts of the Indies they send and plead to the citizens of Trujillo to send them *papagayos* from the said island because they are so good. And the Indians of the said island knowing that there is so much demand raise them taking them from the nests when they are almost ready to fly, and they raise them and *gangrenan* [infect them with gangrene, presumably a method of keeping them flightless] to sell them to the Christians. There are also many *papagayos* of the tiny ones [parakeets or white-crowned parrots] almost of the size of *tordos* [thrushes], in such great numbers that they are great pests, eating the corn and wheat crops of the Indians and Christians like *pardales* [sparrows] do here, against which the Indians are armed with traps and other weapons and take them to eat. (Pedraza 1898, 390–91; brackets and italics mine)

Though Pedraza lauded the gold-rich Olancho Valley and its recently founded *ciudad* known as San Jorge de Olancho, he makes no mention of the region's wild fauna. His most significant and fateful remark about Olancho was that the Spanish settlers had brought many cattle that were doing well on its savannas.

Pedraza's prose shows that he had little knowledge of birds. For example, by the time he wrote, hummingbirds were already well known to the Spanish from several glowing descriptions by earlier chroniclers, yet he seems unaware of this. Unlike other writers, he makes no attempt to document local indigenous names, leaving us confused about the identity of most species. Nevertheless, his other descriptions of fauna and flora of sea and land, including wild and domestic species, paint a valuable picture of indigenous landscapes and their conversion into Ibero-American landscapes replete with cattle ranches, wheat fields, and other Old World imports.

Pedraza's *Relación* appealed to certain contemporaneous Spanish narratives about nature. Writers usually stressed birds that, among other things, would be of interest to authorities in Spain by appealing to elite tastes (hawking, for example), encouraging colonization (because of their abundance), and helping the economy (e.g., parrots). The Psittacidae (macaws, parrots, parakeets) received attention even on the first voyage of Columbus. Indeed, they were one of his strongest pieces of evidence that he had encountered Asia, because Europeans had been familiar with parrots as trade items from the East (and from Africa).[10] Peter Martyr, who compiled some of the earliest accounts from Middle America and the Caribbean, mentioned parrots as the most common pets of indigenous people, even in places where wild flocks abounded in the surrounding forests.[11] Other accounts of Psittacidae from the colonial period single out the Yellow-naped Parrots of Honduras and Nicaragua as the best talkers, and even today they have that value, helping to explain why they have been extirpated from so much of the region.

Cristóbal de Pedraza often gives "new" birds the names of similar European types, which was a common practice in the sixteenth-century New World. Though misidentification was sometimes the cause, local Spaniards often pinned Old World names on the birds to make the landscape more familiar, even if they were fully aware that the birds were distinct. For example, *gorrión,* the Old World "sparrow," became the common name for the hummingbird in Honduras.

In their few Honduran enclaves, the Spanish settlers built traditions about their "new" birds stemming from direct observation, local indigenous knowledge, and the old knowledge brought over from Iberia. The latter tradition initially sufficed to describe such familiar birds as the owl, hawk, and sparrow, but the former sources would have been consulted to make sense of motmots and toucans.

Birds in the Weave

By the beginning of the 1600s, Honduran indigenous populations had plummeted from hundreds of thousands to less than twenty thousand by some estimates. African slaves had been imported to work gold deposits in Olancho and silver mines in central and southern Honduras. But there always seemed to be too few people to maintain a productive colonial economy, while the scourges of epidemics and pirates did not help Spain's cause. Other than having a few white Iberians, most of Honduras became a land of mestizos and *mulatos* in a complex blend of African, Indian, and European cultures. Today traditional knowledge, still the predominant way that Honduran children learn about nature, is a result of these braided cultural currents. The general term for Hondurans who do not identify themselves as indigenous is *Ladino.*

The African contribution to Honduran culture has been little studied except on the North Coast, where it is more recent and obvious. But throughout interior regions like Olancho, centuries-old African traditions can be detected through words such as *mondongo* (tripe) and *bemba* (mouth), through gold-mining practices, and through folklore. The widespread Tio Conejo y Tio Coyote (Br'er Rabbit) stories and beliefs in the powers of the Piedra de Rayo (Thunderbolt Stone) may point to an African heritage.

Some self-identifying indigenous groups have survived who share many traditions with the Ladinos but are nevertheless distinct. Honduran geographer Jesús Aguilar Paz's "Zarabanda y Chiligatoro" (pp. 234–36 in his *Tradiciones y leyendas de Honduras*), tells the story behind the place names of an indigenous Lenca landscape in the department of La Paz in southwestern Honduras. Chiligatoro is a lake that takes its name from a giant in local folklore, a hunter of rare plumes and skins who roamed the ancient cloud forests in search of the *coa* (trogon) and *yure* (quetzal). The Ventana de Cuquinca is a hole ("window") in a crag named after a warrior with feathered headdress. Zarabanda, the present-day name of another lake, is the siren of its waters, a princess promised to Chiligatoro but lover of Cuquinca. Chiligatoro, suspecting the worst, takes the form of an owl to swoop upon them while they are trysting. Vengeful, he imprisons Zarabanda in the lake, where her tears become its everlasting source. Chiligatoro opens the *ventana* on the mountainside with a rock he hurls at Cuquinca, who hides deep within a cave. Chiligatoro goes away to stare at the reflections in his own lake, to brood for eternity, trying to forget.

Lenca landscape are saturated with folklore, and most rural Ladino landscapes are also filled with haunted brooks, enchanted hills, caves that lead to subterranean worlds, trees that weep, and pools populated by sirens. Jesús Aguilar Paz dedicates an entire section, "Geografía y Leyenda" ("Geography and Legend," pp. 45–81 in *Tradiciones y leyendas*), to such phenomena. They prevail in regions once dominated by ancestors and relatives of the Lenca.

The Pech (Paya), a nation of around fifteen hundred whose cultural core is eastern Olancho, share some traditions with neighboring Ladinos, while possessing other beliefs that have no analogues among non-indigenous Olanchanos. Ethnologist Eduard Conzemius included several interesting comments about birds among the Pech in his 1928 study,

Los indios paya: Estudio geográfico, histórico, etnográfico y lingüístico, and also incorporated names of birds into his Pech-Spanish lexicon.

The Tolupan (Jicaque) of Yoro department were studied by Anne Chapman, and their beliefs about nature, including the roles of birds, are detailed in her 1992 *Masters of Animals: Oral Traditions of the Tolupan Indians, Honduras.*[12] Other indigenous groups are the Garífuna or "Black Caribs" of the North Coast, whose knowledge and traditions involving waterbirds are quite extensive; the Tawahka (Sumu) of the Patuca River; and the Miskito of the Moskitia. Conzemius (1932) is an authoritative source for the latter two groups, mentioning, for example, how they fear and abhor the Red-throated Caracara — a bird that is respected if not overly important among Ladino Olanchanos (see chapter 7).

The sharpest lines demarcating bird traditions in Honduras are not those between ethnic groups, or between Ladino and indigenous, but those that partition city from town and town from countryside. They are the lines that mark off Lucita from her *montaña,* that separate social classes and determine "levels of education." Impoverished rural people tend to have less formal schooling but live closer to the land. Often, they possess great empirical knowledge of birds while at the same time exploiting birds to a degree that may shock urbanites. Townspeople, in contrast, have little regular contact with any but a handful of birds, and they dilute traditional knowledge with what they learn in school (often about birds not even found in Honduras). Many city dwellers, such as people from Tegucigalpa, have almost no interaction with the countryside and little empirical knowledge of birds. They are, however, the people most active in the upper echelons of conservation planning and management.

Except in the most remote rural places, the reach of modernization is such that younger generations are turning increasingly to television and schoolteachers and away from folklore and direct observation for education about their landscapes; away from place-based traditions and toward generic facts. But despite the erosion of certain aspects of the sense of place, Honduras remains one of the most rural and traditional countries in Latin America. In Honduras, more than in many other countries, one often encounters vibrant traditions connecting town and rural people to the landscape and its birds.

🌿 *A Profusion of Landscapes*

New patterns of land use became established in Spanish Honduras even while ancient fire-fallow (slash-and-burn) systems, gathering, and hunting endured. Ibero-American geographic creation drew from older indigenous practices but instituted novel systems as well. Before the 1700s, there were never more than ten *ciudades* (Spanish administrative centers), with ever fewer Indian settlements paying them tribute in chickens, maize, beans, and other necessities. Many of the tribute towns also supplied labor to silver mines that dominated the economies of central and southern Honduras. Indians, as well as other non-Spanish castes (mostly *mulatos*), performed additional duties as seasonal laborers or militiamen. From the early 1600s into the nineteenth century, most of the country was a wilderness sparsely populated by tiny mixed villages and cattle ranches connected by tenuous mule trails and footpaths that inscribed the endless mountains and plains. The journey from Tegucigalpa to Juticalpa in Olancho, which today takes less than three hours by car, took seven days.

Much of eastern and northern Honduras, known in colonial times as the Taguzgalpa (including today's Moskitia), was beyond Spanish control and became the refuge of apostate and unbaptized Indians as well as escaped slaves, convicted criminals, and other renegades from Church and State. They had contact with other colonial powers, especially the English, who employed them to obtain mahogany and traded them arms and other goods in hopes of destabilizing the Spanish Empire. From the early 1600s to the eve of independence in 1821, Franciscan missionaries, with the help of the military, attempted repeatedly to settle the remaining unconquered Indians of the Taguzgalpa in missions within the colonized part of Honduras. Franciscan missions played an especially important part in the colonial history of Olancho.

Hondurans of all castes owned cattle ranches, and the landscapes created by and for this practice predominate in interior plains and mountains even today. As Pedraza foreshadowed in 1544, peoples such as the Olanchano elite, whose destinies were supposed to be "golden," ended up becoming wealthy in cattle instead. Other land was given over to staple crops—plantains, tobacco, beans, maize, and squash—while some areas were dedicated to products such as agave, indigo, and wheat, which were favored by the colonial economy but have long ago faded in importance.

The Spanish, like the civilizations that preceded them, favored the flat, dry, and fertile interior plains for settlement, agriculture, and cattle ranching. The piney hills that predominate over most of highland Honduras were valued not for agriculture but for purposes such as white-tailed deer hunting, firewood extraction, pitch production, and mule logging. Settlers generally avoided the highest, steepest, wettest mountains, because cattle tended to do poorly in those areas. (Coffee, which thrives better in such areas than on the plains, did not begin to take on economic importance until the mid-1800s.) Certain mountain soils and slopes were good for crops such as maize, beans, and wheat, but outside the mining zones and the relatively populous western highlands, where low-lying plains are few and far between, people visited the *montañas* — montane rain forests — only occasionally, to gather and hunt.

In the twentieth century, many *montañas* underwent conversion to shaded coffee. Others became pastures and bean fields. A few grew back after being exploited intensively during earlier mining or logging booms. Today, each *montaña* is a heterogeneous landscape resulting not only from human use but also from natural factors such as slope, elevation, and geology. Most Honduran montane rain forests have been affected by humans even if only lightly; the dense forests covering the highest and most rugged mountain ranges in thinly settled areas are the rare exceptions. These blanket the Cordillera Nombre de Dios along the North Coast, the Cordillera de Botaderos south of the Río Aguán, the Cordillera de Agalta running through central Olancho, and several more remote ranges that run west to east to become lost in the rugged hills and pine savannas of the Moskitia, beyond all road termini. The settled edges of these eastern forests are known to geographers and conservationists as the "deforestation frontier," a complex space where rain forest two hundred years old and older is giving away rapidly to cattle pasture and subsistence agriculture.

 Olancho

I am concerned primarily with Olancho, a department larger than the country of El Salvador but containing a small fraction of the latter's population. In 2000 Olancho had approximately 420,000 people in 24,351 square kilometers. It is part of highland Honduras but is divided by the rain forest frontier and feels the humid breath of the northeast trade winds. Central Olancho, where I have done most of my research, is dominated by a southwest-to-northeast-trending range known to geographers as the Cordillera de Agalta. No equivalent local name exists for the 150-kilometer chain; each group of peaks and the steep ravines that approach them are known as individually named *montañas*. The cordillera's most extensive forests cloak the high peaks of the Montaña de Babilonia that soar 1,500 to 2,000 meters above the surrounding plains. This area was denominated the Parque Nacional Sierra de Agalta in 1987.

While the *valle* plains of central Olancho have contained important settlements for many centuries, the mountains, by virtue of their remoteness and abrupt topography, have been impacted heavily by humans only in the last hundred years. The Valle de Olancho south of the Cordillera de Agalta contains the major towns of Catacamas and Juticalpa as well as many villages and ranches 400 to 500 meters above sea level. Human activity has reached the tops of nearby summits and has climbed to within 800 vertical meters of the highest peaks (which range from 2,000 to 2,354 meters above sea level). Roads now penetrate deep into the cordillera's southern flanks, and colonist villages founded since 1950 are peopled by immigrants from the adjacent plains as well as from distant parts of Honduras.

On the northern side of the cordillera, the Valle de Gualaco and Valle de Agalta are still rough-hewn, connected to Juticalpa by one dirt road and hooked up to the national electric grid only in the mid-1990s. These two plains are much less populated than the Valle de Olancho, and as yet there are no permanent villages within the cordillera. Road access to Gualaco's Montaña de Babilonia remains minimal, reaching into the pine zone but rarely as far as the rain forest. However, unequal access to land, combined with desire to get away from conflict, has forced many local farmers up into the forest on a seasonal basis, where they inhabit small settlements.

By the 1520s, the central plains of Olancho were being converted to the domain of Spaniards. Thousands of indigenous people died of diseases and in wars or were captured and sold as slaves. Indians became tribute payers; those who would not heed the Church and Crown fled

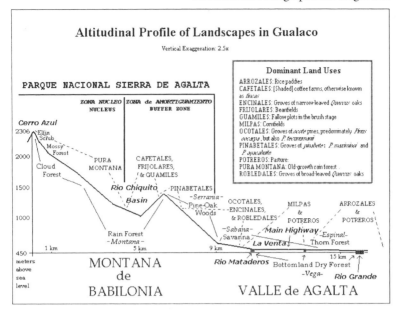

3. Altitudinal profile of landscapes in Gualaco. Based on a sketch by Mary Lee Eggart.

east to the Taguzgalpa. A few tribute towns, most notably Catacamas, were fortunate to be situated on the larger plains where farming was better. The presence of the Catholic Church sometimes served as a palliative for dispossessed local people, whether indigenous or, as the centuries wore on, *mulato,* mestizo, or other castes. In various ways, the king and the Church helped to stem the ascendant power of the ranchers, partly by forcing them to sell their cattle in far-away agricultural fairs, from which they profited little (contraband trade down the big rivers to the English and their minions waiting on the Caribbean coast was thus a quite viable option for one and all). The Church-driven system of *cofradías* (religious brotherhoods) allowed indigenous groups such as the Indios de Catacamas to obtain vast landholdings on which uncountable herds of feral cattle roamed. In 1677, for example, the few hundred Indian families in Catacamas owned three large ranches, one of which contained, by their estimate, sixteen thousand head. A century later, the Indios de Catacamas had expanded their holdings to include close to forty thousand hectares of ranch land, while also holding usufruct rights to much of the Sierra de Agalta. Though by law they could still be whipped in the public square for not keeping their houses clean, the Indios de Catacamas possessed a wealth of resources nearly unparalleled

among tribute Indians (or indeed among any category of landholders)
in colonial Central America. Their wealth, like that of the private land
barons, helped define Olancho in the Honduran imagination: a territory
fecund almost beyond belief. The many social problems were mitigated
by the seemingly endless rich native grass prairies and the river bottomlands ideal for plantains and cassava, while the wild harvest of the plains,
pine forests, and rain forests included mahogany, honey, beeswax, sarsaparilla, sweetgum resin, vanilla, and numerous other valuable natural
products.[13]

The Spanish colonial system gave way to independence in 1821. To
impoverished Olanchanos, this meant the loss of their *cofradías* and
even their supposedly sacrosanct *ejidos* (communal town lands) in the
rush to privatize resources; the winners were the land barons who had
arisen and consolidated power during the late colonial period. In Olancho, throughout the nineteenth century, local and outside large landowners not only gained almost complete dominion of the plains but also
won generous government concessions to exploit natural resources as
Honduras opened its doors to British and U.S. capital. During each
year in the 1850s, for example, thousands of deerskins were shipped from
Trujillo to Boston, and most of these originated in the departments of
Yoro and Olancho.[14]

The nineteenth century saw frequent wars and scuffles between Olanchano rebel factions and the central government, which was constantly
destabilized from within and by other Central American republics. The
endless conflicts were not without rhyme or reason, as they were sometimes portrayed by outsiders seeking to denigrate the region. As Olanchano author José Sarmiento maintains, the wars were in large part, at
least in Olancho, manifestations of unequal access to the land and its
resources.[15] The plains were not only the domains of large ranches; they
also were the staging ground of the government's wars. Wide, flat, treeless expanses were perfect for the displacement of troops and the fighting of battles. Rain forests, on the other hand, were places of refuge for
guerrilla factions, who refused to fight on the plains, preferring to rely
on brief and bloody sallies from the depths of the *montaña*. The small
towns of Olancho rose up continually against the government but were
finally crushed in 1865 when defeated rebels were hung from trees and
their families were exiled. Several towns were burned as well, and memories of this ancient cruelty still afflict the northern towns today.

Even with Liberal reforms and new land laws in the latter part of the nineteenth century, the marginalization of poor farmers in Olancho continued, as did the move toward farming remote, infertile, but safe edges of the deep forests. As recently as 1975, ranchers and the military perpetrated a massacre of *campesino* (poor farmer) land rights activists and Catholic priests. Land rights are still highly conflictive, though there are also titling programs, *campesino* cooperatives, and ranchers who have become export farmers. Advocated by numerous government and nongovernment organizations, "sustainable development" has made modest advances. Gold, which lured Europeans to Olancho, never sustained more than a few. These days, one of the quickest ways to make money in the Valle de Olancho is real estate speculation and development: subdividing ranches into urban subdivisions. Others make their millions buying and selling coffee, cattle, clothes, and other merchandise.

Why do such issues merit attention in a book concerning birds? Because they affect habitat. The fate of the land is the fate of its species, so understanding how a culture perceives and treats its environment is key to understanding relationships between people and birds. The land in Olancho, as throughout rural Latin America, is an absolute, abiding presence — one is born in it and either escapes to the city or deals with it. The land saturates one's being on an intimate level and a grand scale.

Olanchanos, according to Honduran stereotypes, are lazy (a lazy person is known as an *olanchano*), gold-hungry, extremely family-centered, and more than anything, violent. Vendettas between families do indeed run for decades, claiming numerous casualties. But the stereotypical identity of Olancho as "backward" and ultraviolent obscures the actual day-to-day worlds of average everyday people with their everyday jobs, their families, their landscapes, trying to get along. These ordinary citizens, who share a profound sense of place and special relationships with birds, are the Olanchanos celebrated in this book. They are the types of people who make conservation geography possible.

Women, Children, and Birds

Olancho is dominated and controlled by a minority, grown men. Women, especially in the countryside, remain largely within the domestic sphere, and their relationships with birds are quite different than those of men. Women, much more than men, raise their children, especially their girls. Something wonderful happens between children and birds: a depth of feeling and experience that often fades with adulthood, perhaps to be recaptured in old age. How this majority in Olancho relates to birds is underexposed.

When there is talk in the world of conservation about a "culture" of bird killing, the reference is to young males. In my experience, it is the male family members who take on the tasks of stoning and later of hunting. It is the young boys who pluck the beating hearts from hummingbirds and eat them raw, following the age-old belief that their slingshot aim will be magically improved. Women and girls show more protective attitudes and less destructive tendencies toward the avifauna. Girls are socialized into the domestic world centered on the house, the river washing place, and other women's spaces. They are unlikely to be found roaming the hedgerows with slingshots. Such behavior would be frowned upon, like women on a deer hunt. Girls and their mothers have greater opportunity to observe the everyday comings and goings of wrens, swallows, orioles, and other common birds that inhabit the domestic sphere. And it shows. Men can often provide an exhaustive list of the local avifauna but do not know what individual birds are doing from one day to the next. Women, on the other hand, have given me intimate details of avian life histories, though they are less familiar with the men's spaces of field and forest.

How do Honduran *campesinas* manage their domestic spaces? Everywhere in every village, one finds pride in place. Kitchen gardens run riot, flowerpots hanging from the porch overflow with greenery, vines twine along the walls, a crush of fragrant flowering shrubs buzzes with hummingbirds and sphinx moths, fruit trees of all descriptions droop with frugivorous avifauna. Though only a few people have told me they plant certain flowers or fruit solely to attract birds, most are effusive in their praise of those birds that visit their gardens, whether planned for or not. At certain times, *tres pesos,* Short-billed Pigeons, come down from the cloud forest into the yards of Comunayaca, saddening the women with their calls. People are welded to their homes and to the cloud forest *montaña* through the echoes of such calls year after year, through a nostalgia that reverberates in their souls. And there are the *viuditas,* the Blue-gray Tanagers that gladden the gardens of Juticalpa. How must they sound to lonely expatriate Olanchanas who smuggle these birds into their Miami apartments?

I remember an old woman who lived in a cottage in the village of Las Delicias off the north side of the Parque Nacional Cerro Azul-Meambar in north-central Honduras. With eyes alight, she told me of the orioles, tanagers, toucans, and motmots that frequented her lavishly landscaped garden. Most of all, she cherished the daily visits of the *urraca,* the Green Jay, and she knew its schedule perfectly. It is impossible for me to do justice to the depth of feeling with which she expressed her love for this sublimely beautiful bird, but it is a feeling I have encountered in certain types of people in every village I have visited, though not in every house, nor only in women: an ornithophilic dialogue as deep as a lifetime of watching, one that does not grow old, one that can be renewed every day.

The Mendozas of El Boquerón

From youngest to oldest, they are Denis, Norma, Carolina, Nahún, Edin, Geraldina, and Antonio (Tonito). They live with their mother Margarita and father José in the village of El Boquerón off to the side of the great and productive Valle de Olancho, a two-minute walk from the highway between Catacamas and Juticalpa along which buses and pickups race at suicidal speeds. Their wattle-and-daub house perches on a pebbly bluff twenty meters above the Río de Olancho and its rich bottomland pastures, maize fields, and woods. Behind the village, soaring eight hundred meters above the stream, twin peaks define the gaping maw of Boquerón, its crumbly limestone precipices streaked by seeping minerals and draped in agave. Invisible under the thick canopy of the gallery forest, imagine a rocky trail threading the gorge, emerging several hours later on the upper side in the cul-de-sac vale of La Avispa, "The Wasp," where more Mendoza families live. From El Boquerón village, another trail scrabbles to get above the canyon walls, zigzagging through the giddily tilted pastures of Cerro Agua Buena and into the clouds enveloping thirty-four small coffee *fincas*. The Mendozas, like other families in El Boquerón and La Avispa, spend most of the year on the hot, dry plain but periodically escape to the cool mountain refuge of Agua Buena. The village, the canyon, and the mountain are their boundaries of home.

The youngest Mendozas attend grade school in the village, and the next older ones bicycle an hour to middle school in the larger settlement of Jutiquile. The oldest children ride the bus to high school in Juticalpa. Most of *doña* Margarita and *don* José's extra income goes toward defraying the expenses of educating their family.

Beginning the rainy season in June, 1998, the Mendoza girls tended a fledgling *frijolera* (White-winged Dove) they called Julia. The bedraggled creature had tumbled from its arboreal nest down by the river. The children raised it as a pet after clipping its wings. Julia slept inside the Mendoza house, in a *zorzal* (Clay-colored Robin) nest they had procured. But in a destiny typical of childhood treasures, the neighbors' children stole Julia later on that year. Meanwhile, the *zanates* (Great-tailed Grackles) nested as usual in the scarred old yucca tree by the fence, and the Mendozas repeatedly rescued the gawky nestlings that kept toppling out and plunging into their mud yard.

Torrejas (Masked Tityras), *tilises* (Collared Aracaris), and other frugivorous birds visit the luscious hog plum trees in their yard from time to time, and the *nichos* (Great Kiskadees and Social Flycatchers) never let up with their racket. The Mendozas suffer a Striped Cuckoo to eat some of the grain scattered for the chickens. They don't know what the bird is called but think it is a relative of the roadrunner.

Unlike Juticalpa urchins, the Mendozas are not hemmed in by high walls or threatened by busy streets. They have the run of fields and woods that resound with bird calls and cicada buzz by day, amphibian hiccups and Double-striped Thick-knee cries by night. They take every opportunity to be in the river, where they play and bathe. The girls have to help wash clothes in the current and carry brimming buckets on their heads back up to the house whenever the village water system goes out of service. Most of the year, the Río de Olancho is a shallow, limpid creek, a perfect place for human and bird activity. The *zórzalo* (Black Phoebe) can often be seen flitting up and down the river, and the Mendozas know where it nests up by a popular swimming hole. *Garcitas* (herons) are common; *pájaros pesqueros* (kingfishers) include the smaller green ones and the large and raucous blue ones. Occasionally, a *pespita* (Spotted Sandpiper) teeters along the bank.

The *rínzon* (Royal Flycatcher) frequents the middle part of the gorge, making its nest in vine tangles overhanging the current. It is a favorite with the children, who try to observe that bird's special characteristic, a beautiful red crest. Its *turbante* is usually tucked against its head, giving the *rínzon* a hammer-headed appearance. However, when the children are patient and curious, they get to see it flip its "turban" in a courtship display or while it is bathing. Seeing the Royal Flycatcher do this is as spectacular an event for the Mendoza children as glimpsing a male quetzal in full breeding plumage (something they are privileged to witness from time to time up on Agua Buena). They are depressed by the treatment the *rínzon* receives at the hands of unscrupulous youths who attack its easily accessible nests with their machetes, just for the fun of doing something malicious.

I came to know the Mendozas in 1992 through an environmental project that sought to aid local people who wanted to protect the area. El Boquerón, now part of a *monumento natural*, contains patches of endangered tropical dry forest, important flora and fauna, and historical and archaeological sites. The present-day village, founded in the mid-twentieth century, is located on top of the ruins of the Villa de San Jorge del Valle de Olancho, one of the original Spanish administrative centers of Honduras, founded in the early 1540s. For a few decades it had around forty Spanish families who sustained themselves on their tribute Indians and are said to have grown wealthy off the gold panned by African slaves and Indian laborers in the nearby Río Guayape. Owing to constant uprisings and Indian attacks, the town did not last long; it was abandoned around 1590. Legend has it that the twin peaks are remnants of a volcanic eruption that did away with San Jorge and its residents in 1612. Archaeological evidence of San Jorge is abundant in the village. After hard rains, shards of sixteenth-century blue glazed pottery turn up, along with copper weights, spoons, and other artifacts. Precolumbian relics are abundant as well, with mound sites in the village and floodplain and in the area of La Avispa. Caves also usually contain evidence of ancient burials (the three-thousand-year-old Talgua Caves ossuary is not far away).[1]

Since the Monumento Natural El Boquerón was established in 1993, it has become known as an attractive area of easy access for urban Hondurans and foreign ecotourists. Its scenery is spectacular, and the protected dry forest river corridor often affords views of monkeys, trogons, anteaters, and squirrels. Clouds of salt-seeking butterflies dance around those who come to swim or wash their pickup trucks in the torrent. Smartly attired city slickers look askance at the semicircle of silent, ragged, and slightly muddy village children, some malnourished, some naked. Outsiders accustomed to such villages, to the flies, to the mud or dust impregnated with cattle dung and human fecal matter, penetrate the barriers of wealth, class, and silence, finding someone — more often than not a Mendoza — who will take them to the Tepescuintle Cave, to a better swimming hole, or to search out birds. We outsiders, lumbering after the children, find ourselves clumsy and ignorant of the Mendozas' countryside in this minute corner of Olancho with all its secrets. Nor do many visitors suspect that the Mendoza children have been the backbone of several environmental projects and are members of an NGO that has coordinated youth camps, teacher education workshops, and trail building.

When conservationists became interested in Boquerón back in 1992, José Mendoza was the first person we met. *Don* José, like most other local farmers, had been active in fire-fallow agriculture much of his life and was in part responsible for the stripped hillsides. But he found an easier and less conflictive employment in COHDEFOR, the government forestry agency, as guardian of an expensive radio relay station on the top of Cerro Agua Buena. In his youth in Guacoca, a village on the far side of the mountain, *don* José had trailed along behind gatherers and hunters who delved into the forests for sarsaparilla, vanilla, medicinals, honey, and meat for the table. He learned considerable lore from the old-timers and possesses a knowledge of the woods that is all too rare these days. Of all the Olanchanos I have met, he is among the most entwined with the forest, the most married to it—Agua Buena is almost all he talks about. This spirit, to a greater or lesser degree, has permeated the rest of his family.

Doña Margarita is from another part of Olancho but has also lived her share in the forest. When she and *don* José began their life together, they homesteaded on Agua Buena, growing chickens and vegetables and starting their coffee farm. But for Margarita, the *montaña* was not a place to raise children: too far away from medical care and schooling. She still loves it all the same and, like the rest of the family, sometimes thinks that she would rather live up there than on the plains.

Excursions with the Mendoza children are educational for me, because they know the current hideouts of numerous birds. One suffocating April morning in 1996, Edin, Nahún, and I set out upstream along the trail to La Avispa in search of roosting *bujajas* (night-herons). In one shady copse, hundreds of *zorzales* (Clay-colored Robins) flocked on the ground, the river banks, bushes, and trees. Nahún and Edin told me that they would soon be nesting.

We lingered at a spiny *coyol* palm in a pasture. Calling my attention to a fist-sized hole near the crown, they informed me that it held the nest of a *hueteté* (White-fronted Parrot) they had been watching for several weeks. A few days after they pointed out the nest to me, the *coyol* was cut down. Someone wanted the nestlings for pets, meat, or sale.

We rambled on from nest to roost. The children pointed out an oriole nest swinging over the river here and a new *urrupa* (Chestnut-headed Oropendola) colony there. I was infected by Nahún and Edin's vocal enthusiasm for nature. This reached a fever pitch when we heard screaming from the other side of the river and were alerted to the presence of monkeys. None of us had ever seen *micos* (white-faced monkeys) so close to the village, and we tore off through the slapping brush to get closer glimpses of a large troop feasting on wild figs.

After we returned to the house, they recounted our adventures to the rest of the family. In this way—by traversing the land again and again, then telling stories about their exploits, and having these repeated—the children of El Boquerón become inextricably entangled with their landscape. After that hike, the places where the *huetetés* nested, and where we saw the monkeys, became new significant places on their mental maps. Memorable experiences with animals, and especially their retelling, are the ways that avian landscapes become inscribed in the souls of children.

🐝 *White-eared Ground Sparrows in the Coffee* Montaña

In May, 1997, Nahún Mendoza discovered a White-eared Ground-Sparrow nest up on Agua Buena. It was important evidence of a breeding population of a Middle American highland endemic that had never before been recorded in Honduras. We were on an overnight excursion to the peak in search of an elusive eagle that was said to be hanging about the coffee farms. The first afternoon, I glimpsed a ground-sparrow flitting off through the coffee bushes, and though we pursued it to the edge of a dark thicket, I couldn't snap a photo as scientific proof. As dusk set in and their calls resounded from all about, we realized that there was a population of the elusive birds on Agua Buena. The following morning, Nahún flushed an individual from its nest, which contained a naked nestling and an egg and was woven into the herbal tangle on the ground in the middle of the trail. Because I couldn't take a photo without moving the nest, we returned several months later and Nahún encountered the abandoned nest still intact.

Observant local people like the Mendoza's are aware of the White-eared Ground-Sparrow, though they have no name for it and did not know that they owned its only known habitat in Honduras. Is this population threatened by their practices? Its penchant for nesting on mule trails could certainly put nestlings at risk. The birds might also be threatened by dogs that accompany families during the December to February coffee harvest. As for habitat fragmentation, often cited as a primary reason for avian vulnerability, the bird will probably thrive as long as traditional, shaded, chemical-free coffee remains the dominant use of land. Since 1989, no one has burned their land on Agua Buena, and a tenacious cattle rancher was finally dissuaded from allowing his animals to trample and chew up the coffee farms.

A landscape containing many small coffee farms tends toward complexity and diversity, especially in highly irregular terrain that is not yet (and may never be) accessible to motor vehicles. While the coffee stays, biodiversity has a chance, despite the isolation of Cerro Agua Buena's forest, ringed by pastures. However, a narrow corridor still connects the humid coffee forests of Agua Buena with the tropical dry forest in the canyon of the Río de Olancho. From the canyon, a ribbon of forest ascends the tributary Quebrada de Avispa to rendezvous with the vast rain forests of the Sierra de Agalta, which in turn share an unbroken canopy connecting the Honduran and Nicaraguan Moskitia. Agua Buena, though not old-growth forest, can still be reached by monkeys, jaguars, and tapirs. Three-wattled Bellbirds, probably from Agalta, still appear occasionally during the coffee harvest. The Mendozas, and most of the rest of the owners of Agua Buena, are hoping that the old pastures will all return to woods. They want new forests for coffee, cooler temperatures, and thousands more *zapotillo* trees, an Agua Buena specialty, sustaining even greater swarms of pacas and agoutis, succulent game animals that have been on the increase in recent years. Birds such as Agua Buena's signature quetzals and guans will also thrive and prosper. This is the current hope of three generations of small coffee farmers.

Agua Buena holds a prominent place in the lives of families like the Mendozas. They have spent many harvests there in their small tin-roofed houses, suffering from weeks of cold rain and clammy mud, thousands of swarming ticks, *chuluyos* (assassin bugs that carry the deadly Chagas disease), coral snakes, and other curses. In 1999, I was haunted by a girl whose leg had withered from the bite of a *barba amarilla* (fer-de-lance), the deadliest snake in Honduras. She was not bitten on Agua Buena, where *barbas* are unknown, but she was condemned to spend the year there, out of school, cooking and washing for her father, who made a pittance maintaining other people's coffee farms. Eventually, the doctors who saved her life adopted her and took her away to live, with the father's consent.

Is Agua Buena just where the poor are condemned to end up because the good land on the plains is all taken? Is the coffee harvest — three months out of every year of the Mendozas' lives — part of the abject cost of survival, or are there benefits to spending Christmas vacation in the *montaña*? The Mendoza house perches on the edge of a thrust fault, and they can gaze down into the Valle de Olancho spread out like a map, waking up to what most plains dwellers never see in a lifetime, the cartography of a world. In the east, the sun rises from behind the mountains that stretch toward Nicaragua. On clear mornings, Agua Buena is already alight when the plains are plunged in shadow; during the day, while the lowlands swelter, the *montaña* is always cool. In the mountains there is no malaria, scourge of the plains. Down below are the paved road, the big haciendas and agribusinesses, and other reminders of the Mendozas' position at the bottom, backward, marginal, underdeveloped. When they go to the *montaña,* some of that oppressive feeling dissipates under the spell of the power they hold over the one place that belongs to them. Agua Buena holds them and sustains them in far more than simply coffee and bush meat.

Carolina Mendoza has her own mountain garden, the guava trees by the house bedecked in bromeliads, orchids, and ferns, tied in place with strips from plastic bags. Antonio is studying to become an agronomist. Nahún would rather live in the forest than on the plains. The White-eared Ground-Sparrow has a future on thirty-four small coffee farms.

The Urbinas of La Venta

On the edge of the village of La Venta in the Valle de Agalta, Esteban Urbina and his wife *doña* Edita have been raising a large family for over two decades on a fifteen-acre plot they bought back in the days when land on the plains was cheap. Their oldest son, Francisco, now in his early thirties, and his wife Fausta, have four children of their own. A few years ago, *don* Esteban and *doña* Edita gave their son a corner of the farm on which to build a house. The younger sons, Esteban and Lucas, still live in their parents' house, while the daughters, some of whom are also married and have children, live elsewhere and visit on weekends.

Francisco Urbina, who is now a conservationist and one of Honduras's leading bird experts, spent his early childhood in Santa María del Carbón, a Pech Indian village northeast of the Valle de Agalta, where his grandfather had made a living as a homesteader and schoolteacher. There, in the 1960s, the Urbinas' poverty was absolute: they barely survived from their farming, gathering, hunting, and fishing. The family often went hungry, and Francisco mentioned to me that it is amazing he is still alive after contracting so many diseases — diphtheria, whooping cough, measles, mumps, malaria, dengue, and the intestinal parasites. *Doña* Edita and *don* Esteban longed for a better life, which began in the more fertile and less remote Valle de Agalta. During the first few years their land, part of a former hacienda, was covered by open fields. White-tailed deer were abundant, emerging from the woods at dusk to feed on the pasture edges. Scarlet Macaws plied the gallery forests in large flocks; *cacaos* (Red-throated Caracaras) were as common as Black Vultures. Today, the Valle de Agalta is almost completely subdivided by barbed wire, pastures are saturated with pesticides, and deer have been hunted so heavily that they only come out at night, up in the steepest pine forest ravines on the slopes of the Montaña de Babilonia. Macaws and *cacaos* are all but gone.

During their decades in La Venta, *doña* Edita and *don* Esteban raised a family of three boys and five girls. Their ever-expanding gang of rambunctious grandchildren are raised fully immunized, with outhouses, electricity, and a nearby main road. Most will graduate from high school, and perhaps from college. But like their parents, aunts, and uncles, they still find joy among the woods and hedgerows. *Doña* Edita and *don* Esteban would never consider subjecting their families to life in a city as so many others have done. Both have told me they hate cities because there are no orchards, rivers, birds, cattle, or deer.

While *don* Esteban, like his neighbors, initially thinned out the *monte alto* (high forest) of the bottomland along the Río Mataderos, simultaneously he encouraged reforestation of the pastures to provide his growing herd of livestock with shade and browse. The open woods and savannas that the Urbinas favor for their cattle also yield fence posts, firewood, medicinal plants; provide cover for *codornices* (Crested Bobwhites), *chachalacas,* and other game birds; and give many other benefits that a pure grass pasture would not. They have planted or protected so many different kinds of fruit trees that ravening birds and children are rewarded on almost any day of the year. The Urbinas have a mango grove in the bottomland that yields thousands of fruits in June and July. During good years, hundreds of fallen mangos are devoured by maggots, wild and domestic mammals gorge themselves, and birds feast in the canopy. Even after this "natural tax," enough fruits remain for the Urbina children to keep busy every morning carrying armloads back to their houses. But because families can never consume all the fruits their mangos produce, children are also frequent envoys to the neighbors. Here, as everywhere in Olancho, the gift of mangos is also a show of neighborhood solidarity. *Don* Esteban has devised a management system to ensure that the neighbors are not offended but that they neither steal all his fruit nor take potshots at the doves, parrots, saltators, and thrushes that make easy targets. Every morning of mango season, during his daily rounds of the property, he heaps three or four piles of ripe mangos in places where neighbors' children will come across them, knocks down fifteen or twenty more for his own family, and leaves the rest to the birds and animals. As he has commented to me, woe unto any neighbor's child who passes the limit!

Certain boys in La Venta, with the implicit consent of their parents, enjoy killing birds and other fauna whenever they have the opportunity. *Don* Esteban was raised that way and used to tolerate this behavior in his children. In recent years, since their son Francisco has become an influential conservationist, the Urbinas have tried to keep slingshots off their property, teaching their ever-growing number of grandchildren to tattle on neighbor children who break their rules. The land is now a de facto nature reserve, with over ninety species of woody plants and abundant herbaceous growth hosting a rich faunal diversity.

For the Urbina children and grandchildren, the biodiversity of their farm has provided endless educational amusement. Besides birds and fruit, there are frogs and toads, water opossums and tamandua anteaters, beetles and squirrels, crayfish and mushrooms, crabs and fish. One can always discover something, protect it, or perhaps bring it home for the soup. The Urbinas' youngest daughter Edita once bragged to me of a tiny *cucarachero* (wren) nest tucked off in a hedgerow. She was the wren family's protector and monitored the nestlings in secrecy, afraid to betray their hiding place to boys. In 1995, a Tropical Pewee established its territory around *doña* Fausta's house, and in the dawn hours her family could observe it making the rounds of accustomed perches, calling. One morning, when the bird strayed across the fence, it was caught by children from the neighboring house, strangled, and tossed back over into the Urbinas' yard. Francisco told me that his children were devastated.

I have often wondered about the fate of Honduran children's games in the age of television. In Juticalpa, children rarely play together in the streets any more, and even the diversions of Luz's youth are losing out to video games and cartoons. But in the countryside, the culture still is strong. I was thrilled one day, watching the Urbina grandchildren playing El Gavilán, "The Hawk." This is a popular role-playing game with many variations in Honduras, involving a hawk, a chicken, and her chicks. Elvin, energetic and talkative, was asked by his exasperated mother Fausta, "Comiste pía? Comiste loro?" (Did you eat a Brown Jay or a parrot?).

The grandchildren are too young to roam far from the yard. On the other hand, Lucas and Esteban Junior know the good swimming holes, every fruit tree and when it fruits, how to milk cows and rope calves, and myriad other tasks and diversions. Lucas seems most like his father of all the siblings and hangs on every word of the elder Urbina's hunting stories, which include harrowing encounters with jaguars, mountain lions, white-lipped peccary, and white-tailed bucks with large racks.

In June, 1998, I spent a morning with Lucas looking for *aguiluches* (Ornate Hawk-Eagles) that had been hanging around the farm and whatever other birds we could find. In a newly sown maize field below the house, we visited the *espantapájaros* (scarecrow) Lucas had made to frighten *huachires* (Melodious Blackbirds)—devastating pests—away from the field. It served its purpose well and was a better tactic than throwing stones or setting off firecrackers.

An awkward escape of vultures indicated the carcass of one of the Urbinas' calves that had wandered into a neighbor's pasture and been poisoned by chemical-saturated grass, an all-too-frequent hazard these days. We encountered Esteban Senior and Junior down in the *vegas* (bottomlands) planting corn at eight in the morning. They had arisen several hours earlier and were ready to eat the breakfast Lucas had brought them. They would continue for a couple more hours before moving on to other tasks. *Don* Esteban suggested we try out a backswamp where the *cocoleca* (Gray-necked Wood-Rail) had been in evidence.

There were no *cocolecas* to be seen, so we decided to walk in the current of the Río Mataderos, which reaches two feet in depth. Lucas told me that when his parents first arrived in La Venta, the river, which rises in the Montaña de Babilonia, had been deeper and colder. *Jicoteas* (river turtles) abounded in the old days, but a man came in and harvested them to sell their meat, virtually extinguishing the local population. Larger fish had been common as well—once, Lucas had caught one of the coveted *cuyamel*. Nowadays, a rare "big" fish is around ten inches, and the main attractions are *camarones* (crayfish) and *canechas* (crabs). *Canechas* became our special mission: Lucas needed some for a medicinal soup his mother was making. We hunted at the ford of the trail from La Venta to the nearby hamlet called El Ocotal, and there was frequent traffic, including a riderless horse galloping at full tilt, pursued by angry wasps.

By this hour of the morning, birds were becoming scarce. Lucas pointed out the cavity nest of a *chaco* (Golden-fronted Woodpecker) high in a riverside walnut tree. Because he had observed parent *chacos* during previous breeding seasons, he could predict when this brood would hatch and how long after that they would fledge. Lucas knew of many other birds along the river—when and where they nested, what they ate, and what ate them.

After Esteban showed up to join Lucas in the swimming hole, we went back to the house to rest. The family talked of how they give common animals many names. They call the Black Vulture *zopilote, zope,* or *cabeza pelada* ("bald head"). "Bird" can be *ave, pájaro, pajarito,* or *pajarraco.* The dewlap has two names: *güergüera* and *charcha.* They quizzed me on six names for one animal, none of which I knew: *ñanca, ñura, tendones lisos, guángara, clinuda,* and one that they were too embarrassed to mention. These all referred to the Central American agouti or *guatuza,* one of the most common mammals in the area. The Urbinas used the example of the agouti to underscore their firm belief that local people know much more than what is in Francisco's guidebooks. Of the people I know in Olancho, the Urbinas are among the most secure about the validity of their own ways of knowing. Even Francisco himself, who interacts with conservationists and biologists from around the globe, still holds firm to this world of empirical evidence and tradition. As has been the case for Lucas, Francisco's primary source of knowledge as a child was direct experience and his father's and mother's wisdom. But even *don* Esteban is not immune to Lucas's questing mind, when the true facts about some bird or other creature are in doubt. As Francisco did before him, Lucas has learned the value of arguing and asserting his own view. If he has seen something his father has said couldn't be, then this may be cause for revision of their canon. The Urbinas are a family who reach their truths through long and sometimes contentious discussion, believing little about nature that they haven't seen or can't verify.

🐦 Two Olanchano families live intertwined with their landscapes of home, attentive not only to domestic flora and fauna but to wild species as well. The Mendozas and Urbinas are not mavericks. They stand for an aspect of rural Honduran culture about which little has been written: people's love of nature. This does not mean they let blackbirds destroy their crops or let hawks prey upon their chickens. Their ornithophilia is practical, founded in management of the land, *their* land. Birds are still abundant precisely because La Venta is a village of gardens (to which I return in chapter 6), and Agua Buena a forest of coffee. In villages such as these, many people appreciate birds and maintain abundant habitat on the small pieces of land that belong to them. Their children are raised on this land, and its birds are their birds.

Think of what a conservation project would miss by not hearing the voices of the household, not recognizing the feelings that common garden and field birds can summon. I wonder about the wisdom of conservation projects that focus primordially and sometimes exclusively on male farmers and hunters in or near old-growth rain forests. Can that be effective in a country where biodiversity and people are spread evenly across a patchwork of arid and humid habitats? Why not begin at the fulcrum of everyday life, the home and its surrounding landscape? This would entail working with women, encouraging them to do more of what they are already doing — attracting and protecting birds, and teaching their children. Women and children are the majority, and recognition of their efforts could work wonders for conservation.

Children are the guardians of nests more often than the persecutors. In their trespasses through hedgerows and mango orchards, the landscape gets written all over them. They are haunted by birds and other beings, even as they learn to possess and manage the land. I suspect that in due course many will be like the old woman in Las Delicias, watching for the gorgeous *urraca*.

Counterpoint of *Zorzal* and *Zopilote* in Juticalpa

[In the old days], clouds of loras, guaras, garzas, *and other birds could be seen at dawn crossing the sky, and returning to their roosts at dusk. As winter approached, great numbers of* golondrinas *would swirl over the city, announcing the rainy season. Under the eaves of the tile roofs, tiny brown birds called* cucaracheros *made their nests.*

Victor Rubí Zapata, from *Mi Juticalpa y yo*

Latin American urban areas may not seem likely candidates for havens of biodiversity. Given their pressing social problems, it may appear pointless to write of the relationships they foster between birds and people. However, for many city dwellers, wild things hold great significance: birds are not taken for granted as they might be in the countryside. Birds are not irrelevant to urban society but are part of a city's environmental well-being, a phenomenon that is taking on more and more importance in Honduras these days. Not only do wild species reflect the environmental health of the city; they also impress their value into the minds of decision makers who hold sway over the fate of the countryside and the rain forests.

The Greening of Juticalpa

As the decades pass and the world comes ever more quickly to Juticalpa, it grows in size and density, each year more clogged with pickup trucks and supermarkets, dust and street crime. During the lives of its octogenarians, Juticalpa has burgeoned from a tranquil, colonial-style town to a boisterous city of thirty thousand with glistening modern banks, paved streets, throbbing nightclubs, a GMC dealership, two universities, and more and more modern houses replacing the traditional whitewashed adobe and *bajareque* (wattle-and-daub) dwellings. Juticalpa continues to expand into the surrounding countryside, making strolls out of town more difficult and less desirable. What were once shaded country lanes are now dusty thoroughfares devoid of trees, offering views of scrubby fields awaiting real estate development. The conversion of cattle pasture to subdivision reflects an economic shift for Olancho's wealthy class from an increasingly outmoded and impractical pastoralism to land "development" and "improvement."

The Río Juticalpa, which meanders through town, was once a wide, deep current bordered by giant *gualiqueme* trees. It is a shadow of its former self, a mere trickle most of the year, but a muddy behemoth during the rainy season. The peak of Candeleros north of town was once a forested *montaña* but is now pasture. The great clouds of parrots that cast shadows have been reduced to seasonal flocks of a few hundred, while the *guara roja,* the Scarlet Macaw, is gone altogether.

Many long-time Juticalpa residents are unequivocal in their condemnation of modernization for its effects on the natural environment, even while they recognize the benefits of synthetic medicine, piped water and sewage, and ample educational opportunities. But the pastoral idyll of earlier days, when town gave way to country only a few blocks from the plaza, when the river was clear and deep and the backdrop of peaks was cloaked in a deep blue canopy, is a subtle presence in the lives of many who remember. Others perhaps have less reason to cherish memories of a rigid, impoverished past and hold positive visions of a clean and shining future. However, the nostalgic and the progressive also meet: Juticalpa's Sociedad Cultural (cultural society) and its city government have supported several architectural restorations, schools have carried out small reforestation projects, and the Parque Central (plaza), still the heart of town, is cleaner and greener than it has been in many years. In one notable episode in 1999, local employees of the Honduran energy authority, ENEE, pruned branches away from electric lines along the main highway. Immediately, many citizens complained to city government officials, who in turn appealed to the forestry agency, COHDEFOR, for help in applying a fine to the "destructores del medio ambiente" (destroyers of the environment). Meanwhile, concerned *juticalpenses* continued searching for solutions to the problems of an overflowing municipal garbage dump and undersized community slaughterhouse.

It might be thought that current environmental consciousness is a recent import in the wave of *ambientalismo* (environmentalism) cresting over Honduras. But Juticalpa's "green" pride has antecedents in its own cultural history as well. A set of municipal environmental restrictions from the 1870s included strict control of the river as well as maintenance of *fajinas* (greenbelts) that bordered the town, protected for their firewood, fruit, and other natural products.[1] Nor were municipal decrees frivolous or unheeded — *doña* Clara, Luz Bonta's mother, remembers the strict control that authorities exercised over the use of the river in the 1950s. People were not allowed to bathe or wash clothes immediately upstream from where the community's drinking water was drawn.

Visitors often comment on the lack of huge trees in Juticalpa, and while the casual outsider might attribute this to a generalized "deforestation," it also has a specific history. During the Second World War, the military intruded into people's backyard *patios* and cut down their tall trees, supposedly to deprive terrorists of perches from which to shoot down planes. One of the few old trees saved was "hugged" in desperation: the historic tamarind that still stands in the yard of a local high school survived because the director refused to budge and preferred to risk being shot.

World War Two is not the only reason that few large trees have existed in Juticalpa until recently. Many types of big trees are anathema because of damage from their roots and danger of falling branches. In an ink sketch of the town from the 1850s, the central plaza is bare, whereas today it has a nearly closed canopy.[2] It is probable that the proximity of town and countryside in former days, and the availability of fruits and other tree products in the *fajinas,* meant there was formerly no need for the intensive use of private space that we find today. As Juticalpa grows, vacant lots between houses fill in, and as land values rise, owners subdivide their lots, while individual families wall in their backyards. Two generations ago, a backyard *patio* was a common space used by a block of homes; now, each home has its own private *patio.* In addition, recent *ambientalismo* in Honduras has favored public and private reforestation, though narrowness of streets and sidewalks precludes most tree planting in public. City government officials, aware that they might be targeted as destroyers of the environment, no longer force people to shave their

1. Francisco Urbina discusses birds with the Santos family
outside their house near the headwaters of the Río Chiquito.

2. Lucas Urbina with the scarecrow he made to
frighten away birds from his father's cornfield.

All photos by the author unless otherwise noted.

3. View of La Venta from a nearby Sierra de Agalta slope. The main highway through the Valle de Agalta cuts across the top of the photo. Vegetation shifts from open *sabana* to thick *vega* along the Río Mataderos.

4. Mangos, plantains, and *coyol* palms in and above the *vega* of the Río Mataderos at La Venta.

5. Two Urbina children and a friend go off to round up the family's cattle.

6. View of Sierra de Agalta and a corner of the Valle de Agalta. Open plains alternate with strips of pine forest in the *valle*; the mountain slopes contain pine at lower elevations and broadleaf higher up.

7. El Encino, a village in northwestern Olancho. The view shows the prevalence of thick vegetation near houses, the fields and *guamiles* surrounding the village, and the pine on nearby slopes.

8. A house in the municipality of Esquipulas del Norte. The pattern in earthen paint on the wall represents the mountainous landscape. House is constructed of wattle-and-daub (*bajareque*) with a combined tile and thatch roof. To the left is a dense dooryard garden.

9. North slope of Cerro Agua Buena during the burning season. Cattle and agriculture have stripped the mountain of vegetation, but shaded coffee farms (behind and above the photographer) have helped prevent a similar fate for its highest reaches.

10. A representative nonfrontier landscape of the Olancho Mountains, showing a mixture of land uses including dense forest, pasture with *coyol* palms, pine woods, *guamiles,* and grain crops. This region, in the municipality of Yocón, has been ranched and farmed since at least the 1700s, according to land titles.

11. View from Las Delicias del Murmullo across the gorge of the Río Catacamas to the *pura montaña* of the Sierra de Agalta. Here Three-wattled Bellbirds and howler monkeys can be heard almost every day.

12. The taming of the *montaña cruda:* a settler cabin deep in the Sierra de Agalta above the Planes de Babilonia. Workers had been observing the nesting habits of a White-crowned Parrot at the edge of their clearing. Using chainsaws, they had created the clearing for a coffee farmer who had paid them to deforest within the nucleus of the Parque Nacional Sierra de Agalta.

13. Social marginalization leads to the farming of "impossible" slopes. Farmers from the Gualaco village of Linares at the very edge of the Parque Nacional Sierra de Agalta nucleus have founded a seasonal community at the ecotone of *serranía* and *montaña*. They have nowhere left in their home village to grow their subsistence crop, beans.

14. Outlier of the deforestation front in the Río Chiquito watershed above the Valle de Agalta. Behind the near ridge the high peaks of Cerro Azul and Pico de Agalta, cloaked in *pura montaña*, rise 2,300 meters above sea level.

15. A Valle de Agalta thorn *sabana* at the onset of the rainy season. This cattle ranch is prime habitat for the Honduran Emerald.

16. The Sabana de La Lima, first confirmed recent site for the endemic Honduran Emerald in Olancho, converted to rice paddies. In the background, the Valle de Agalta gives way abruptly to the Sierra de Agalta. Though rich in rails, whistling-ducks, and other waterfowl, the rice paddies replace the native thorn forest and its compliment of biota. Since this photo was taken in 1996, the paddies have been abandoned.

17. *Vega* forest along the Río de Olancho at El Boquerón village glistens in the June sunlight. The limestone cliffs of the Cerro del Boquerón soar 800 meters above the water.

18. A Magnolia Warbler in a coffee bush along the Río Mataderos at La Venta.

19. A feral Rock Dove has been attracted to nest under the eaves of a house in El Encino.

20. An *alma de perro* (Lesser Roadrunner, center left) blends into the cinder-strewn landscape near Las Lomas. Honduran folklore describes the bird as an accursed woman "with the soul of a dog" forced to roam the desolate hillsides forever unable to quench its thirst. Conservationists interpret the expanding range of the Lesser Roadrunner as an omen of desertification.

21. A Violaceous Trogon (*coa*) during mating season in the El Boquerón gorge near La Avispa.

22. Cattle Egrets (*garcitas bueyeras*) near a farm pond in La Empalizada.

23. Lucita in her mother's *jardín* outside their house in Juticalpa.

24. Francisco Urbina on a birding trip to the Río Chiquito. He is standing on a notch in a *liquidambar* (sweetgum) that has been tapped heavily for its resin.

25. This Rufous-capped Warbler, known locally by the generic name *chipe*, is a common and tame denizen of the humid *guamiles* on the lower slopes of the Sierra de Agalta.

26. Nahun Mendoza sips coffee on a foggy afternoon at his parents' wattle-and-daub house on Cerro Agua Buena.

27. Midriff of the Valle de Olancho, traversed by the Río Guayape. This rainy season panorama was taken from the Mendoza house on top of Cerro Agua Buena. The most distant mountains rise near the border with Nicaragua.

28. Berta Muñoz
in her garden in Juticalpa.
Photo courtesy of
Daniel Graham.

29. Dolores "Lolita" Mayorquín in her backyard in Juticalpa.
Photo courtesy of Daniel Graham.

30. The coffee *montaña*.

31. El Boquerón: Gorge of the Río de Olancho.

32. Julia the *frijolera* (White-winged Dove), cared for by the Mendoza children of El Boquerón.

33. *Pichiches* (Black-bellied Whistling-Ducks) kept as pets in Gualaco.

34. Francisco Urbina chats about *cacaos* (Red-throated Caracaras)
with Olivia García in Las Lomas.

35. *Tincute* (Turkey Vulture) on a pine forest perch.

yards bald. They encourage spraying campaigns and other measures to combat the hazard of malarial and dengue-ridden mosquitos that thrive in thick, dank growth.

Black Vultures and Public Space

Contemplated from any hill above town, Juticalpa appears forested, owing to the vegetation bursting out of almost every backyard. In stark contrast, the person in the street sees little greenery outside Parque Flores, popularly called Parque Central, the town plaza. Without probing into *patios* and the occasional front garden, one may remain unaware of the many birds that inhabit and visit Juticalpa. Most of these are familiar local species, but Neotropical migrants can also be found, and some even spend their nonbreeding seasons here. For example, in 1991 and again in 1992, a Hooded Warbler spent several months in the undergrowth at the back of the *patio* of the house I rented as a Peace Corps volunteer.

Our only fondness for the (now demolished) open-air restaurant across the street from *doña* Clara's house, which blared music and occasional gunfire until the wee hours, was the row of four African oil palms out front. For three consecutive years, I observed a "wintering" Yellow Warbler that gleaned in the palms all day long, despite the dust and noise of the street. Luz and *doña* Clara noticed the bird as well, even though neither they nor anyone else had a name for it other than *chipe,* which translates as "small chipping bird." Nevertheless, the Yellow Warbler meant something to Luz and to her mother, a small consolation for the decade-long crucible of the restaurant.

The built environment of Juticalpa favors certain nesting birds. Most notable are the feral *palomas de Castilla* (Rock Doves) and the House Sparrows. The latter are recent arrivals to Juticalpa, and there is no local name for them even though they are among its most boisterous urban residents. People are aware, however, that House Sparrows are steadily replacing the *cucaracheros* (House Wrens), a trend that local historian Victor Rubí attributed to the loss of open eaves through the switch from tiled roofs to modern, sealed structures. *Cucaracheros,* as their name suggests, prey on cockroaches and other common household pests, traditionally nesting in eaves and coming and going at will inside and around dwellings.

Other structures provide special niches for birds as well. The 1847 Catholic cathedral, with its twin belltowers, has provided nesting habitat for swallows and Barn Owls as long as anyone can remember. The various commercial radio and TV antennae are perches for Tropical Kingbirds and Blue-gray Tanagers throughout the day. But the most ubiquitous "public" bird is the *zopilote* (Black Vulture), synonymous with urban areas in Central America, both cherished and reviled by local people throughout the centuries. Indeed, the *zopilote* was abundant even at the time of Conquest. Early Spanish chroniclers of natural history in the New World mentioned that the bird was an important sanitation agent, and indigenous people did not bother it for that reason. *Zopilotes* lived everywhere people did in 1492, and little has changed since. Though they are associated with death and decay, and have the unsettling habit of perching on church steeples, they are not feared.

The *zopilote* is a surprising candidate for "most folkloric" member of the Honduran wild avifauna. Its ubiquity and tameness, hopping gait, and "baldness" (as well as its eating habits, of course) are construed as comic but slightly sinister and have inspired Hondurans to enshrine it in popular songs, dances, sayings, and place names.

Honduran folklorist, agronomist, and teacher Pompilio Ortega, who wrote during the first half of the twentieth century, was fond of the avifauna and appreciative of Honduran culture. Nevertheless, he despised vultures, as evidenced in his summary of beliefs about the feast of the vultures where the *rey zope* (King Vulture) feeds first. He writes, tongue-in-cheek, that the only redeeming characteristic of vultures is this social order. Ortega states that neither cyanide nor strychnine will kill the beasts, and going against the grain of traditional knowledge, he says that the birds spread disease rather than contain it, especially because they defecate on the roofs of houses. He mentions that if, as rumored, laws have existed protecting vultures, then similar measures should have been taken with flies. Ortega claims triumphally that at least they do not eat each other, invoking the common saying *cute no come cute* ("vultures don't eat vultures"; *cute* means "buzzard").[3]

Latin American popular opinion goes against Ortega. Since precolumbian times, vultures have not only been highly regarded as sanitary agents but have also been used in medicinal concoctions. *Zopilote* medicine was used in both Peru and Mexico. Indeed, of the medicinal birds recorded by early Spanish chroniclers, the *zopilote* is the most often cited (others include the Magnificent Frigatebird, Brown Pelican, Andean Condor, Inca Dove, macaws, rheas, and hummingbirds). Bernabé Cobo, in his 1653 *Historia del Nuevo Mundo,* writes of a curious use of the *suyuntuy,* the Black Vulture, in Peru: "The vulture has been proven to be medicinal, because in the year 1614 it befell in this city of Lima, while I was here, that a young student, from too much study and devotion to which he gave himself without the restraint of prudence, came to lose his reason; they cured him by giving him to drink for fifteen days the distilled water or broth of a vulture; and with this cure he regained his sanity and became so healthy that, afterward, he took holy orders" (in Cobo 1956, 318).[4]

Francisco Hernández, in the 1570s, recorded *zopilotl* medicine in his accounts of the natural history of Mexico: "It is said that the burnt feathers, reduced to ash, prevent the regrowth of hair . . . and when applied half-burnt, cure wounds, if at the same time one eats the meat, which also usually cures syphilis. It is also said that its sun-dried heart has a strong odor, and that its droppings taken in the dosage of one drachm are useful for the bad-tempered" (Hernández 1957, 343).[5]

Jesús Aguilar Paz gives a Honduran analogue. Citing the *zopilote, tijul* (Groove-billed Ani), and *tincute* (Turkey Vulture), he indicates that the birds can be cooked down and the broth used in poultices or inhaled as a cure for asthma.[6] If the idea of medicinal birds seems strange, think of chicken broth, considered excellent for sick people in Honduras, the United States, and elsewhere. In Juticalpa, hot liquid chicken fat is commonly used as an effective decongestant. As for *zopilotes* in Olancho, it seems that their old medicinal value has been forgotten, though boiled *zanate* (Great-tailed Grackle) fumes are still inhaled by a few older residents.

Zopilotes have inspired an intriguing literature in Honduran popular culture. Consider the following enigmatic children's round:

El Zopilote

Whence do you come *zopilote*
Walking with that [swaggering] gait?
I come from the courthouse,
Because they've made me Justice of the Peace.
Whence do you come *zopilote,* with your yellowing beak?

I come from the rocky hills where I was searching for beehives.
Now the vulture is dead, [shoved up] against a stone wall,
And to the old people he has left,
The gray hairs of his staff.
Now the *zopilote* has died, in the middle of the passageway.
And to the young girls he has left
His beak as a brooch.
Now the *zopilote* has died, from a meal of cheese,
And for all of you he left,
The wrinkles on his neck.
Now the *zopilote* is dead,
Now they're taking him to be buried,
Four *zopilotes* and a mouse.[7]

Jesús Muñoz Tábora, who transcribed the round, describes an imitative folk dance called *El Zopilote,* a "jocose dance, inspired by the bird's hopping gait."[8] The *zopilote* was also the star of a children's game:

Boys and girls formed a circle, each one taking the name of a bird, in order. The instigator, boy or girl, asked the *"zopilote,"* another player:

—*Zopilote,* did you go to the *campo* [countryside]?
Zopilote: Yes, I went.
Other: And what did you see?
Zopilote: I saw a *chorcha* [oriole] (or any other bird).
Chorcha: Zopilote, did you go to the *campo*?
Zopilote: Yes, I went.
Chorcha: And what did you see?
Zopilote: I saw a *zorzal* [Clay-colored Robin].
Zorzal: Zopilote, did you go to the *campo*?

The game continued, each player following the order previously established. If anyone made an error and named the wrong bird, they had to donate a personal article such as a comb or earring. At the end of the questions, the instigator collected all the personal articles, and asked about each one in turn: "Should this be burned?" The owner of the article answered: "No, don't burn it, it's mine." The instigator turned to another, and asked: "You who are a most dispassionate witness, what punishment do you give?" This child then meted out the punishment, which could be, for example, that the owner of the article dance like a *jolote* [domestic turkey].

The owner would have to imitate the dance of the *jolote,* because not doing so meant he or she would lose the article. The most engaging aspect of this game was how the punishments were carried out. It was hilarious watching each of the players imitating a *chompipe* [turkey]; observing a "tom" calling to a "hen"; or acting as a prop for drunks; etc.[9]

Childrens' games such as this one required the kind of public space that has all but disappeared in Barrio Las Flores of Juticalpa, where Lucita grew up. Luz Bonta, like many adults, fondly remembers playing games like this out in the street or in nearby vacant lots. Today, the busy streets no longer suffer children to play, while TV and other indoor diversions compete for their time.

🐦 *Clay-colored Robins for Clara Luz Rojas*

To glimpse what goes on behind the walls of Juticalpa, in the private worlds of kitchen garden *patios,* we start at *doña* Clara's house, then make a visiting circuit of relatives and friends to discover a human geography of birds in narrow domestic quarters.

The lot on which *doña* Clara's house stands once formed part of a larger property dating back to the nineteenth century. Some of the adobe bricks left over from the construction of the now vanished ancestral house built by her great-grandfather Jesús Alemán are still stacked in a corner of the yard. As far back as records go, this branch of her family belonged to Juticalpa's middle class, town born and bred, seamstresses, shoemakers, and schoolteachers. *Doña* Clara's street, two blocks from Parque Central, is populated by families who own small stores and cars; almost all have outside walls that flank the street. *Doña* Clara's house is somewhat unusual in that like her mother before her, she has maintained a small garden in front, defending its flowers and greenery from the grabby fingers of children and the pore-clogging street dust.

The long presence of *doña* Clara's family in central Juticalpa has produced in her a rootedness and sense of place that is apparent in her intricate knowledge of neighborhood happenings and her appreciation of the gentler aspects of living in an ever more chaotic and dangerous town. Like many older *juticalpenses,* she bemoans the absence of quiet and tranquility. Nowadays, she can't go for a stroll along the polluted river, nor up to the Cerrito de la Cruz, a nearby hill with a large cross erected at the turn of the twentieth century and once a favored place for excursions but now frequented by muggers. But she can still bask in the shelter of her *patio* and make the rounds to those of her friends and relatives. *Doña* Clara's *patio* is eight by eight meters, with only one tree of any size, an avocado. Unfortunately, she had to get a tall *macuelizo* tree removed in 1998 because its root system was heaving up the floors. Most of *doña* Clara's more than forty plants are ornamental shrubs and herbs.

The shade, seasonal fruits, and leaf duff of *doña* Clara's *patio* provide attractive habitat for the *zorzal* (Clay-colored Robin). This brownish tan thrush, one of Honduras's favorite birds, is often seen unobtrusively scratching for worms and other food. During good avocado seasons, so many *zorzales* show up that Clara must scare them away to get any fruit for herself, but she bears the birds no ill will. Instead of using an alarm clock, she is awakened by the *zorzal*'s dawn song that "heralds the beginning of a new day."[10]

While the *zopilote* is the quintessential bird of urban public space, the *zorzal* is the most cherished backyard bird in Honduras. In the countryside, town, and city, the *zorzal*'s popularity is due to its song, ubiquity, and tameness. The following anecdote by Pompilio Ortega helps to reveal what the *zorzal* expresses in Honduran culture.

In his "El Pájaro Anacoreta" ("The Anchorite Bird"), he tells of a particular *zorzalito* that has lived for five years in the eighth of a *manzana* (areal measure equal to 1.75 acres) Ortega has dedicated to the cultivation of ferns.[11] He describes how *zorzales* (thrushes in general) are migratory birds of much interest for bird enthusiast societies: in Indiana, a birdwatchers' society predicts with great accuracy, down to the exact hour, the annual return of a type of *zorzal*. He writes that he has seen a white-collared variety in Honduras only in the high *montaña cruda* (cloud forest), though he has recently been told that they migrate to lower altitudes and damage seedbeds.[12] But "his" common *zorzal* is another kind, an untiring songster, especially when the *zorzala* (female) is nesting. During these periods, the male is known to sing from three in the morning until ten at night, barely interrupting himself to catch an insect for his companion. In Coyocutena (Ortega's country home and experimental farm), they stay six months, "but because we have no bird societies in Honduras yet, we don't know where they spend the other six. . . . We have often speculated on the motive for which the hermit *zorzal* has stayed alone in the ferns without ever leaving."

Ortega wonders whether the bird might be a widower, quipping that perhaps his wife left him for another. Perhaps his promised bride deserted him. Should the bird be pitied or congratulated? Ortega observes that the bird can certainly not be said to lead a happy life, if we measure felicity by the common Honduran belief that a bird sings when it is happy: this one never sings nor even warbles.

The family treat the Anchorite *zorzal* with great familiarity, and he returns the favor. They give him food to get him through lean periods, because despite the fact that something is always fruiting on the Ortega farm, the bird limits himself to what he can glean within his small retreat. Not far away is a grove of Japanese plums, and one morning Ortega hears a great number of birds there, especially *chorchas* (orioles), singing boisterously as if saying, "Give us some more, because this kind of feast is not something you see every day." Nevertheless, the *zorzal* refrains from taking part: "from pride, abstinence or humility — who knows?"

The *zorzal* sometimes misbehaves. Once, after his farm had become a type of experimental school, and he worked around the country in agricultural extension, Ortega returned with some special orange seeds the president had given him, very excited to see if he could germinate them, since he had never been able to graft the variety. While he was preparing the soil, he left the seeds on a planter, but he returned to find that they had disappeared. He sat down to contemplate his ill fate, and realized that the *zorzal,* with little food and perhaps resentful that Ortega had left him alone for the cold season, had eaten them. "The *zorzal,* perhaps forgetting his situation, or remembering what he once was, sometimes began to make a nest, but he never finished it, and instead would shred it impatiently, scattering the little vines to the winds with his bill and claws."

Sometimes, the bird would take on the task of ripping the moss from the orchid flowerpots, while at other times he would scratch like a chicken, even destroying the roots of the most delicate ferns. When Ortega found him out in these antics, the bird would hop onto a branch or frond, tilting his head to observe the author better, "as if to ask, 'What do you think of my handiwork?' I look at him with warmth and tell him that between those of us with similar luck run great currents of sympathy."

In towns, where most birds are the familiar ones, people tend to notice the strange and exotic, the birds for which they have no names. When *doña* Clara's mother Eva Maradiaga was still alive, they were visited by a scarlet bird they couldn't identify. It showed up one day and took to eating hot peppers from a bush in the *patio*. The family observed it in amazement, but they never determined what it was called. *Doña* Eva thought that it must have come "from some *montaña* somewhere." Though it stayed but a brief time, the unknown scarlet bird brought a bit of mystery into their everyday lives. Something exotic had tinged their *patio* and had been worth more to them in its ephemeral visit than any talking *lora* or plaintive *paloma* they might have bought and kept.

Doña Clara has never liked caged birds. They sadden her, because birds should always be allowed to fly free. She cannot but think of how she would feel, locked up in such a prison. She keeps no parrots, birds that grace almost every Juticalpa household. On one occasion, her house did play host to an egret, but it had the run of the place.

Lucita cherished odder sorts of animals around the house — goats and other things that reminded her of the countryside. Her most interesting acquisition was a *garcita* (Cattle Egret, in this case), a bird that abounds in cattle pastures throughout the plains. They named it Tijuana, and it made a great sensation among friends and neighbors. She was kept busy procuring it fish to spear, and she had to be careful not to approach its stabbing beak too closely. Lucita would drag her grandmother down steep banks to get to a certain pool called Poza de la Gorda up the river, where the best minnows could be found for her pet. She was heartbroken when Tijuana, wings unclipped, eventually flew away.

Doña Clara's front garden has changed form over the years with the family's fluctuating tastes in decorative shrubbery. It is only two by eight meters but is crowded these days by several bird-friendly flowering shrubs such as the *Niña de Guatemala* and hibiscus. Over against the neighbors' protruding wall is a spreading and thorny *limón del norte,* a tree that bears tiny orange citruslike fruits most of the year. It attracts small flocks of *viuditas* (Blue-gray Tanagers), one of Juticalpa's favorite birds, at predictable intervals during the day. Occasionally, if one scrutinizes them closely, one can pick out the rarer Yellow-winged Tanager. The *viuditas* always make their presence known by their characteristic squeaking. After they have eaten their fill and one has had time to admire their beautiful blue plumage, they fly off squeaking to another garden or to perch on the tall radio antenna nearby.

Doña Clara's cousins Berta Muñoz and Juana Gutiérrez, like many *juticalpenses,* have cherished the visits of *viuditas* to their own *patios.* The late *Doña* Juana, whose daughter and grandchildren live in south Florida, said that it is not uncommon for Juticalpa immigrants to smuggle up a *viudita* or two to keep in cages and remind them of home.

Another regular visitor to Doña Clara's front garden is the *colibrí* (Cinnamon Hummingbird). *Doña* Clara notes that the hummingbird's "tiny size reminds us that it also fits into God's plan; it is always active sucking the nectar of flowers." Though this most common kind of visiting *colibrí* is plain in comparison to other species, its movements enliven her garden. A North American friend of mine who was a Peace Corps volunteer in rural Olancho observed a hummingbird one day at Clara's house. He was quite surprised to see such a bird in what seemed to him an avian desert. Indeed, to anyone living in a rural area, an individual hummingbird can pass entirely unnoticed among the multitude. But to an urbanite like Clara Luz Rojas, it is a special and notable being.

Many of Clara-the-retired-schoolteacher's opinions of birds center on what they can teach us of living honest lives in the eyes of God. The woodpecker, she says, "is constantly working, setting an example in its labor and affirming as well the greatness of the Creator." And "when we hear [the parrot] talk, we think of the love and presence of Jehovah in giving each and every one of His creatures separate abilities" (a "tongue," in the parrot's case). Swallows "remind us of our youth, when, on arriving from their journeys, they made their homes under the eaves of our houses." For *doña* Clara, who spent part of her youth in the countryside, the mention of certain birds evokes nostalgia, perhaps because she is mostly city-bound now and too old to tramp for a morning along the hedgerows and through the woods. "The melancholic song [of doves] reminds us of when we were young girls, of our frolicking play in the countryside."

To *doña* Clara, birds are far more than pretty things to look at. They inspire emotions, enliven our days, spark remembrance, and teach us values. They are feeling beings. This is the message of Pompilio Ortega's Anchorite *zorzal:* to many Hondurans, birds are sentient fellow beings with which we can empathize and which can empathize with us. If we look closely at *zorzales,* we may find them scrutinizing us with interest.

🦋 *The Dooryard Garden of Berta Muñoz*

Doña Clara's cousin Berta Muñoz lives on a narrow lot down the street with her grandson Mauricio. Despite being only three meters wide, her property contains herbs and vegetables such as tomatoes, green peppers, and cilantro that are molded around the walls in a well-tended garden. Larger shrubs are clustered in small groups toward the back kitchen. Overhanging her property is a venerable mango tree belonging to the neighbors. Most of its branches droop into *doña* Berta's *patio*.

Making the most of their limited space, *doña* Berta and Mauricio have become intensely aware of the avian goings-on in their *patio*. During May and June, the mango season, Mauricio frequently scales the high wall to get to the tree, and while he is harvesting fruit, he checks on the status of its nests.

On May 16, 1998, the *zorzales* had just hatched after what *doña* Berta remarked was an incubation period shorter than that of chickens. She is not bothered by the fact that the *zorzal* nest technically belongs to the neighboring lawyers' office. She has no doubt that the nest is "hers," since the male *zorzal* made it with materials from *her* garden, a process that she observed closely. He wove it from the fibers of her *patastera* (cucurbit vine), cementing them with moss-covered mud from around her flowerpots.

She and Mauricio cherish the song of the *zorzal* and keep a couple for that purpose. When the nestlings are big enough, Mauricio will capture one or two and clip their wings, so that they stay in the yard. Meanwhile, *doña* Berta and her grandson maintain their vigilance against Juticalpa's many famished cats.

Doña Berta adores wild birds, clipping their wings to "domesticate" them so that they will stay around and keep her company. However, she never puts them in cages, preferring to let them hop around the garden and the kitchen, eating scraps and keeping her place bug-free. Other than *zorzales,* their favorite "domesticate" is the *turca* (White-winged Dove), which also nests in the mango and is monitored by Mauricio. At any given time they have small numbers of *turcas* and *turquitas* (Ruddy Ground-Doves) pottering around the dirt, accompanied sometimes by the larger, feral *palomas de Castilla* (Rock Doves) that she also allows to range freely.

The casual visitor to *doña* Berta's home is little aware of the mango, but on this afternoon I have sat down and tried to understand the significance it has for its "owners." Besides yielding a seemingly endless supply of *zorzales* and doves year after year, the tree also shelters a nest of the *viudita* (Blue-gray Tanager) in its upper branches, a bird that Berta appreciates for its brilliant colors. Another common bird that is nesting right now high in the branches is the *dicho feo* (Social Flycatcher], which she describes as insectivorous, with a tiny crest. Of the explosively active *dicho feos,* she comments that they "dance in the air" above the trees.

In her narrow domestic sphere, little bird activity escapes *doña* Berta's observation. Green and brown hummingbirds get scrutinized minutely when they make visits to her flowers. Though they are not found in her yard, she is familiar with hummingbird nests from visits to her family in El Plomo, a village out on the plains. She describes them as woven from fine fibers and bark of the *carnezuelo* (a type of acacia). Speaking of nests, *doña* Berta comments that one of her favorite pastimes in the countryside is searching for them in the dense hedgerows.

Of the people I know in Juticalpa, Berta Muñoz is the most orni-thophilic. She openly admits that she adores birds because of their beautiful songs and colors and their ceaseless and always engaging activity. In her carefully cultivated garden, they are a prized bonus, a lush and en-riching presence among the greenery, denying her poverty of space.

Other older Juticalpa residents whose children have long since moved away have different types of intense relationships with birds. Emilia ("*doña* Mila") Cardona tended a spacious house quite close to *doña* Berta's and lived awaiting the weekend visits of her progeny from distant points of Honduras. During the weekdays, however, *doña* Mila's house was anything but silent and solitary. Rather, it reverberated with the din of her aviary. Her favorite caged birds were an old, restless, and ex-tremely noisy Mealy Parrot with a considerable vocabulary and a Gray-chested Dove with a soothing, deep coo. Both birds were brought to her from the *montaña* (rain forest)—she named the parrot, but not the dove. Within their counterpoint resounded the chittering and whistling of sev-eral dozen Budgerigars and Old World finches, paired and enclosed in a dozen hanging cages. To round out the diversity were a quieter native Short-billed Pigeon and Red-lored Parrot. Throughout her lonely weeks she was surrounded by talk and song, while visitors were made distinctly uncomfortable by the jealous stares of her favorite Mealy Parrot.

Doña Mila passed away in 1999. Among her last wishes, faithfully respected, was that her children would release all her birds, that they could be as free as she.

Doña Clara's next-door neighbors Dolores ("*doña* Lolita") Mayorquín and her husband Alfonso Bardales keep a clipped, talking parrot named Panchita in their *patio,* pampering it with food scraps. They are also fond of a wild *zorzal* that is almost as tame as the parrot. The *zorzal* sleeps in a shrub in the tiny garden, keeping their plants free of insect pests but not disdaining scraps, for which it ventures onto the kitchen floor. In the past, *doña* Lolita had caught wild birds to put in cages, but *don* Alfonso wasn't keen on that, so now she contents herself with the Red-lored Parrot, making Panchita practically a member of the family, as they put it. Meanwhile, the *zorzal* maintains its freedom outside the captive sphere but well within their domestic realm. In Olancho, one often finds this pairing of parrot and *zorzal* in an intriguing dialogue of wild and domestic.

How widespread are expressions of ornithophilia among townspeople? Local doctors Uniberto and Lesbia Madrid think that many people in Juticalpa cherish birds, even while others are oblivious. They told me of their own curious experience. One day, a wounded *zanate* (Great-tailed Grackle) fluttered into their *patio,* victim of a ravenous mutt. Their maid, whom they describe as a great bird lover, tended the bird and made a splint for its broken wing. Their children were fascinated with the showy *clarinero* (male grackle) and named him Sipiti. Uniberto retold with an edge of amazement how the bird would call out to its "brothers and sisters," who would show up bringing food for their wounded "sibling." The human family nursed and nourished the *zanate* well, and eventually it recovered and flew away.

🐦 *Octogenarian Juana Gutiérrez's Comments about Birds*

Luz is enthralled by the reminiscences of Juticalpa's octogenarians and nonagenarians. Clara and Luz frequently used to visit Juana Gutiérrez, a cousin and their closest family in town. *Doña* Juana, who passed away in 2001, was born in 1912. She lived in a new house her children built, filled with modern appliances her daughter brought back from Miami. Nevertheless, *Doña* Juana ignored the modern gas stove and preferred to cook her simple meals with firewood. She continued her mother's tradition of keeping a spotless house and did not get rid of her carefully fenced chicken yard, fruit orchard, and ornamental garden in the spacious *patio* seven meters wide and sixty long.

Doña Juana, wrinkled, frail, but loquacious, was one of the most opinionated people in Luz's Juticalpa and had many interesting things to say about birds:

> When ground-doves come here, I throw them corn so they won't leave. They drink water I put out by the kitchen. But we hardly see pretty birds: orioles, those yellow ones, don't come at all. We do get wrens and grackles. The most common ones are the *zorzales,* which nest here. I always told those kids [her grandchildren] to leave them alone, because they don't do us any harm. Yapa [Suyapa] used to like to take out the nestlings, but I think they are repulsive-looking. Ah, *zorzales*! But there are fewer these days: those [neighborhood] kids have killed so many of them with slingshots. One time a little kid killed a dove at my house, then he roasted it to eat.
>
> Three little *zorzales* fledged in May from the *zorzal* nest here in the mango. The *zorzala* comes back at dusk—there she is right now! I once had a *zorzal* in a cage. But my mother chewed me out—"Would you like to be a captive?"

Doña Juana's *loras* (parrots) were prominent members of her domestic community, keeping her company in the intervals between her childrens' visits.

> My *loras*—those animals last a long time! That one they brought me from Choluteca—she's called Panchita. The other one is Rabi—she gave herself that name. I give my *loras* coffee and tortillas in the morning—coffee makes them talk more. Chicken makes them talk more, too—but salt is bad.
>
> I don't like macaws—they're too destructive. They eat doors, shoes . . . they've been offered to me, but I always refuse. You know, flocks of macaws used to show up right over there in Sabanetas [a nearby *barrio*]. But they don't come any more—who knows where they've gone? I think the kids ate them all. There used to be so many, and *loras,* too—at times, their flocks were so large they cast shadows.

The woodpecker comes here — he eats my oranges, grapefruit, and *guanábanas.* Yes, I have to protect my fruit from all those birds.

Do you know the *dicho feo?* He says, "Fuiste al río? Sí, fuí" [Did you go to the river? Yes, I went].

Whenever I see a great swirling mass of *zopilotes,* I always think that there's some dead guy, because over in that direction is where they [criminals] go to dump dead people [their victims].

Along the Río Guayape, there used to be flocks of guans in those huge old trees. A long time ago, I had a pair of guans, but an opossum ate them. I also had an *alcaraván* [Double-striped Thick-knee]. They're very intelligent — if you speak to them, they understand, just like a dog. "Get over here right away!" [one says], and they come. They sing at dusk, at midnight, and at dawn, right on schedule. The wild ones lay their eggs in the middle of the fields; there used to be flocks right around here.

Doña Juana did not buy into a popular characterization of owls as malignant: "*Lechuzas* [Barn Owls] feed on mice and lard. The other morning we woke up to find one in that tree — and the chickens all terrified. But I don't believe that they're evil — I'm not a believer in any of those legends about spirits. Have you heard the *estiquirín* [Great Horned Owl]? You know, the one that eats cats? I have."

Nicolás Mayorquín Remembers
Slate-colored Solitaires

The Gutiérrez's next-door neighbor Nicolás Meza Mayorquín ("*don* Colacho") has lived much of his life in Juticalpa and worked for many years in the banana plantations on the North Coast. In the old days, he had maize fields on the hills outside Juticalpa and hunted widely in the nearby forests. *Don* Colacho is fascinated by animals and plants of all kinds and tells endless anecdotes:

You don't know the *Santa Cruz?* They come here all the time, those little reddish brown *turquitas* [Ruddy Ground-Doves]. The people say, "Here come the *palomas de Santa Cruz!*" Both the *Santa Cruz* and the *frijoleras* [White-winged Doves] have made nests here in the *patio.* Another bird that comes here a lot is the *cucarachero* [wren]. They clean the houses of pests. Why are they called *cucaracheros?* Because they eat insects, mosquitos, spiders, cockroaches. But with all the noise from the cars in the street, they don't often come this far into town any more.

You always see the swallows — they cross the seas, they fly very long distances. And the herons — there's a dark one, and a white one.

I'm eighty-six or eighty-seven. I used to go out and work my fields; I've killed many snakes and deer and other animals. [He tells several hair-raising hunting stories.] In the old days, this *barrio* was all pasture and scrub. The birds such as sparrows that live in those areas, you don't see them around here any more. And the hummingbirds — when the pastures flowered, they would come to suck the nectar.

We had a pretty bird in a cage once — we never knew what it was, but a farmer told us. You do sometimes see birds, and you don't know their names. Sometimes, right here at our house, birds show up from who knows where. One time I found a little dead bird here in the *patio,* very pretty. I stuffed it, but I finally lost it: but, you know, all things come to an end.

There used to be tall forest right over there by La Lima [a nearby village]. There were *comelenguas* [supernatural "tongue-eaters"], like snakes, but with wings. And the Barn Owl — it's so ugly! They found a bunch of them in the municipal building when they refurbished it. Those owls go into the cathedral to eat lard from the candles.

Don Colacho is the only person I have encountered who explains the name of the *torreja,* tying it to the bird's wandering in search of food (the Masked Tityra is one of the few arboreal birds in central Olancho that can be found from the plains up into the high mountains):

Torreja flocks show up on the plains around Semana Santa, that's why they are called *torreja* [a popular pastry confected only during Holy Week]. Their call also goes *torreja.*

In the countryside, the *pía* [Brown Jay] always announces someone's arrival. When you're out working, and someone comes bringing the lunch, you already know when they're going to arrive, because of the *pía's* calls.

Other birds of the countryside? There's the *picapiedras* [Ferruginous Pygmy-Owl] — it makes nests in trees like the *bombón.* It has a sad but pretty little song. Then there's the *pucuyo* [Pauraque]—he was made an example of. What happened is that he was a rich man who stole money from a poor man, then he lost it. So now he comes out on the trails ahead of people, [calling] *"mi dinero, mi dinero!"*

There are two kinds of hawks—one that hunts chickens, and another that calls in the pine forests [he imitates the call of the Red-tailed Hawk]. In the *montañas,* you hear the *jilguero* [Slate-colored Solitaire]. It has a pretty little song, like a whistle. In the old days, the rich people here used to keep them in cages to liven up their houses. They could cost as much as one hundred lempiras.

The macaws, they say, have all been taken away. There used to be a great multitude of them right around town; they would eat pine seeds. Did you know that the squirrel and the macaw are friends? One day, the macaw was eating a cheese [*queso*]. "What are you eating?" says the squirrel. And the interrupted macaw dropped the cheese. He says, *"Queso!"* [in a macaw-like voice]. The squirrel grabs the cheese, turning it in his paws, but he doesn't let it go—eating it, saying, *"Quesito, quesito, quesito"* [in a squirrel-like voice].

There are many more birds—the *cacao* [Red-throated Caracara], it calls in the *montañas.* The *guardabarrancos* [Turquoise-browed Motmot], the one with the racket tail that puts its eggs in holes in the banks.

Do you know the eagle? I don't, but I've seen it on TV. The quetzal? I think I know it, but I can't remember.

🐦 Why include relationships between birds and people in urban areas in a conservation geography? Because people who live in towns and cities in Latin America are owners of large ranches, and they are teachers, politicians, professional foresters and agronomists, and others who have a great impact on rural places. Because urban areas are not desert islands but are characterized by their biological and cultural interconnections with the countryside. "Urban" birds come and go from town to country, continent to continent. Their human counterparts come from and go to the villages, the deforestation frontier, the United States. Towns and cities are integral nodes in the fabric of the cultural and natural landscape.

Large Private Landowners as Conservationists

Large landowners, known as *terratenientes,* hold most of the fertile land on the plains of Olancho and own vast properties in the mountains as well. By virtue of the amount of land they control, their management decisions are important to birds and other wild fauna. Some are grass-only cattle ranchers, investing large sums in chemicals to ensure that their cattle are healthy and fat and their pastures are weed- and tick-free. Others let their pastures grow into brush, providing minimal management for their land and fostering chemical-free environments. Still other *terratenientes* are not ranchers at all but have decided to convert their land to agribusiness. Some own large coffee farms in the *montañas.*[1]

The centuries-old tradition of the Olancho cattle baron—master of all he surveys—is fading. There are as many self-made wealthy landowners as there are heirs of ancient cattle fortunes, while corn and watermelon are proving more lucrative and dependable than meat production. But land distribution on the plains is still highly skewed, and the villages of the peons become ever more crowded as their populations grow with no room to expand. Land reform has been sporadic and dangerous, with the memories of two brutal massacres in the 1970s still fresh in the minds of rich and poor alike. It is safer for the poor to farm steep mountain slopes beyond the reach of large landowners, to work as day laborers, or to emigrate to the cities, the North Coast, or the United States.

There is no stereotypical *terrateniente.* Many are rich only in land and cattle but otherwise live the lives of poor farmers. Some flaunt their wealth, with expensive cars, mansions, and important political posts. A certain sector loves the land and its wildlife, as I show in the course of this chapter. Others value their land almost solely for income generation.

Terratenientes who protect wildlife are in effect owners of private nature reserves, whether or not conservationists recognize them as such. The fates of some species rest on their management strategies, as is the case with the Honduran Emerald, a hummingbird endemic to the thorn forest that survives on large and neglected ranches in the Valle de Agalta and Valle de Aguán farther north. In other cases, a local bird population thrives thanks to the efforts of several neighboring landowners in the Valle de Olancho, where cattle ponds shelter hundreds of Black-bellied Whistling-Ducks. In the first example that follows, a large landowner controls the fate of a small watershed and its wildlife, while bringing his protective tendencies to bear on an entire village.

Elmer Maradiaga in Comunayaca

Clara Luz Rojas's brother Elmer was active in the government's land reform program back in the 1960s. Although he has a house and many influential connections in Tegucigalpa, he prefers the role of gentleman farmer in the remote village of Comunayaca. *Don* Elmer is somewhat unusual because he lives for extended periods on his hacienda (most of the Olanchano landholding elite live in towns or cities, leaving a ranch manager in charge of day-to-day operations and visiting on weekends). He maintains excellent relations with local peasant farmers, who hold him almost universally in great respect. This has helped him develop a great sensitivity to their beliefs and practices.

In June, 1998, we sat down together in Juticalpa to talk about the avifauna on his land:

What I explain to people who kill them is that birds are creations of God. I came [for the first time to Comunayaca] in 1965, and in those days, they killed everything that moved. They killed animals not just to use, but for the fun of it. They fished in the rivers with explosives. Every little boy went around with a slingshot. But there are many more birds now in Comunayaca, because many people have changed their ways. Not as many kids have slingshots now. In any case, I protect my land. I've chased out hunters by firing shots in the air—

people don't hunt on my property any more. There is no permission ["No hay permiso"].

There has certainly been a regeneration of the fauna. I explain to people that even snakes are useful, that they serve to maintain equilibrium by controlling populations of agoutis. People continue to learn.

Scarlet Macaws used to be abundant here in certain seasons. They ate pine seeds, and you'd find them mostly up in the *ocotales* [pine groves]. Do you know the *cocoleca* [Gray-necked Wood-Rail]? I just saw one the other day for the first time in ages. They used to be abundant.

I'm wondering whether there's been some climatic change. You see, every year during the coffee season, thousands of *palomas de montaña* [Band-tailed Pigeons] come down to eat those *capulín* berries — without fail. But last year, they didn't show up.

Cacaos [Red-throated Caracaras] used to abound, but now they're quite rare. That's the black bird, like a *zopilote* with a red dewlap. I also have the *guaco* [Laughing Falcon]; that's another raptor which has a very loud call. And the *rey zope* [King Vulture]—we see a good number of those, even ones that are all black [immatures]. And then there is the *tera,* the one called the *quebrantahuesos* [Crested Caracara]. I have all of those.

Talking about changes: there used to be a lot of birds that didn't make it up to Comunayaca from the Río Juticalpa valley. Now ones like the *clarinero* [Great-tailed Grackle] and *fuiste al río* [Social Flycatcher or Great Kiskadee] are abundant. It's just that they don't sing as much up at my place. And the *zorzales* [Clay-colored Robin]— there didn't used to be many of them, and now they're abundant, too.

You know, I get two kinds of orioles. There's the one that makes the bag nest, and another one, the *chorcha cajetera,* which makes a nest like a little box; it's a songbird.

My neighbors are not native Olanchanos, they're from the South. You can tell by a lot of their beliefs. They call the woodpecker *güis.* They believe strongly that it announces a visit. If they're out in the fields and they hear one call back at the house, they know that someone stopped by while they weren't there. They believe, also, that the *guaco* [Laughing Falcon] announces a death. "Muerto va," it says. And they firmly believe that!

Serenqueques [Bushy-crested Jays] are very common, and the *paloma chinga* [Little Tinamou] is abundant. It sings around midnight with a voice that sounds like a whistle. Yes, we have *pavillas* [Highland Guans], but they're quite scarce now. Recently, one was killed up in my coffee farm.

Are you familiar with the *tres pesos*? No? It's a beige-colored bird, a little bigger than a *zorzal* but not as plump. It flies rather slowly. *Tres pesos* go in pairs, down in the vine tangles, and whistle in tandem: "tres pesos pido!" What a pretty song, like a harmonica! But it makes some people sad. They come down from the *montaña,* showing up in people's yards at the height of the dry season.[2]

What else? There's the *torreja* [Masked Tityra]—it's lead-colored. And a type of dark-colored parrot we call *pico blanco* [White-crowned Parrot]. It lives up in the *montaña,* but loves maize, and it used to show up in the maize fields in thousands during the coffee season. Not any more.

One bird I see a lot is a kind of large, all-black *aguiluche* [Common Black-Hawk] we call the *cangrejero.* It eats almost exclusively the crabs down in the river. *Quetzales*? Yes, they live up in the *montaña* — sometimes they come down into the pines near the house. Occasionally, local people kill them because they are pretty. Generally, people leave them alone — they're no big deal.

Let's see — the *alma de perro* [Lesser Roadrunner] is abundant, and we have the *picapiedras* [Ferruginous Pygmy-Owl] and a lot of *pucuyos* [Pauraques]. Lucita, you remember that tree full of *oropéndula* [Chestnut-headed Oropendola] nests? That colony is gone.

Down in the river, the *ajoque* [Green Heron] has come back; it was gone for several years. The heron we get the most of is the *garza morena* [Little Blue Heron]. But the *bueyera* [Cattle Egret] only shows up at my place during the summers. You should have seen the Valle de Lepaguare back in the fifties, when I was young. For several years there were some big lakes out there, and you'd see flocks of that huge heron, the *garzón moreno* [Great Blue Heron].

Elmer Maradiaga is aware that many birds migrate altitudinally in search of food, nesting in the cloud forest and moving down to the valleys at times. In an earlier conversation, we had talked of the adjoining cloud forest, the Montaña de Comunayaca, which contains about a thousand hectares of forest. He and other coffee farmers control access to cloud forest through their buffering shade coffee farms, thus helping to prevent its wholesale conversion to subsistence agriculture. The difference between this privately protected *montaña* and the Montaña de Candeleros above Juticalpa is stark. Under the mandates of powerful cattle ranchers, Candeleros was converted almost entirely to hillside pastures in the last decades of the twentieth century. Indeed, the mountains near Juticalpa have been so heavily deforested in recent years that the Montaña de Comunayaca is now the only well-forested area in the entire drainage basin of the Río Juticalpa. The drastic effects of reduced forest cover became evident in October, 1998, when the rains from Hurricane Mitch swelled the river more than at any time in living memory, sweeping away dwellings all along the old road and destroying the floodplain neighborhoods in Juticalpa. Meanwhile, *don* Elmer's land, under its protective cover of vegetation, was left almost unscathed.

Who Guarantees the Future of Thorn Forest Species?

But what of landscapes scorned by their owners? The Honduran Emerald (*Amazilia luciae*), as far as we know, depends for its survival as a species on scrub that most ranchers consider worthless.[3] Unfortunately for conservationists, it is not a high profile bird in local culture; it is merely one of several *gorrioncitos* (little hummingbirds) that inhabit the thorn woods of the plains and is among almost thirty hummingbird species found in central Olancho. But Olanchano ranchers have not been the only ones oblivious to the unique bird that inhabits their land. Not until 1988 did ornithologists realize that the emerald is a denizen of thorn forest. Previously, they believed it was a rain forest native.

Ornithology's mistake came about because the natural history of the Honduran Emerald had never been studied. Collectors had taken skins for over a century but had not described the bird's habitat. Burt L. Monroe, Jr., in his 1968 monograph *A Distributional Survey of the Birds of Honduras* (the authoritative ornithological text on the country), assumed that the Honduran Emerald was a rain forest species because the place names on museum specimen tags suggested that the birds had

been collected in the vicinity of humid forest. Working solely from specimens, Monroe assumed that this rare endemic inhabited the rain forest.
But in 1988, when experts Steve N. G. Howell and Sophie Webb visited
the place described by the coordinates of an old collecting site in the
Valle de Aguán, Yoro, they found themselves in a desertic landscape that
received less than 800 millimeters of annual precipitation. Burt Monroe's error is understandable, however, because montane rain forest in
the Cordillera Nombre de Dios is found only a few kilometers away.[4]

Howell and Webb discovered not only that the four male Honduran
Emeralds collected in the Valle de Aguán by Arthur Twomey and Roland
Hawkins in June, 1948, and June, 1950, were from its thorn forest but
also that an endemic subspecies of the White-bellied Wren (*Uropsila
leucogaster hawkinsi*) lived in its undergrowth in the vicinity of terrestrial
bromeliads. They noted that plantation agriculture threatened the remaining thorn forests. Howell and Webb searched out the Honduran
Emerald in its two other historic collecting locales in central Honduras
(near the town of Santa Bárbara and near Cofradía, Cortés) and found
that these had also been thorn forest. Unfortunately, in these areas the
species' habitat had been completely erased, and no emeralds could be
found. The only historical collecting spot they failed to investigate was
the Valle de Olancho.

Conservationists in Olancho took up the search for the Honduran
Emerald in 1992. Though we were unaware of Howell and Webb's 1988
article, we had read Burt Monroe's description of collector extraordi-
naire Cecil Underwood's 1937 foray into Olancho, during which he collected the Honduran Emerald. We thought it would be important for
our bird inventory project if Honduras's only endemic bird still existed
in Olancho. Because we did not know that the bird was a specialist in
thorn forest, we searched without success in humid gallery forest, in vine
tangles, and around houses. Several years later, after we read the literature and found out what the emerald's true habitat was, we concluded
that the bird had been extirpated, because the Valle de Olancho has virtually no areas of thorn forest left. If the Honduran Emerald was to be
found in Olancho, we would have to look in other, less populated plains.

The Valle de Agalta, wilder and less developed than the Valle de Olancho, still contains large patches of thorn forest. It seemed the most likely
candidate for an emerald population, and in 1994, Francisco Urbina,
Parque Nacional Sierra de Agalta employee, with his Peace Corps vol-

unteer co-worker Robert Gallardo, located the bird in a patch of thorn forest within the Sabana La Lima. Not only was the endangered Honduran endemic present — it was quite common in what had once been an open plain and now consisted of thick woods of thorny leguminous trees and arborescent cacti. Conservationists like Francisco Urbina and I were interested in preserving the emerald, especially because one of only two known remaining sites is but a few kilometers from his village. In addition to looking for other sites, we have discovered more about the thorn forest, itself a unique habitat. In the 1930s, botanist T. G. Yuncker found plants unique to the Aguán thorn forest, though little work has followed this study.[5] The Aguán and Agalta plains share an endemic hummingbird species, and an endemic race of the Green-backed Sparrow, *Arremonops chloronotus twomeyi*.[6] These and the endemic race of the White-bellied Wren found in the Valle de Aguán (which does not occur in the Valle de Agalta), point to the thorn forests on the Honduran Caribbean slope as areas of local endemism. This was by no means a new discovery; rather, it was a rediscovery of a fact that had been unknown or ignored in present-day Honduran conservation efforts to save rain forests. It is worthwhile outlining here how the emerald's forest came to be and why cattle ranches may be the key to its survival.

It seems likely that the Honduran thorn forests are relics of a formerly more widespread habitat, probably dating from the Pleistocene.[7] In the 1960s, three herpetologists described a Pleistocene corridor of biotic dispersion through dry plains and valleys along the northern Middle American Caribbean slope, largely independent from the Pacific Coast dispersion corridor.[8] Dry forest biota emigrated from their evolutionary core or refugium of arid western Mexico, becoming isolated in certain areas that are dry thanks to microclimate and topography. During drier epochs, thorn forests may have been more widespread, existing in Honduras in areas where habitats such as rain forest, cloud forest, and pine woods thrive today.[9]

Why do thorn forests subsist only as the disjunct patches we encounter today? On the Honduran (and Guatemalan and Nicaraguan) Caribbean slope, areas that receive less than 1,000 millimeters of precipitation a year — the quantity necessary for tree cacti and other typical species to flourish — subsist only in interior plains under severe rain shadow. The rest of the explanation for the thorn forest's present relict distribution lies in geomorphology and human culture, as geographer

Carl Johannessen showed in his 1963 *Savannas of Interior Honduras*. His detailed study includes the plains of Agalta and Olancho as well as several other seasonally dry regions around the country.

Johannessen's text does not celebrate the thorn forest.[10] Faithful to local opinion, Johannessen described it as the scourge of Olanchano ranchers and the result of range degradation on the open prairies of the past. He wrote that ranchers had been battling thorny and otherwise unpalatable growth for centuries. During certain periods in certain areas, thorn scrub was reduced to copses on great native grass plains, but it could never be eliminated entirely. In the 1950s, when Johannessen did his research, Olancho's savannas had been swallowed up by thorn forests and other undesirable "scrub" habitats, owing to poor range management. Since he wrote, however, thorn forest has receded with the advance of modernization. Today, the thorn forests are giving way to irrigated fields of melons, sorghum, and cotton for export; to fish ponds and rice paddies; to "improved" pastures grazed by genetically improved cattle. This development takes place on the land of *terratenientes* who have access to credit, capital, and labor. (Smallholders have rarely found the clayey savanna soils suitable for their staple crops of maize and beans, making the issue of thorn forest preservation chiefly the provenance of large landholders.)

Where thorn trees are removed wholesale from the savannas, grass rhizomes become established, and as many Olanchano ranchers know well, under careful range management rich native short-grass prairies take the place of thorn scrub. The balance is delicate: where grass cover is degraded by too many bovine hooves and mouths, or is allowed to grow rank and overshade itself in the too-frequent absence of mouths, thorny growth takes over. The speed at which woody species invade is astonishing. This occurs not only in thorny savannas but throughout the dry interior of Honduras. In much of the Valle de Olancho, the most noxious species is the *carbón* (*Mimosa tenuiflora*), a thorny leguminous tree or shrub that forms impenetrable stands. Ranchers detest it and burn it out annually. Nevertheless, the thorn forests that ranchers find undesirable do have their benefits to local people. *Carbón* is one of the most valuable species for firewood and charcoal in the Valle de Olancho, while leguminous *Acacia* and *Prosopis* trees characteristic of the diverse Valle de Agalta thorn forests are quite useful for this purpose as well.

Furthermore, the thickest thorn forests are havens for game species such as quail, doves, white-tailed deer, and collared peccaries.

The Honduran Emerald is common in the remaining patches of thorn forest on the Sabana La Lima (and at several other sites around the Valle de Agalta). We have observed it feeding on *Opuntia* (prickly pear) flowers, and Howell and Webb observed the birds on the flowers of *Pithecelobium lentiscifolium, Aechmea bracteata, Pedilanthus tithymaloides,* and a *Lemairocereus* or *Cephalocereus* organpipe cactus. The males vociferously defend their territories around *Mimosa* and other thorny trees on the grassy edges of glades. Somehow, this hummingbird has weathered the past four centuries of range management. The present threat to the emerald's habitat in the Sabana La Lima is not old-style cattle ranching — which never conquers all scrub at all times — but the changing culture of *terratenientes,* who are moving into irrigated export crops, most notably rice. The Sabana La Lima forests are now isolated remnants because most of their former extent of several square kilometers has been bulldozed into heaps, the ground furrowed into ridges and trenches and sown in rice. Not even fringes of thorn forest have been spared. The result is a plethora of migrant and resident water birds but no emeralds. The paddies are beautiful, their glistening green rows stretching back from the road toward the lowering Sierra de Agalta. The air is abuzz with swallows, the water plied by egrets, herons, Wood Storks, and whistling-ducks. Uncommon species such as migrant Wilson's Snipe and secretive rails also hide there.

The La Lima thorn forest, beautiful in a very different way, is also rich in fauna that seek tangles so dense that neither human nor domestic animals can disturb them. We have encountered large flocks of migrant wood-warblers, vireos, gnatcatchers, and buntings; several species of raptors; many other local resident birds; and tracks of opossum, white-tailed deer, eastern raccoon, and collared peccary. One day in late July, 1998, Francisco Urbina and I took a botanist there, and we were pleasantly surprised to find that one of the largest rice paddies showed signs of disuse, as if it had not been farmed the previous season. We poked about a small island of thorn woods adjacent to the paddy, flushing out hundreds of White-winged Doves. The thickets were alive with birds, as they usually are, but we arrived too late in the morning to detect Honduran Emeralds, which seem to be active primarily at dusk and dawn.

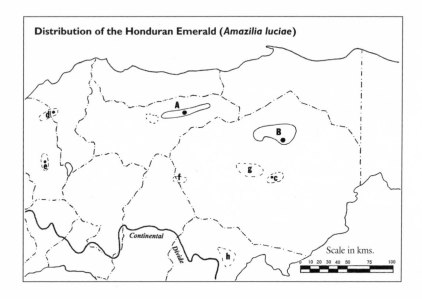

Distribution of the Honduran Emerald (*Amazilia luciae*)

Distribution of the Honduran Emerald

Current known distribution:

A. Valle de Aguán, Yoro. Extant populations in *espinales*. Thorn forests of upper Aguán also harbor endemic races *Arremonops chloronotus twomeyi* (with Valle de Agalta and Valle de Gualaco) and *Uropsila leucogaster hawkinsi* (range isolate).

B. Valle de Agalta, Olancho. Extant population at dot (Sabana La Lima); remaining area indicated contains extensive, unmonitored *espinales*.

Historical collecting sites:

c. Valle de Olancho. Two collected near El Boquerón in 1937. Virtually no *espinales* left in area.

d. Cofradía (Cortés). One collected in 1935. Virtually no *espinales* left in area.

e. Santa Bárbara (Santa Bárbara). One collected in 1935. Virtually no *espinales* left in area.

Possible emerald sites containing unsurveyed thorn forest remnants:

f. Terraces above the Río Guayape in the *municipios* of Guayape (Olancho), and Orica (Francisco Morazán).

g. Valley of the Río Telíca and tributaries, especially in the *municipios* of Guarizama and San Francisco de la Paz.

h. Valle de Jamastrán, El Paraíso.

Further possible sites include *valles* in the headwaters of the Río Coco, Department of Madriz, Nicaragua, particularly near El Espino.

The hacienda owner's venerable ranch manager showed up, barefoot and on horseback, curious about who was poking around on private property. He told us that the neighboring rice paddies had indeed been abandoned, because their owner had lost them to a company in payment of a debt. We have heard other rumors that the savannas are simply not productive for rice (Johannessen noted this as well). Does this signify that the Honduran Emerald's habitat is not doomed? It depends on the personalities of the landowners, some of whom seem quite unapproachable. Nevertheless, COHDEFOR forestry employees and other conservationists in the Valle de Agalta have begun efforts to woo the more receptive *terratenientes,* and a few are already preserving patches of thorn forest they had slated for destruction. What about the possibility of the state or a private group buying up thorn forest remnants and perhaps establishing an ecological corridor to the Parque Nacional Sierra de Agalta only a few kilometers away? This viable option would demand large sums of money as well as alienating the land from the people who have owned it for centuries. If the Honduran Emerald can thrive on the right mixture of scrub and pasture, then its future depends on a truce between modernizing ranchers and thorn forests before the Valle de Agalta becomes as developed and unforested as the Valle de Olancho.[11]

Tomás Guillén, Bird Protector

There is at least one *terrateniente*-conservationist in the Valle de Agalta. *Don* Tomás Guillén, native of the town of San Esteban, protects his land vehemently, trying to attract both waterfowl and terrestrial species. In 1995, Francisco Urbina and I visited his ranch, but he was not there. On that occasion, there were few birds on the three-acre pond, but the ranch manager assured us that at times it was full of whistling-ducks, Muscovy Ducks, herons, and many birds he couldn't identify, which might have been sandpipers, gulls, and pelicans. In June, 1998, we had the opportunity to interview Tomás Guillén at his house in town.

I made my lake in the 1950s. It's about two *manzanas* [3.5 acres], and my whole property is about 140 *manzanas*. To give you an idea of the birds I get: three years ago, *águilas pescadores* [osprey] nested in a *quiebramuela* tree up above the lake. The young fledged in July.

Most of the water birds come in after the cold fronts in January and later, when it rains for days. The migrants start arriving in September. I get birds from both coasts, and from the Moskitia. Some stop here on their intercontinental migrations.

We pulled out a bird guide, and he pored over the unfamiliar plates, mentioning some of the aquatic birds that have stopped at his pond. He has had groups of up to seven gulls (probably Laughing Gulls), rare vagrants in central Olancho. He also described what sounded like terns, and others that were probably different types of sandpipers and plovers. He once had two Brown Pelicans, another exceedingly scarce visitor to central Olancho. Various *patos aguja* (Anhingas) have resided in his pond briefly, while the *espátula* (Roseate Spoonbill) was a common visitor. *Cigüeñas* (Wood Storks) were not uncommon, and kingfishers were abundant.

Perhaps the most frequent birds were herons of many different types. He was fascinated by the "large one that eats carrion." He also spoke of a "garza blanca con alas negras" ("white egret with black wings") that Francisco and I identified as the locally rare Black-necked Stilt. Tomás Guillén didn't own a bird guide himself and was quite confused by the difference between ducks, American Coots, and grebes, all of which visited his pond. We asked him about two easily identified birds, the *pichiche* (Black-bellied or Fulvous Whistling-duck) and the *pato de monte* (Muscovy Duck): "The *pato* comes here, yes. It has nested, and a few years ago they mixed with my domestic flock, they came to eat the food here. *Pichiches* have nested, too. This year I've watched eleven adults with twenty-two young — I haven't seen the nests, and I don't know if different ducks put eggs in the same nest. I gave them some feed, but they were killed by my neighbors. You see, I protect my birds, but as soon as they leave my property, they get shot. I hear them fly over the Ramirez's pond, and "boom, boom!" You go look at their pond — nothing, no birds. I'm the only landowner around here who protects birds."

We wanted to find out about the Honduran Emerald, because we knew he was familiar with it through his contact with Francisco Urbina and Peace Corps volunteer Robert Gallardo several years before.

I don't have any emeralds on this property. It's not the right kind of woods, though I've searched. You'll find the emerald in the *espinales* [thorn forests] farther out on the plains. But I get a lot of other birds in my woods. Do you know the *bruja* [White-tipped Dove]? We have a huge quantity of those. And the *loro negro* [White-crowned Parrot], a parrot that's all dark, that comes down from the *montaña*. There are a few *cacaos* [Red-throated Caracaras] around occasionally too, and yes, I know the *pájaro campana* [Three-wattled Bellbird], the *campanero:* from my place you can hear it up in the *montaña*.

I used to get great flocks of macaws, but they dwindled year by year, and the last one of all came in four years ago. I still have the *carpintero grande* [Lineated Woodpecker], the one with the crest. But there are a lot less now, because the people kill and eat them. I also have the *chorcha corralera* [Black-headed Saltator].

We were curious to know about *don* Tomás's attitude toward birds, why he protected them, and what he thought about other landowners. Though he was evidently proud of his birds, and displayed a genuine love for them, he was clearly on the defensive against prevailing local opinion. When I wondered aloud whether landowners who had Honduran Emeralds would be interested in protecting them, he thought it would be completely worthless to talk to them. They would seem interested at the time, act excited for the moment, but would ridicule you behind your back. "If you want to catch the interest of ranchers," he told us, "talk about cattle. They never lose interest in that subject."

Tomás Guillén did not characterize himself as a rancher (*ganadero*) but rather as a sort of gentleman farmer who wanted to protect his land. He told us that when he had made his pond back in the 1950s, the land was all barren pastures, and there had been virtually no birds. He allowed much of it to become tree savanna or woods. He strictly controls access to his hacienda but still notices loss of birds, mostly to subsistence hunters. We all agreed that his was the richest pond for waterfowl in that part of the Valle de Agalta — there are plenty of other small bodies of water, but their owners rarely protect them to any great extent. *Don* Tomás protects birds, he says, just for the sake of preserving them.

Why Terratenientes *Protect Whistling-Ducks and Howlers*

Oscar Flores Pinot, a local teacher and agronomist, collaborated with us on the Honduran Emerald project. When he first learned of my interest in birds, he suggested I visit a ranch of some friends of his, the doctors Uniberto ("Beto") and Lesbia Madrid (husband and wife). They reside in Juticalpa and maintain a small hacienda with several ponds near the village of La Empalizada. Oscar and I drove to their hacienda several times when they were not there, and the ranch manager let us walk around. On my first visit to their land I saw two Masked Ducks, which are rarely recorded in Honduras. There were also Least Grebes, American Coots, Common Moorhens, and the *pico de oro* (Northern Jacana) in abundance; a group of *alcaravanes* (Double-striped Thick-knees) standing in a field; clouds of migrating swallows, Dickcissels, and Indigo Buntings; and a few score *pichiches* (the onomatopoeic local name for whistling-ducks). The evidence of faunal protection was everywhere — the Madrids' ponds and a neighbor's protected lake provided refuge to these and to many species of herons and egrets, to Wood Storks, White Ibis, and Roseate Spoonbills.

In early 1995, Oscar and I hosted three geography professors from the University of Texas, seasoned birders who had already been to Costa Rica and around the world. At dusk on the twenty-ninth of December, 1995, we drove the dusty track to the Madrids' ranch. Upon hearing a great noise emanating from the other side of a rise, we left the pickup and crept up on foot. There, on neighbor "Beto" Pagoada's lake, was a huge flock of adult and juvenile Black-bellied Whistling-Ducks. We counted six hundred and were told later that they sometimes occur in even greater numbers. This encounter was one of the most spectacular birding experiences for my professors in Honduras, especially because the *pichiches* were thriving on private land. In Texas, like in Central America, the conservation possibilities of private land, particularly cattle ranches, are still becoming appreciated.

In 1998, after five years of sporadic visits to the Madrids' ranch, I finally had a chance to interview the owners, whom I had never met. Besides wanting to learn about their motivations, I was curious to find out about a neighboring property from which the roars of mantled howler monkeys emanated. Oscar and I sat down to talk birds at the Madrids' house in Juticalpa. They were pleased to meet me finally, because they had been hearing about the "gringo birdwatcher" for several years. They mentioned that with the passing of time, other foreigners had come to see the *pichiches*. Their ducks were becoming "famous."[12]

We often ask ourselves how these birds benefit us. It's a really interesting question, but you know, I don't think they really benefit us at all. Just to look at, I guess—they beautify the place; they're very beautiful.

We have four larger ponds and a smaller one. Two are about a hectare each, and the others are smaller. We also have cattle pastures, tilled fields, and *carbonal*. We hate the *carbonal*, we always get rid of that. It doesn't qualify as woods, that's for sure.

We started renting the property in 1990, and we bought it later. The ponds were already there. When we arrived, there were virtually no *pichiches*, and hardly any trees. It was pure pasture. So we've let some trees grow. We have also left a *montañita* [wooded grove] to regrow, maybe two hectares. Most other landowners don't leave anything at all.

The *pichiches* are migratory—right now you hardly see any, because they're on their nests. Some of them aren't even afraid of people any more. Sometimes hunters get into our property, but I run them off. And my neighbor Beto Pagoada doesn't allow hunting, either. Those ducks like his lake a lot, too. But on other ponds they hunt the ducks, so *those* landowners don't get any ducks at all. They all come to our ponds.

Back when we got the property, the *pichiches* were heavily hunted, I guess because they're easy to kill and great to eat. But I talked to the locals *very seriously*. I said, you can use traps, but no guns. If you want to trap the ducks, just bait with corn. There's a plague of rabbits on our property, so I let people trap *them*. There are so many rabbits we can't even raise beans.

The ponds are really for cattle, yes, but the cows don't disturb the nests. The *pichiches* nest in the reeds around the ponds. You see, the cows don't like the reeds—they'll go through the open parts, straight to the water. Each *pichiche* raises around twelve ducklings, it seems to me. Every year there are eight to ten broods born in each pond. They'll be getting big in July, August. So I guess we have the biggest population of *pichiches* in the whole Valle de Olancho? That's great, isn't it?

Another bird we have a lot of is the *alcaraván*. It's also called the *tera*. Sometimes, you see eight at a time, and they follow tractors to get the grubs that are tilled up. No, I'm not talking about the caracara,

I mean the thick-knee, the *alcaraván*. But isn't that the same as the *tera*, the caracara? No? Now we're all confused. You see, we are really *town* people. You know, before we bought the property we hardly knew anything about birds, except grackles and pigeons and so forth. The first time Lesbia saw *taragones* [motmots], she thought they were quetzals. "Beto!" you said. "We have *quetzales* on our property!" "No, love!" I said. "How are we going to have *quetzales* out here in the middle of the plains?" What we have most of are *guardabarrancos* [Turquoise-browed Motmot], the ones that sit on the barbed wire, switching their tails.

Oscar, do you remember how abundant the *golondrinas* [swallows] used to be? At times they were so thick you could grab them with your hands. I'll tell you, they hardly show up any more. Mark, what *about* migrations? You say *golondrinas* are migratory—do birds only migrate over land? I've always been curious about that. You say they also go over water—don't they get hungry? Where do they stop to eat?

We get very few *zanates* [Great-tailed Grackles]. But one bird we have in abundance is the *pico de oro* [Northern Jacana], and we get large numbers of the *pispitas* [sandpipers], as well—they're not really that interesting, but they're there. We also get big flocks of some kind of little yellow bird in the fields [Dickcissels?].

You know that *garzón* [large heron]? It's really incredible how he hunts. Stands stock-still in the water, and suddenly spears a fish with that beak, never seems to miss. And those *patitos*, those *pollas de agua*, the ones that dive [Least Grebes]? They've got some beaks, too. The other day one of my workers was pecked pretty hard by one that he tried to pick up.

We're starting to get those big, wild *patos*, the black ones with white on their wings [Muscovy Ducks]. They haven't nested, though.

We get two types of *lechuzas* [owls]. One is gray, and eats chickens—the ranch manager killed one last week. The other one is all white, really ugly.

Oscar mentioned that the white one was the *lechuza de campanario* ("belltower owl": Barn Owl); we agreed that the gray one was the Mottled Owl and chided the doctor for letting such a beneficial bird be killed. Generally, however, Beto and Lesbia displayed no animosity toward birds; in fact, they were interested in learning how to attract more and quickly took to Oscar's idea of planting certain fruit trees.

You know a black-billed, small parrot [White-crowned Parrot]? We get incredible numbers of those. They're the biggest pest of the corn crop when it matures. We hire local kids to make a lot of noise, setting off firecrackers and yelling. Those *pichiches* give us problems, too, and they're harder to scare off than parrots. The *pichiches* just fly up and alight a little way away.

How do birds benefit us? You know, they don't, really. Of course, there is the *garcita bueyera* [Cattle Egret], which eats ticks. . . .

We get a lot of animals out on the plains, too. We even had a puma — we were seeing its tracks all over the place. One day, the beast flushed right out of that little patch of thick woods. I saw it right in front of me, I swear! Couldn't believe it. We have lots of animals — *mapaches* [eastern raccoons], *zorrillos* [skunks] *cusucos* [nine-banded armadillos]. But no *guatuzas* [Central American agoutis] — it's too dry. We do get the *gato de monte* [gray fox]. And lots of snakes.

Doña Rosa, Lesbia's mother, has no less than one hundred *olingos* [mantled howlers] on her land. Those were definitely the ones you guys heard from my property. On their hacienda, my in-laws left some jungle, with several fig trees — that's why the monkeys are there. Those animals also love the plantain fields. That hacienda goes all the way to the edge of the Río Telica. And we have another neighbor, Rigoberto Mercado, who protects his land, too. Between Beto Pago-ada, my mother-in-law, Rigo, and us, we protect about six hundred hectares.

I'll have to take you out to my mother-in-law's hacienda so you can see the *olingos*. You should also come out with me to our place when you can. I can show you the *pichiches* on their nests. But don't drive out to my mother-in-law's unescorted — you could get shot at. More of a precaution, with all the cattle thievery and strangers around.

Oscar and I went to look for *pichiches* and *olingos* in early August. We arrived at the Madrids' ranch one day at four in the afternoon, and even though it was raining we saw and heard a fair number of birds. In one field, thirty to forty *pichiches* were standing around, while a Fork-tailed Flycatcher swayed on a grass stem. At the first pond, fringed by abundant rushes, were Northern Jacanas with young, and a Purple Gallinule. Tropical Kingbirds were abundant, and there were the usual buzzing *saltarines* [Blue-black Grassquits] and *semilleros* [White-collared Seedeaters]; we heard the frequent two-note call of the *codorniz* or *mascarita* [Crested Bobwhite]. A small ranch building sheltered several workers who had just finished a long day of castrating calves. As we waited for the doctor to arrive, they told us about the myriad *pichiches* that showed up on occasion. We asked if they hunted the ducks, but they said it was not allowed. When the doctor came, we lamented the state of the weather and decided against tramping out to look for *pichiche* nests. "But the birds are here," he said, taking in his property with a sweep of the arm. "Everything is here—*chiras* [Eastern Meadowlarks], *garzas*, *patos, pichiches*—everything but people. That's what we keep out." Everyone agreed vociferously.

We drove to his mother-in-law's property, an agribusiness of high-yield maize grown on a fertile natural terrace above a backswamp of the Río Telica. A swampy grove of wild fig trees was the attraction for up to forty howlers at a time, but they were not in residence that day. According to the doctor, they were on a neighboring hacienda downstream. He told us that his mother-in-law's family protected the howlers out of curiosity, since these were very likely the last ones left in the entire Valle de Olancho. In the old days, howlers were abundant in the Valle, but today they subsist only in thick rain forests of the Sierra de Agalta and other areas. These howlers, so close and accessible to Juticalpa, drew visitors who often scrambled down the bank into the swamp to get a closer look and perhaps throw stones at them. To solve this problem, the family had erected a type of gazebo to keep visitors away from the howlers; *don* Uniberto told us that one of his brothers-in-law planned to install a viewing telescope.

Lesbia and Beto Madrid, with their relatives and neighbors, have shown me a world of faunal protection parallel to that of the official governmental and NGO conservation movement. Nobody came and told them they had to protect habitat, nor did they do it for legal reasons. They learned what they know about local biota on their own, without field guides or contact with the Honduran protected areas movement. The Madrids, like Elmer Maradiaga, are conservationist landowners who strike a balance with the needs of impoverished local people. As with *don* Elmer, most of what the Madrids know about the birds on their hacienda they have learned from local farmers who grew up there. They neither exclude local livelihoods entirely nor allow flora and fauna to be extirpated. The Madrids, Tomás Guillen, and Elmer Maradiaga are only a few of the *terratenientes* in Olancho who zealously protect the biodiversity on their properties. If and when private nature reserves are recognized in Honduran protected areas legislation, such landowners will benefit considerably from incentives such as tax alleviation, and there is little doubt that they will go even farther to make their haciendas ecologically friendly.

Pajarales in Human Landscapes

Latin America is home to more bird species than any area of similar size on the planet. Countries such as Honduras have almost as many species as all of North America north of Mexico. Central Olancho — one mountain range and surrounding plains — has more than five hundred species of birds (the entire province contains around six hundred). In Olancho, as in many tropical mountainous areas, bird diversity is related in part to landscape complexity. Along a five-mile transect between plains and high peak, habitats vary from the tropical dry forest mosaic to pine woods and midlevel rain forest to cloud forest, each with distinctive avifauna. People have affected all but the remaining old-growth montane rain forests of the high Sierra, and in many areas human use has resulted in patchworks of savannas, woods, coffee farms, beanfields, fallow scrub, and artificial lakes. In heterogeneous, humanized landscapes, such as those owned by small farmers who maximize their survival strategies — a little bit of coffee, some beans, a grove for firewood, a *guamíl* or plot of fallow scrub — one may come upon a rather remarkable type of place referred to casually as a *pajaral* or place of many birds. The *pajaral* is rich in avian diversity and contains many rain forest as well as non–rain forest species.

The overwhelming abundance and diversity of birds in the *pajaral* is not lost on Olanchanos, even on those one might think would become blasé about birds through daily exposure to toucans, trogons, motmots and other such colorful species. In villages like La Venta in the Valle de Agalta, one grows up with the *pajaral,* with its calls and hues, its rush of wings. Village children use the term *pajaral* nonchalantly, because in their world where everything is new and urgent, there is no place yet for nostalgia. Their elders scoff at the *pajarales* of today, reminiscing sadly about times when parrots came in clouds, not flocks. They remember when macaws would change the color of the woods and when there were more orioles, saltators, hawks, woodpeckers, chachalacas — when there were more birds everywhere. The *pajaral,* to urban dwellers and farmers alike, has become a sign of what is being lost, but even in its current reduced state it is still an inspiration for what can be brought back: the avian diversity of the human landscape.

This chapter is about the *pajaral* in the landscape of the small farmer: the village of gardens and its surrounding mosaic of fields and woods. How and why does this type of landscape foster so many birds, and why is it of paramount importance to Neotropical avian conservation? How does the landscape of small farmers bring birds and people together, even while putting some species at increased risk? Below, I continue the train of thought from chapter 2 in a celebration of rural places and lifeways, exposing the possibilities of the present and future *pajaral.*

The Scarlet Macaw as Symbol of the Pajaral

A few years back, Honduran schoolchildren elected the *guara roja,* or Scarlet Macaw, as the national bird. It seemed a marvel that a bird most young people outside the Moskitia have never seen in the wild would become Honduras's premier avian symbol. Tegucigalpa conservationists joked that the *guara* is not at all uncommon. It can be found in cages everywhere! Indeed, the bird has declined drastically in the wild, a victim of the pet trade and habitat destruction, and perhaps for other reasons as well. The Scarlet Macaw is the preeminent symbol of the fading *pajaral,* and in Olancho villages where it was common only two decades ago, it is almost inevitably the first bird people mention when talking about the way their *pajarales* used to be. Francisco Urbina and I have made a special effort to understand why the *guara* has disappeared, and what this means to local people. We have found that almost invariably the *guara roja* is the first bird out of the mouths of Olanchanos when they are discussing what has been lost: it is used to prove the widespread belief that the environment is severely damaged.

Guaras, once common in most of Honduras, claim an important place in Honduran culture. Even though they are recognized to be flashy and intelligent, they aren't well liked as cage birds because they are raucous and destructive. *Guaras* are most often kept by well-to-do families who cherish them more as status symbols then for their conversational abilities. At the gates of Copán Ruins, captive macaws have been photogenic tourist attractions, while in some outdoor restaurants of the North Coast they sidle up to diners to demand handouts. They are as common as quetzals on the promotional brochures of Central American ecotravel outfits. But long before ecotourism, *guaras* stimulated the Honduran imagination, as folklorist Pompilio Ortega captures in "Razonan las Guacamayas?" ("Do macaws reason?").[1] He wrote that in his village, as in all Honduran villages, pigs roamed free, going wherever they chose. One woman had a partly finished fence around her yard, and she was frequently invaded by piglets that came from neighboring houses to raid her garden. She would retaliate by beating the animals with a pole. The result was that every time the squeals of a piglet were heard in the neighborhood, women up and down the street would rush out to save it from a beating. The vengeful woman's *guara,* observing all this from a fence post, learned to imitate the squeals of a piglet, causing an uproar, whereupon the bird would laugh raucously in a human voice.

From his perch, the *guara* in Ortega's village was close enough to the jail to talk with the guards. One day, during a jailbreak, the *guara* guided pursuers of an escaped prisoner: "Corran, allá va abajoooo!" ("Run, there he goes down that way!").

This particular captive bird was allowed to fly free, leaving its domicile for long periods. One day, an individual bird left a wild flock to perch on a sack of coffee on the back of a mule headed out of town for San Pedro Sula. It began a conversation with the muledrivers. "Nicolasa?" it said, appearing to search for its owner, the piglet-beating woman. After repeatedly querying "Me vas a dar pan?" ("Are you going to give me bread?") to no avail, it returned to its adoptive flock.

"Psychologists," Ortega wrote, "tell us this is neither reasoning nor intelligence, but only pure instinct." He thought this a poor word for such an animal, and that the lexicon lacked an appropriate term to describe it.

The *guara roja* is common in Honduras today only in the eastern lowland rain forests and pine savannas, where the globally threatened Great

Green Macaw is also found.[2] On the central plains of Olancho, *guaras* are still seen occasionally — the Urbinas, and Oscar Pinot in Juticalpa, report high-flying pairs and trios from time to time. In 1995, a farmer from the village of San Buenaventura in the Valle de Gualaco flushed two *guaras* out of his coffee farm on the edge of the Parque Nacional Sierra de Agalta. But, as one hears people lament again and again, the *guaras* have effectively vanished from central Olancho, after dwindling to a trickle over the last twenty years.

Francisco Urbina's mother *doña* Edita has not made up her mind about the reasons for the *guara's* disappearance. She can hardly believe they're gone. In the 1970s, the piney slopes a kilometer from La Venta blushed with them. They descended on the forests to eat pine seeds. She recalls that though the *guaras* roosted in the pines, they also abounded on the plain, where they ate the fruits of the *piñón,* a shrub in the Euphorbiacae family commonly used in live fences (almost every person I have interviewed in Olancho mentions *piñón* and pine seeds as the *guaras'* principal sustenance).

Doña Edita, having observed the *guaras* dwindle and disappear, thinks that they have gone elsewhere. No one in her family witnessed their wholesale slaughter or massive capture in the Valle de Agalta. Francisco says that local people in his area don't like them as pets — they are too destructive, too loud, and not very good talkers. If *guaras* were extirpated thanks to the pet trade, the Urbinas were never aware of this practice in or around La Venta.

The Urbinas do remember that boys with slingshots persecuted the magnificent birds. Dead *guaras* had various uses. They were large and easily approachable targets, their meat was appetizing, and their feathers could be used for decoration. Nevertheless, Francisco and his parents do not believe that such actions explain the *guara's* extirpation from the Valle de Agalta. What happened to the "thousands" and "great flocks" that persisted even into the 1970s?

A few people theorize that the *guaras* were wiped out by some disease. Others think they were not destroyed but forced to go elsewhere. People remember that macaws came in flocks to eat pine seeds and *piñón* during the rains but were absent during the dry season. That they were migrants and not residents is supported by the fact that nobody remembers having seen nests, even though young birds have been observed.

Perhaps the macaws that visited central Olancho were persecuted on their nesting grounds (wherever those were), since a popular way to harvest members of the parrot family is to chop down a tree with a nest and take the nestlings that survive.

Based on the evidence we gathered, Francisco began to wonder whether the disappearance of the *guara* was related to changes in the pine forests combined with direct persecution and loss of nesting habitat on the lowland rain forest frontier. National and foreign lumber companies have extracted most of the large pine timber from Honduras, and the normally rapid regeneration of pines has been retarded in many regions by the ever-spreading use of uncontrolled burns for richer pastures. Furthermore, the pine bark beetle infestation that swept through Honduras in the mid-1960s caused up to 70 percent tree mortality in some areas.[3]

Macaw conservation is an important issue in many Neotropical countries. Our own investigation in Olancho has served to underscore the value of local knowledge, key in a historical and geographical analysis of the species' place in the *pajaral*. Conservationists should be aware that the Scarlet Macaw was once a leading member of the *pajaral* and a cherished part of the Honduran avifauna. Efforts to bring it back, at least in places like Olancho, should be based in this cultural appreciation.

Why Local Names Matter

One way to gauge local knowledge and awareness of the *pajaral* is to find out about names. The fact that people give names to many of their birds signifies a cultural understanding of the roles of the *pajaral* in their lives, and gives the lie to any assumptions outsiders may make about local disinterest in or ignorance of biodiversity. Rural Olanchanos possess an intricate lexicon of bird names, as they do for other fauna and for the flora. When talking to rural Olanchanos, one enters a labyrinth of meanings that at first bewilder and confuse the newcomer. After hours of patient discussion, one comes out on the other side of the labyrinth with a far richer knowledge of the meanings birds have for people. I can but scrape the surface of this lexicon (additional local names are listed in the appendix).

Local knowledge about parrots and parakeets far surpasses that possessed by a casual birdwatcher armed with guidebooks and binoculars.

The identification of *loros* (parrots) and *pericos* (parakeets) often demands an acute awareness of habits and habitats, calls, and flight pattern. The three common *loros* of La Venta — what the Urbinas call *frijol* (Red-lored Parrot), *fueteté* (White-fronted Parrot), and *come-maíz* (White-crowned Parrot) — can be identified by their wingbeats and flight patterns. The *fueteté* has shallow, rapid wingbeats and a straight flight path, while the *frijol* has deeper, stronger strokes. These two commonly fly in small family groups and nest on the plains, while the diving and swooping *come-maíz* descends from the mountains in large flocks.

The *frijol/Cristobal/licoy/picoy,* or Red-lored Parrot (*Amazona autumnalis*), is also known as the *pico rojo* ("red beak"), while the *fueteté/hueteté* is the *naranjero* ("orange eater") and *guayabero,* because it descends in great flocks on *guayabo* (guava) forests during fruiting season. Two similar long-tailed species are the Green Parakeet and the Olive-throated Parakeet. The Green is known as *ocotero* ("pine parakeet"), *pecho rojo* ("red throat"), and *barba roja* ("red beard"), while the Olive-throated, which people describe as frequenting abandoned termite nests, is the *chocoyo* or *chocoyito*. The smallest local parakeet is the *periquito de montaña* (Barred Parakeet).

Loros and *pericos* are often named for their calls, which people hear a little differently from place to place. The onomatopoeic *frijol* (Red-lored Parrot) of La Venta is *Cristobal* in El Boquerón, *licoy* in Gualaco, and *picoy* in San Esteban. This geographic variation is surpassed by that for the Social Flycatcher, which is called *nicho, nicho feo, dicho feo, bicho, bicho feo, Luisito,* and *fuiste al río.* The Groove-billed Ani is *tijúl, tíjul, tijuíl, tijulio,* or *Tío Julio;* the Melodious Blackbird is *huachír, huachíl,* or *huachín.*

Local names also carry significant information about birds by pointing to salient aspects of their natural history. Take the example of the "White-crowned Parrot." The single English name describes a physical characteristic but tells little of substance about the bird. On the other hand, a plethora of local names describe the bird's feeding habits, colors, and common habitats. It is called both *pico blanco* (white bill, for its white crown) or *loro negro* (because it appears all dark when seen in flight). *Lora de montaña* signifies that it is native to the montane rain forest (where it nests), and *come-maíz* declares it a pest of maize crops. Careful questioning reveals that populations of the White-crowned Parrot have diminished in both the Valle de Agalta and the Valle de Olancho. Most people believe that the reason is destruction of its nesting habitat in the *montaña* combined with its persecution as a crop pest on the plains. Local experience suggests that scarecrows can help preserve the bird and avoid wasting precious funds on birdshot. Slingshots are ineffective against flocks large enough to destroy a family's livelihood within a few hours. Shouting and setting off firecrackers, as the Madrids have done, can probably solve the problem.

Seventeen species of pigeons and doves (family Columbidae) inhabit central Olancho. The number of names for them indicates the importance they are accorded as food sources, pets, and symbols of secular and religious devotion. The dove is the dominant bird image used in Honduran poetry. In popular culture, names for doves are tied to meanings ranging from the divine to the obscene. They are the only wild birds for which rural Olanchanos build habitations. These are inverted half-cylinders of thick, dry bark hung from under the eaves of houses, and they are quite attractive to the feral *palomas de Castilla* (Rock Doves). Luz Medina comments that townspeople often view houses with feral doves as a sign of poverty, perhaps because doves are stigmatized as meat sources by people who can afford "better."

The mournful calls of the *tres pesos* (Short-billed Pigeon) in Comunayaca and *doña* Clara Luz Rojas's *paloma* can evoke sadness and nostalgia, while to Emilia Cardona in Juticalpa, dove calls were not sad but beautiful. Jesús Aguilar Paz records a rich onomatopoeia among the Honduran doves. The *palomas franjoles* "dan las horas" ("give the hour"); the *palomas de montaña* go "adiós ooh . . ." or "tres pesos ooh . . . ," and the *palomas guamileras/comunes* say "Muchachos, qué hacemos, se va el cura" ("Boys, what shall we do, the priest is going away").[4]

The White-tipped Dove is known as *barranquera* or *barranqueña* because it is common in forested gullies. But Tomás Guillén assured us that its real name is *la bruja* ("the witch"), which another resident of San Esteban also told us was its "true name." Neither had ever heard it referred to as *barranquera*, even though this is what it is called in La Venta, a village only a few kilometers away.

Sometimes, local bird names capture the poetic quality of a species far better than any standardized official name (whether in English, Spanish, or Latin). The Striped Cuckoo, a rarely glimpsed denizen of thick brush, is easy to detect thanks to its distinctive two-note whistle. Because we did not know a local name for it at first, we used *cuclillo rayado*, which made little sense to Olanchanos, who do not apply *cuclillo* (a Castilian Spanish term) to any members of the cuckoo family. We finally encountered a village where people were not only familiar with the bird but had a name far more evocative than ours. They called it *pájaro pichete*, "lizard bird," because they had observed its reptilian style of running—slithering along the ground and up into the vegetation; perhaps the name was inspired by the bird's color pattern as well.

Some bird names come from folklore that can be encountered across Honduras and beyond. The *alma de perro* (Lesser Roadrunner) is common in burned fields and pastures, and its name is used all over Honduras, though few people can recount the story behind the origin of this name. According to Jesús Aguilar Paz, the *alma de perro* ("soul of a dog") derives its name from an old tale about some debauched women who would abandon their small children at home for long periods. Upon returning from one extended vacation in sin, they found their children dead of hunger and thirst. Divine wrath condemned these women "with souls of dogs" to wander perpetually among the most hellish, burned landscapes, unable to drink from streams. If they tried, the water would turn to blood. And so these "souls of dogs" run about with their beaks raised to heaven, waiting for the first drops of water from the sky after the long summer drought. The *alma de perro's* infinitely sad song is heard at dusk, when it has given up hope of water for the day and pours forth its shame and bitterness.[5]

The *pájaro león* ("lion bird": Squirrel Cuckoo), cousin to the roadrunner, is known far and wide. According to an oft-mentioned bit of Honduran bird lore, it is thus named because it announces the hidden presence of a mountain lion. Folklorist Antonio Osorio Orellana relates a story told to him by a farmer new to an (unnamed) Honduran village, who entered the nearby forest and heard the calls of the *pájaro león* or *tubuca*.[6] He fled fearfully back to the village, and the neighbors told him that indeed a lion had been lurking about in the forest, coming out at night to take calves. They returned with firearms but found no trace of the animal. The farmer related to the folklore collector that his experience had left him doubting the veracity of any connection between the presence of the bird and the predator. After all, the *pájaro león* is a common bird across the country, and its call is frequently heard. The *león*, on the other hand, is all but gone from large areas of Honduras. Even in

Olancho, where the puma still roams, many farmers comment skeptically that "wherever the *pájaro león* calls, it is said that the mountain lion is close by," with emphasis on "it is said."

Birds that have local names seem to be the ones local people know best. These are usually the common, everyday species such as the *chorcha loca* ("crazy oriole": Black-headed Saltator), *pico de oro* ("golden beak": Northern Jacana), and *paloma chinga* ("tailless pigeon": Little Tinamou), but they include scarcer species like the *pájaro estaca* ("stick bird": Northern Potoo) and *estiquirín* (Great Horned Owl). Certain highly visible bird groups, like the toucans, doves, parrots, and woodpeckers, have more than one name for almost every species. Other groups, like the woodcreepers, have one generic name, *trepapalos,* and most local people are unaware of the subtle differences by which outsiders with binoculars and bird guides distinguish them. The extreme example of this is the *chipe,* essential to the concept of *pajaral,* and applied to over a hundred "indistinguishable" species of arboreal warblers, vireos, greenlets, and gnatcatchers, among others. *Arrocero,* "rice eater," has a similar semantic function for terrestrial finches, sparrows, seedeaters, and so forth. Overall, since 1991 we have recorded names for more than two hundred local bird species. In the village *pajaral,* the percentage of known and named birds is highest, while in the old-growth rain forest many fewer species are recognized. The vast majority of species in the rain forest have no local names (including, for example, all the ovenbirds and antbirds as well as most tanagers).

🐦 The Pajaral *at La Venta*

Villagers have names for the birds of their *pajarales* because they spend so much time on this most familiar terrain. To understand how the rural domestic landscape created by small farmers in Olancho (and by extension throughout many similar parts of Latin America) is favorable to avian biodiversity, I have made many visits to the Urbinas in La Venta. The Urbina farm is a fine example of a *pajaral* and is a model for rural bird-friendly landscapes.

The Urbinas do not depend entirely on what their farm can produce. *Don* Esteban has a variety of sidelines, including the repairing of mechanical devices and shoes. In *doña* Edita's ancestral town of El Pedrero, northeast of the Valle de Agalta, *don* Esteban has a coffee farm to which he and certain members of his family relocate during the harvest. But the major income sources for the Urbina family are from the son and daughters, who work outside La Venta.

Before 1994, the Urbinas were political activists, securing the vote for the *Nacionalista* party in their corner of the plain. They were known as voracious deer hunters by night, campaigners by day. All that changed when Francisco, the oldest son, became a Baptist in 1993. He brought his family into the faith, wed his common-law wife Fausta in a religious ceremony, and became a minister. The Urbinas are now pillars of their church in La Venta and work hard to evangelize the local population. Every evening, and almost all day Sunday, the family dresses up in their best clothes and goes to *culto,* where fervent worship and song fill their hours.[7] Their lives are replete with religious discussion, missions by bicycle to remote villages, and verbal crusades against the stark varieties of "sin" that proliferate in the Valle de Agalta — blood feuds, alcoholism, drug abuse, and homicide. When I asked Francisco if he feels they have made progress in La Venta (because converts often backslide), he mentioned that one of their strongest members was the *estanquera,* the woman who had owned the village's drinking establishment, which used to claim at least one homicide victim monthly in drunken brawls.

The Urbinas' faith is a hedge against the harsh social reality of the Valle de Agalta. It is a constantly reiterated barrier of piety that keeps them all, especially the small children, inside an almost hermetically sealed world. Outside, they risk being drawn into circles of political alliances and never-ending conflicts, where not owning an AK-47 assault rifle is an unwise and unmasculine choice. Out there, they say, people exist who will shoot you point-blank because you "looked at them wrong." Even more frightening, if your family does not retaliate in kind, the enemies will usually get away with their crimes in a frontier society where law enforcement is minimal at best. Rebelling against such a world, the Urbinas need a hedge of faith that is strong and reliable. But they have more than songs and prayers to keep the evil at bay. Their land itself is a physical barrier, a private sphere respected by others, where children can delve for nests and climb for fruits in relative safety. Their ten hectares provide a refuge for childhood innocence and everyday sanity.

Casual visitors to the Urbina farm might gaze at the vegetation and see only a maize field, some scrub, a big tree, a little coffee. But the microgeography of a farm is far deeper and more complex. Every patch of vegetation has specific meanings to its farmers. Most plants have several uses. A tree can provide fruit, medicine, shade, fence posts, and firewood. Certain trees and patches of vegetation have secret as well as public meanings — specific histories known only to one person, and others shared by members of the family. From family to family, farms differ both in their biophysical composition and in what they mean to their owners. The *campesino* landscape as a whole is an ongoing composition that each person creates and experiences in a different way.

Domestic animals help to shape the landscape. Pigs traverse networks of trails to and from rooting places, from outdoor latrines to riverside tuber-filled mud sloughs. Chickens scratch their way across microfaunal landscapes; ducks shovel out oozing springs. More than anything, the microgeography of farms like the Urbinas'—the shapes and sizes of plants, species composition, the look and smell of the land—has to do with the grazing, browsing, resting, watering, and defecation of cattle. Parcels such as the *arboleda* (wood lot) are crisscrossed by cattle paths, and the animals "hollow out" the vegetation from beneath. These hollows make perfect diurnal resting places for the *pucuyo* (Pauraque). In the Urbinas' management scheme, cattle must be carefully penned and herded, since they tend to overgraze succulent food plants and avoid unpalatable growth, thus encouraging the latter to flourish. The diets of cattle help determine floral composition of the *campesino* landscape on the plains of Olancho.

Cattle need quality pasture grass. The Urbinas are intimately familiar with the lush types of African grasses (for example, *jaraguá* and *guinea*), which despite good yields they regard with some suspicion as "foreign" and "invasive." They prefer the delicate mat of aesthetically attractive grasses such as the *zacate estrella* and *zacate gallina* that grace the *sabana* ("savanna," in this case meaning rural grass yard) between the houses. *Don* Esteban and Francisco know how to avoid undergrazing and overgrazing of each kind of grass and have designed a careful system of day-to-day livestock rotation, while also using their cows to fertilize fallow fields and clean out corn stalks. They work continually to maintain their barbed wire fences around every parcel. Cattle are extremely important to the Urbinas, and their landscape changes and improves through new techniques resulting from frequent family discussions about management strategies.

On the Urbina farm, wild birds, small mammals, herpetofauna, invertebrates, and others also find their places. The Urbinas memorize the Circadian and seasonal rhythms of many wild birds just as they know the fruiting and flowering of the birds' preferred plants. Many of their birds are residents and regular visitors to the immediate vicinity of the dwellings, which includes the *sabana* between the two houses, the vegetable gardens, the *huerta* (kitchen garden), and some widely spaced trees. Francisco's rapidly growing *chincho* trees in front of his house are refuges for nesting birds such as the *turquita* (Inca Dove, in this case), while the protective foliage brings migrant *chipes* (e.g., wood-warblers and vireos) close to the porch. Esteban Jr. told me that Inca Doves nest in the *chinchos* every year. These tame ground-doves are highly regarded in La Venta, and several families kill them to eat. *Barranqueras* (White-tipped Doves) are not shy, either. They often come to eat grain with the domestic fowl when it is tossed out in the morning.

The territory right around *doña* Fausta's house is staked out by several varieties of small *mosquero* (flycatcher), by a *gorrioncito* (hummingbird), and by the ubiquitous *cucarachero* (House Wren), which goes up and around the walls and inside the house, as well as along the fence posts and through small shrubs. The tops of the *espino blanco* trees often host the larger *mosqueros,* including the *dicho feo* group.[8]

The *huerta* next to *doña* Edita's house dates from the late 1980s, and in its present form contains *achiote* (annatto), avocados, mangos, and *coyol* palm trees, with cacao, coffee, and ornamentals in the understory. The Urbinas tap into La Venta's water system here, and the runoff from showers and other washing helps to create a moist, humid understory favored by *zorzales* (Clay-colored Robins) during the long, hot summer. The *coyol* palm has provided nesting habitat for different types of doves, while an entwining *maracuyá* (passionfruit) vine sees the visits of many frugivores as well as hummingbirds that come to suck the passionfruit flower nectar. Thrushes and tanagers frequent a nearby coconut palm, nesting among its fronds. *Don* Esteban is most proud of the birds that use his fruit trees back by the vegetable garden. He has taken me out at night to show me Clay-colored Robin, Melodious Blackbird, and Spot-breasted Oriole roosting spots, secure from house cats among the protective foliage of the oranges, lemons, and tamarind.

In the stretch of land between the houses and the river are several large *guanacaste* trees, their great, spreading canopies heavily laden with epiphytic *gallitos* ("little roosters," bromeliads), orchids, and ferns. In addition to hosting flocks of migrant and resident *chipes* and other gleaning birds, the giant trees may harbor *chachalacas* and a wide variety of raptors, including vultures, *guacos* (Laughing Falcons), *cacaos* (Red-throated Caracaras), various types of hawks, and in 1998, a family of *aguiluches* (hawk-eagles). *Don* Esteban, always the protective farmer, sighted them from his house and blasted away, killing one. His conservationist son Francisco was not present at the time. On retrieving the massive bird, he and *doña* Edita were chagrined to find that they had made a mistake. This was no *gavilán pollero* ("chicken hawk," a generic designation) but a type of crested eagle. It was the first time anyone could remember seeing such a bird in La Venta. These are known to be rare denizens of the *montaña,* and it is still unclear to them why such a magnificent *cazamicos* ("monkey-hunter," any large rain forest raptor) would show up on the plains at the very edge of a large village. The other two members of the hawk-eagle family stuck around at least until May, roosting in the tall trees and hunting in the nearby *vegas* (bottomlands). The Urbinas concluded that the eagles were taking advantage of the high number of small mammals in the *vegas* that year. Francisco, who was angry that his father had shot a threatened Ornate Hawk-Eagle, made sure that the others were protected. His parents held onto the massive talons and crested head of the bird, all they could salvage from voracious recycling agents.

Several of the fruit trees scattered across the Urbina property become aviaries in certain seasons. There is a type of *Genipa* tree called the *jagua* right behind the *huerta,* and its gray and pulpy fruits, ripening in July and August, are devoured by blackbirds, orioles, thrushes, tanagers, parrots, and saltators as well as by children. Frugivorous birds eat most of the *ciruelas* (hog plum) before they fall, while also gorging in the mango grove several times a day during the May apex of fruit production.

Some of the Urbinas' most attractive birds stay in the *vega* bottomlands, where there is a partial evergreen canopy of walnuts and figs heavily laden with epiphytic plants. The *vega* trees are safe and rewarding havens for such species as Masked Tityras, Blue-throated Motmots, Chestnut-headed Oropendolas, and the three toucans: the large *pico navaja* (Keel-billed Toucan) at times in groups of eight or more, the smaller *tucanillo verde* (Emerald Toucanet) on occasion, and the *tilís* (Collared Aracari). The *tucanes* are absent for long periods, and the Urbinas know that during those times the birds are feasting up in the *montaña.*

In the dense, moist, and insect-rich undergrowth of the *vegas,* Neotropical migrant wood-warblers such as the American Redstart and Hooded, Yellow, Chestnut-sided, Magnolia, Blue-winged, Worm-eating, Kentucky, and Black-and-white warblers are abundant during migration; some stay several months. Migrant vireos are common as well. The Streak-headed Woodcreeper, a *trepapalos,* is a permanent resident, and its downsliding trill can often be heard.

In a corner of the Urbina property is a small grove of *guácimo* trees, also known as *tapaculo* or *caulote.* This tree, characteristic of Middle American dry forests, is known for its dry, black, and succulent fruits, efficacious remedies for diarrhea. The *soldadito* (Crimson-collared Tanager), *viuda* (Blue-gray Tanager), and other frugivores are very fond of them. Other features of the *guácimo* are its tangles of evergreen, parasitic *muérdago* (mistletoe), which glow red with berries during the height of the dry season, at a time when the deciduous host trees and most neighboring trees are leafless. A group of diminutive yellow, black, and white tanagers of the genus *Euphonia* specialize in eating *muérdago* berries.

In January, 1996, Francisco and the three geography professors from Texas encountered in the *guácimo* grove a flock of euphonias that tentatively included a new species for Honduras, the White-vented Euphonia. I visited a few weeks later and confirmed the sighting, finding a single male with the flock of Yellow-throated and Scrub euphonias that spent part of every morning in the grove. Francisco reported that the euphonias stayed around at least another month. The White-vented Euphonia, approximately number 700 on the "official" list of Honduran avifauna, was not unexpected. It ranges from Guatemala to South America, and the lack of a Honduran record had been an oversight, reflecting less its own rarity than a paucity of observers. Significantly, a new species for the country came from its first observer's own backyard.[9]

In the pastures and corn fields between the houses and the *vega,* isolated trees such as the *indio desnudo* take on special significance for perching parrots, doves, flycatchers, raptors, and many others. The *encino,* a narrow-leaved evergreen oak (*Quercus*), is the preferred habitat of several woodpeckers, which also visit the citrus trees and other fruits. The common *chaco* (also *checo* or *cheje:* Golden-fronted Woodpecker) is the tamest and best known. Another, the *chaco naranjero* (Golden-olive Woodpecker), specializes in orange orchards, while a third, the *chaco de robledal* (Acorn Woodpecker), visits the *encinales* (*encino* groves) and *robledales* (broad-leaved oak groves). Local people are fascinated by this woodpecker because it stores acorns in rows of holes that it drills into pine tree trunks.

Two large, crested woodpeckers (Pale-billed and Lineated) are also occasional visitors to the *vegas,* though they are more common in the *montaña.* They are often referred to in the Valle de Agalta as the "true" *carpinteros* or *carpinteros grandes* and in other places as *pito real.* People in the Valle de Olancho know them as *monte zumbas,* after their loud drumming that resounds throughout the woods. Experienced observers know that there are two species, one more common on the plains (the Lineated Woodpecker), with a variety of calls, and another usually found in the mountains (the Pale-billed Woodpecker), recognized by its distinct double drum. Some people kill these large woodpeckers for food.

Francisco has become adept at identifying the obscure *mosqueritos* (small flycatchers) such as the Common Tody-Flycatcher, Slate-colored Tody-Flycatcher, and Northern Beardless Tyrannulet that lurk in the Urbinas' scrub. The best-known of myriad small birds in these scrub habitats are the easily visible *semillero* or *collarín* (White-collared Seedeater) and the *saltarín* (Blue-black Grassquit). Several other types of small birds, generically known as *arroceros* ("rice eaters": sparrows and finches) are usually invisible in the dense, impenetrable brush, except during high summer when most of the foliage has dropped. During the driest months — March, April, and May — the Urbinas glimpse birds unknown to them, some migrant, some resident.

Among the wild shrubs in the Urbinas' *guamiles* (fallow fields grown into scrub), the *pimientilla* and the *madreado* are most attractive to birds. Another, the *fruta de culebra,* is favored by tanagers, while more than ten varieties of hummingbirds regularly visit bramble flowers. In the fields, the corn on the higher terraces and the beans and corn of the *vegas* need to be protected against the visits of avian pests. But other birds are left alone: the *pico de oro* (Northern Jacana) of the *vegas,* and two kinds of *tijerilla* ("scissor-tails": the Fork-tailed and Scissor-tailed flycatchers). By the river, the Urbinas have observed the nesting habits of a *cabezón* ("big head": Rose-throated Becard), numerous *martín pescadores* (kingfishers), swallows, herons, motmots, and sandpipers. Once, after a storm, Francisco found a Sungrebe swimming in a backwater (this species is usually found only on the coastal rivers). And so on it goes — the *pájaro pichete* emitting its ethereal two-note call from a hidden perch, a pair of *pájaros leónes* scrambling up the trees, small groups of Groove-billed Anis bursting out of the hedgerows, and Olive-sided Flycatchers perched on dead snags during migration.

The same day he first glimpsed the White-vented Euphonia, Francisco showed the professors two of the loudest and most attractive scrub denizens, the Barred Antshrike and the Rufous-browed Peppershrike. As yet, we have been unable to encounter local names for either species, even though knowledgeable observers like Esteban Urbina and José Mendoza are familiar with the birds. Both species, though quite secretive most of the year, are among the most ubiquitous dry forest and scrub inhabitants. The Barred Antshrike, in particular, is hard to forget: the male is zebra-striped and has a variety of memorable calls. The peppershrike's monotonous vireo refrain is one of the most often heard sounds on the plains. Nevertheless, for a reason unknown to me neither bird seems to have carved a niche in popular consciousness.

One of the generic *arroceros,* hard to see and drably colored, is the locally endemic race of the Green-backed Sparrow, *Arremonops chloronotus twomeyi*. In the dry season it can be seen in the bushes, and its bouncing-ball call can be heard everywhere. During other seasons the "Twomey's" sparrow is close to invisible and largely silent. As is the case with the Honduran Emerald (chapter 5) and White-eared Groundsparrow (chapter 3), only recently have conservationists singled this sparrow out as an important bird. Otherwise, local people would have been none the wiser regarding its special status. Like the groundsparrow, the Green-backed Sparrow seems to thrive in the human landscape and is not threatened by prevailing cultural practices.

The *pajaral's* vegetative complexity and diversity favors more than two hundred species of birds on the Urbina farm. Except for *don* Esteban's tendency to blast at raptors, the Urbinas generally protect their birds. Furthermore, for a variety of reasons including their own health and safety, they do not believe in using agricultural chemicals. Both resident birds and Neotropical migrants find safe haven here. When the birds leave the Urbina farm and visit another in La Venta, as many do on a daily basis, they are generally protected as well, though some landowners do not restrict human depredation of birds at all.

La Venta and its environs are a cultural landscape knit together through networks of trails, the river, and ties of friendship and kinship. There are stark differences between this village of small farms and the adjacent landscape of the *terratenientes* described in the preceding chapter, where each ranch is an exclusive domain, and only one or two types of vegetative cover dominate large areas. Unlike the large ranches, *campesino* landscapes are crisscrossed by public trails, and one of the few ways that strangers can be kept from trespassing on a particular farm is barking dogs. For example, two main trails cross the Urbina farm, giving people ample opportunity to pilfer domestic and wild resources. Though *don* Esteban and *doña* Edita rarely punish neighbor children who steal their fruit, more valuable resources such as firewood are coveted. It is a serious breach of ethics to remove any tree or shrub from someone else's land without permission. The same can sometimes be said for birds and other fauna. It is ultimately up to the landowners whether "their" birds can be hunted.

The Urbinas are captivated by birds, seeing them as more than mere objects. Their farm is a microcosm of intertwining human and avian cultures. Like almost everyone, they love orioles, tanagers, and toucans for their colors; Clay-colored Robins for their songs; wrens for their inquisitiveness; swallows for their freedom in the air. They express wonder and joy openly when they have close experiences with certain birds, and they admit freely that birds enrich their lives. So often are the same types of feelings evinced by other people in La Venta, and throughout the villages of Olancho, that one feels the *pajaral* has a future.

Biodiversity Conservation, Starting in the Village

What might "biodiversity" and "conservation" mean in the context of La Venta and its *pajaral*? The location of this large Honduran village of three hundred houses, straddling the ecotone of deciduous savanna and semi-evergreen floodplain, clearly contributes to its biodiversity. But the resultant diversity of niches does not come about solely through a combination of natural factors such as elevation, soils, slope, temperature, and biogeographic position. The key factor is the land management practiced by local residents: they are not consciously "planting for birds" but achieve that effect in their agroecosystem. Where one *hacienda* managed for cattle results in only a few types of floral and faunal habitats, the same area occupied by twenty small farmers becomes a biotic mosaic.

Although the attraction of abundant food sources (especially fruits) turns La Venta into a death trap for certain species, many others, such as the Neotropical wood-warblers and vireos, go virtually unnoticed by slingshot-wielding kids and shotgun-toting farmers. Some small farmers apply dangerous agricultural chemicals, but La Venta is largely free of these in comparison to *terrateniente* landscapes, where abundant capital, easy credit, and the need for high production combine to favor chemical saturation.

Close to 250 species of birds inhabit the many niches of La Venta at some point during the year, whether as regular nesters, seasonal inhabitants, or occasional visitors (e.g., Sungrebes and Ornate Hawk-Eagles). This "unplanned" avian diversity results from local cultural practices that tend to favor biotic diversity and complexity. What is *already happening* in so many villages similar to La Venta should be the basis from which to undertake any further conservation-oriented projects. Indeed, such projects in many cases can involve only small changes in the ways that people interact with birds. When Francisco Urbina bore upon his parents to protect hawk-eagles, he was an agent in this process of adjustment and of bird conservation with no need of a budget. A people-centered, village-level conservation strategy for the *pajaral,* just about anywhere in Latin America, should recognize and, if possible, be built on existing cultural and political structures. This type of conservation should be carried out by local extensionists who encourage concatenating "small" actions rather than reliance on experts, fund-raising, and management plans as prerequisites for success. Local leaders such as Francisco Urbina are capable of being the catalysts of conservation in their villages. In his case, ornithophilia has buoyed him at times when not even his employer, the government agency COHDEFOR that manages wildlife and protected areas, is willing or able to give support.

As long as there is some accord between local lifeways and conservationist concepts of the importance of protecting biodiversity, bird conservation can be effective. Outsiders need to realize that many rural people care about birds, individually or as part of their family ethic, and that local knowledge is always important. Outsiders, and local people like Francisco Urbina, may profit from tapping into cultural streams and inserting themselves into specific ongoing situations, rather than imposing a conservation "ethic" coming from above and beyond the village. As a conservationist, Francisco is well aware that La Venta is not "trashed" or "degraded," to use two common outside terms for places that are not "virgin rain forest." He is sure that his relatives and neighbors hold the key to protecting their birds and the environment in general, because the *pajaral* is a human place.

Owls, *Cacaos,* and
Golden-cheeked Warblers

The *cacao* or Red-throated Caracara, though believed by ornithologists to have been extirpated from Honduras, hangs on in the remote hill country of northern Olancho. It is an everyday bird to those living on the margins; in comparatively modernized areas like La Venta, the *cacao* is now a memory.

Northern Olancho contains sparsely populated savannas on the far edges of its remote plains; beyond them the seemingly endless hills contain lenses of fertile soil for agriculture only along intermittent streams; the rest is vast silent pine and oak woods. In contrast, the Cordillera de Agalta rain forest frontier is dynamic and full of promise; coffee, cattle, and migratory agriculture are dependable sources of sustenance and income. While rain forest edges become more crowded every year, fewer and fewer people scrape their living from the sterile northern hills. As logging companies exploit the pines, water sources dry up, forcing ages-old communities to disband and emigrate. Outsiders are obsessed by the rain forest, whether because they want to exploit its resources or protect it, watch its birds, study its biodiversity, or hunt its jaguars. Few other than loggers are interested in the northern hill country, where biodiversity is relatively low and amenities for visitors are virtually non-existent.

Olanchanos who live in the northern hills are considered outdated and their beliefs are seen as irrational by those who live in centrally located areas such as the rich plains, the electrified villages, and the capitals. These "marginal" Olanchanos are at the bottom of a social and spatial hierarchy, the last to receive benefits; only battery-powered radios help them keep up with the pace of the world. This chapter delves into the situations of birds that live in the northern Olancho hills and in other places outside the normal scope of culture and science — birds that are forgotten, misunderstood, and ignored.

The night is another marginal realm that saturates human existence, causing even the most rational among us to begin yielding to superstition, especially when bereft of flashlights. To urban and rural dwellers alike, the night is still mysterious, and its birds, especially the owls, are stigmatized in local culture. Finally, the pine forest *serranía*, biotically impoverished prelude to the rain forest *montaña*, is the ever-present "background landscape" of daily existence in much of Olancho and highland Honduras. Among conservationists at least, the *serranías* hold little appeal when compared to nearby rain and cloud forests. However, the situation of one of its most notable avian residents, the Golden-cheeked Warbler, foreshadows the importance that the *serranía* should have for conservation schemes.

🐦 *Red-throated Caracaras in the Northern Hills*

Throughout northern Olancho, the *cacao* is one of the most familiar birds, though local people always comment on its drastic decline.[1] Francisco Urbina and I have not yet submitted the evidence of our rediscovery to any ornithology journal, for lack of photo evidence. The *cacao* persists in the hill country of northern Olancho and visits villages in the Valle de Agalta infrequently. Francisco has seen it many times, but because my opportunities to visit its nesting grounds have been limited to a handful of brief excursions, I have not yet glimpsed it. After six years of frustration, I finally heard one call in the hamlet of El Rodeo, Gualaco, in 2000.

This story began for Francisco and me when we were comparing notes on raptors back in April, 1994. His question "What about the *cacao*?" confounded me. From his description, we decided that he was talking about the Red-throated Caracara, which the bird guide said was called *cacao* in Panama after its far-carrying cries. Francisco, who had never seen it close up, described it as an odd type of raptor that never soared but perched and flew awkwardly, like a guan or turkey. According to Burt Monroe's 1968 *Distributional Survey of the Birds of Honduras*, the bird had been collected near San Esteban in 1948 and in the Valle de Olancho in 1937. Esteban Urbina, Sr., was quite familiar with the *cacao* and had seen it close up many times. In the old days, this black bird with a red throat had been abundant and had usually been observed feasting on arboreal wasp larvae from the *trompa de chancho* ("pig's snout") and *casco de burro* ("donkey's hoof") nests. *Don* Esteban couldn't fathom why there were fewer *cacaos* now, because these were birds that no one hunted. One could see groups of two or three and occasionally as many as eight. In the old days, the Urbinas recalled, they had been as common as Black Vultures around La Venta.

Checking these descriptions against those of other local residents, we became certain that the mysterious bird was the Red-throated Caracara. The problem for us was that ornithologists considered this species extirpated from Mexico and northern Central America. The relevant literature reported that it had not been recorded north of southern Nicaragua in three decades and was also scarce in southern Central America, hanging on in only the most remote areas. The reasons for the bird's astonishing decline were unknown, and studies were needed urgently. (By contrast, the Red-throated Caracara's range throughout South America has apparently not diminished.)[2]

The Urbinas recall the *cacaos* to have been only seasonal visitors to the Valle de Agalta. Gualaco residents confirmed this for the Valle de Gualaco. The Urbina family did not know where the birds spent the remainder of the year, nor had they ever seen a nest. We assumed that the relict Olancho *cacao* population resided in the nearby *montaña* of the Sierra de Agalta and that family groups made occasional forays or postbreeding dispersals to nearby lowland villages such as La Venta. The *cacao,* according to the literature at our disposal, was a rain forest bird. But, oddly, although this is a difficult species to overlook, no one had heard or seen the bird in the Montaña de Babilonia.

Though nobody found them during frequent trips to the Parque Nacional Sierra de Agalta in 1994, the caracaras were sighted often in the Valle de Gualaco and Valle de Agalta. After December, they disappeared altogether. By August, 1995, *cacaos* resumed their infrequent appearances on the plains. We began to suspect that the birds retreated to somewhere more remote, perhaps to nest, during the dry season, returning to the plains in the rainy season.

In late 1996, Francisco received a report from a friend who had seen *cacaos* north of the Valle de Agalta in the Pacura area. While scouting for timber, he had observed them nesting in tall pines on steep slopes above the Río Grande (see fig. 2; the river is at upper right on the map of central Olancho). He claimed to have approached the birds quite closely, since they seemed to have little fear of people. Following this account, we changed our compass bearing 180 degrees, turning away from the Sierra de Agalta and postulating that the *cacaos* of the Valle de Agalta were emerging from the great fastness of rolling pine and oak forest in northern Olancho, where the human population density is the lowest in Honduras outside the Moskitia. North and northwest of the Valle de Gualaco and Valle de Agalta lie four thousand square kilometers of Olancho hill country with barely a fertile vale to encourage settlement.[3] The primary livelihood in the region is logging, carried out by an assortment of Honduran and foreign timber companies that maintain camps here and there, skidding old-growth pine logs off the slopes and out of the gullies, cutting them, and hauling them to local mills and to other places closer to Tegucigalpa and the coast. Despite the logging, the region remains quite wild, with only one or two families per square kilometer. Indeed, as mentioned, logging and accompanying environmental changes are forcing families and entire communities to abandon the hills.

On June 22, 1998, Francisco and I obtained the loan of a forest service vehicle and driver for a day of *cacao* hunting. Across the highway from the turnoff for La Venta, a road departs northward, skirts a big sawmill, and winds along dissected alluvial fans through the sere hill country along the northwestern edge of the Valle de Agalta. The La Venta–sized village of El Barrero, next to the Río Grande, surprised me in its opulence. This cattle-ranching village was clogged with the dust of late-model pickup trucks; there were satellite dishes and other signs of the *nouveaux riches*.

After El Barrero traffic ceased, and we clambered up and down and around for an hour in empty scrubland, finally pausing at the tiny hamlet of El Zope ("The Vulture"). Francisco talked to an acquaintance who was aware of the *cacaos* but had not seen them recently. We continued, and where we turned off the road onto a dead-end track toward the hamlet of Las Lomas, the landscape became cactus-studded and dry as a desert, even though only a few kilometers away in the Valle de Agalta the rains had commenced more than a month before, and La Venta was

already verdant. Along the Quebrada del Benque below us a tall deciduous gallery forest grew, while the cacti, agave, and acacia on the slopes
gave way upstream to *serranías* (piney hills).

The hamlet of Las Lomas consisted of a handful of dwellings set well
apart from one another on a hill above the Quebrada del Benque. We
lingered briefly at the house of Olivia García, promising to return for
lunch after finding the *cacaos.* She knew them well, even though she had
not ventured up into the hills in many years. *Doña* Olivia commented
that during the winter, the birds came down to the quebrada right below
the village and that a group had shown up several days before. None
were around at present, so it was best we hike farther into the hills.

Eliberto Torres and his son took us on the search. He assured us the
birds had "come down" ("han bajado") in the previous eight to fifteen
days, so they couldn't be too far away or difficult to find. He, *doña* Olivia,
and people we encountered along the trail all knew the bird, its call, its
dietary habits, and its superficial similarity to vultures. In Las Lomas, we
discovered excitedly, the *cacao* was still an important member of the avifauna. *Don* Eliberto outlined exactly when and how many birds usually
showed up at the village; on which trees they would perch; which wasps
nests they preferred. He also saw them frequently while hunting up in
the high *serranía,* where they prefer tall pines.

As we hiked through progressively more secluded *montañuelas*
(groves of thick forest), the tracks of wild mammals became more
common along the creek margins. Deer, coyote, and puma—species all
but gone from the plains—were among the larger fauna. *Don* "Beto"
impressed us with his knowledge of birds, describing minutely the differences between two local trogons, and between the *taragón* (Blue-
crowned Motmot) and the *guardabarrancos* (Turquoise-browed Motmot). Eventually, he and Francisco decided that the *cacaos,* if they were
present, were not along the stream, so we scrambled to a crest of the *serranía* to scout around before angling back to the village. As in most pine
woods in Olancho at the beginning of the rainy season, the understory
here was still open, with sparse, low, herbaceous growth. Fire scars on
the trunks and ash accumulation on the ground indicated that the area
had been burned not long before. In Olancho, subsistence hunters burn
the understory of pine woods almost every year, in part because they
know that their favored prey, white-tailed deer, thrive best on the young

and tender shoots. They also know that if they let the forest go for too many years, the dry tinder will ignite anyway, causing massive canopy fires rather than the customary brush fires.

Don Eliberto assured us that the *cacaos* lived at the headwaters of the Quebrada del Benque year round, and this made sense to us because the hills might be a main source area for the birds that are seasonally present in the Valle de Gualaco and Valle de Agalta. But though our *cacao* imitations resounded across the gorges, we had no luck that day with the species. In consolation, we were treated to a close look at two adult *rey zopes* (King Vultures) and a juvenile in flight. These are not uncommon birds in Olancho (as they are elsewhere in Central America), and from time to time they are seen feeding on carcasses along main roads. Though they seem to have diminished in population, they were never as common as the *cacao;* but their high soaring makes them far easier to detect.

Every faintly usable patch of terrain in the *vega* bottomlands of the Quebrada del Benque had a recognized owner, even if he or she had but claimed it decades before and had never returned. The overhanging *serranía,* on the other hand, because it was useless for agriculture, still belonged to the state. Cattle ranchers and other *terratenientes* were not (yet) a presence in Las Lomas, and village residents scoffed at the peons of villages on the plains, locked into debt and wage slavery on the large haciendas. Eliberto Torres had a vocabulary of toponyms that made the "monotonous" terrain come alive, though none of his names appears on the official topographic map. These were his home places, as familiar to him as his back *patio.* Like other residents of Las Lomas, he still has the self-assurance of farmers who are rarely visited by outsiders. Las Lomas: where the *cacao* perches awkwardly on branches above the stream in which people wash clothes and whence they draw water; where a bird presumed extinct in Honduras is still a prominent part of the avifauna; where "backward" Olanchanos live out their lives beyond the reach of *terratenientes* and electricity and have ten thousand hectares of wild hill country out back that no one else seems to care about, where they are free to do as they please.

Olivia García, who was around seventy, told us how her grandparents, when young, had settled in Las Lomas. She stated proudly that they had been *criollos* from the town of Gualaco — meaning that, make no mistake about it, Las Lomas had been founded by townspeople from the

Spanish-Honduran tradition, not *campesinos* who lived like *indios*. She seemed to have little desire to go elsewhere and commented how people who got a little money became supercilious. Development workers would have called her poverty absolute, because like most other residents, she lived on what her family provided in the way of beans, maize, and *chatas* (a type of Musaceae, relative to the plantain). Her house and yard were immaculately whitewashed and swept, with every plant in its place and every domestic animal well cared for. She laid out a huge lunch for us on a mahogany slab table, refusing Francisco's attempt to pay her, saying that it was she who owed him. Olivia García and her granddaughters were fervent *Cristianos* (Protestants), kept in the faith by Francisco's infrequent bicycle visits. He was one of a handful of outsiders they saw on a regular basis. It was little wonder, then, that the *cacaos* of Las Lomas had remained "secret." In later years, with a vehicle of my own, I was able to visit several similar villages across northern Olancho, all with similar stories about the *cacao*. In 2000, I finally heard it briefly, though did not see it.

If the *cacao* has not yet vanished from Olancho, then why has it not been reported to or by ornithologists during the last forty years? How could such a prominent member of the avifauna have escaped the notice of Neotropical ornithology and the ever greater numbers of birders descending on Central America? The answer is that there *is* no ornithology of northeastern Olancho. It is a blank space with virtually no scientific data collected on it, and no bird tours visit it either. The only published ornithological knowledge about the Valle de Agalta and surrounding hills near San Esteban comes from Arthur Twomey and Roland Hawkins's brief 1948 collecting trip. During that expedition, they shot a pair of *cacaos* on July 2.[4]

Burt Monroe's monograph was so detailed that it became the authoritative ornithological text on Honduras after it was published in 1968. During the 1970s and especially the troubled 1980s, ornithological attention shifted to safer Neotropical regions, and new additions to the Honduran avifauna were few and far between. Areas such as northeastern Olancho, which had never been surveyed adequately, remained obscure. In light of this, our "rediscovery" of the *cacao* did not seem that miraculous. The bird had never disappeared in the first place; it was the observers who were lacking.

Though progress in ornithology and conservation is retarded by such

lacunae, scientists are correct in believing that the Red-throated Caracara
has declined drastically. Local people agree that we are tracking the last
remnants of a population that was common as recently as the 1970s. And
no one, neither ornithologist nor farmer, knows why. Francisco Urbina,
Eliberto Torres, and I discussed possible reasons for the *cacao's* spectacular decline. Had a disease swept through the Central American population? Or was it the impoverishment of the pine forest? Francisco raised
these questions in a paper he gave at the 1998 international congress of
the *Sociedad Mesoamericana para la Biología y la Conservación* in Managua.
He explained that the *cacao* seems to prefer older, mature pines because
of the greater prevalence of wasp nests. Logging and disease have not
eliminated the old-growth pine forests by any means; but these practices
have thinned out these forests considerably in northern Olancho. Meanwhile, the plains to which the *cacaos* appear to practice postbreeding dispersals are drenched with chemicals, especially on the large ranches and
cooperatives. The plains, unlike the *serranías,* are becoming more and
more heavily populated. As yet, we have only the sketchy outline of a
hypothesis adequate for northern Central America. (The geography of
the species' decline in southern Central America has to be different, because the southern limit of highland pine is northern Nicaragua.)

Francisco and I are working on a local distributional survey of the *cacao,* based on a model of nesting distribution in the least populated and
most heavily forested *serranías.* The westernmost *cacao* report was given
to us by a forester from Gualaco who saw some several years ago in western Olancho near the town of El Rosario. He had observed them while
supervising a salvage harvest of thousands of pest-killed pines, and he
queried us as to whether *cacaos* are known to eat insects in dead trees, as
those had appeared to be doing.

There is no reason why Red-throated Caracaras cannot still be found
sparsely throughout their historically recorded range in Honduras,
which includes (ornithologically unsurveyed) parts of the departments
of Yoro and Francisco Morazán. Old-growth pine forests and remoteness from human settlement seem to be the major prerequisites. Francisco Urbina, on a 1999 trip to the depths of the Patuca rain forest on
the border of the department of Gracias a Dios, was told by local residents that the *cacao* is a common bird in ecotones of broadleaf forest
and pine savanna.

Nocturne

The night is a liminal realm where even self-declared rationalists find themselves beginning to believe the old tales, persuaded by the strange calls of owls, nightjars, potoos, rails, and others. To many local people, the avifauna of the night are as little known and little appreciated as the *cacao*'s landscape is among ornithologists.

The *lechuza* (Barn Owl) is without doubt the most hated and feared of Olancho's birds, especially because it has a penchant for nesting in church belfries and roosting on the peaks of houses. It is widely believed that the *lechuza* enters churches to eat the candle wax. Some people claim that one type — the *lechuza mantequera* or *lechuza de campanario* — does this, while another, the *lechuza de sangre,* sucks the blood of infants. The latter is an evil spirit, La Lechuza, a witch in avian form. The belltower owl, on the other hand, is just a flesh-and-blood bird.

Antonio de Herrera, the Spanish royal chronicler who compiled a detailed history of the sixteenth-century New World, provides strong evidence that current beliefs about the Barn Owl have precolumbian indigenous roots.[5] Of an unidentified Honduran Indian group (probably related to the Lenca), he wrote: "If a Lechuza perches on top of the house of a sick person, they believe that death is certain, or even if it perches on another house where all are healthy [someone will die]." This is identical to present-day Ladino beliefs. But it is possible that Spanish settlers imported the same types of beliefs with them from the Old World, where Barn Owls are also found. Today's traditions about such birds are almost certainly derived from a mixture of Iberian and indigenous traditions.

The *estiquirín* (Great Horned Owl) is less feared, perhaps because it is restricted to the pine forests and is not seen in villages. Nocturnal deer hunters consider it bad luck to shoot one. Those who do will not kill any deer the rest of the night.

The *tocolote* or *tecolote* (Mottled Owl), the most often seen of the crepuscular and nocturnal owls in rural Olancho, seems to have no belief attached to it other than its damning reputation as a predator of domestic fowl. There are several other owls as well, most of which are shot on sight. Some residents of Olancho also eat owls. In 1991, the old church in Gualaco was being refurbished, and in an inadvertent action to embarrass the mayor, who was assuring my Honduran co-worker of her plans to be environmentally sensitive in her new administration, an employee walked over and opened a bag for us to glimpse several fluffy Barn Owl nestlings. He was going to cook up "some chicken for dinner." He told us proudly that he had cleaned the nest out of the belfry and had already killed one of the parents. But soon thereafter, Barn Owls repopulated the church.

Better hidden nocturnal owls are not immune to human persecution. For example, our only recent report of Spectacled Owls is a pair killed and eaten by farmers in the rain forest of La Chorrera in the Montaña de Babilonia in 1992. But not all interaction between Olanchanos and owls results in death to the birds. In 1996, during an overnight visit to Ramón Santos's coffee farm in the headwaters of the Río Chiquito deep in the Sierra de Agalta, Francisco and I encountered a relationship more beneficial to owls. Around eight o'clock in the evening, while chatting with the Santos family, we were startled by the nearby call of an owl we had never heard before. The family told us that every night they watched a certain owl that lived in the *pura montaña* looming over the small clearing. It was finely striped black and white, like no other they had seen. Francisco's imitations of its call brought the Black-and-white Owl to a perch at the edge of the clearing, whence it observed us for several minutes before swooping off to another tree. That was one of the few times the species had been recorded from Honduras. The Santos family cherished the owl's visits and evinced neither fear nor any desire to do it harm.

The most common of the diurnal pygmy-owls, the *picapiedras* or *gallina del diablo* (Ferruginous Pygmy-Owl), has a reputation for enchantment and mystery among some people, though it is common and easy to observe in hedgerows and open woods throughout the region. The *picapiedras* gets its name because it sounds like a stonemason exercising his trade. Jesús Aguilar Paz wrote that the bird is believed to be a frustrated lover who, turned into an owl, forever chisels at the statue of its beloved on moonlit nights.[6]

The screech-owls, sometimes known as *orejitas* ("little ears"), are common residents of the *serranías* and plains. In May, 1998, during Semana Verde ("Green Week"), Eliberto Padilla, president of the Grupo Ecológico de Olancho (GEO) in Gualaco, showed one to a throng of school students in the public square. He used the little owl, which had damaged its wing crashing into a wall the night before, to illustrate a point in his environmental presentation. The schoolchildren were fascinated with the bird and crowded around after the speech to get a closer look and to stroke its feathers. The Vermiculated Screech-Owl, obviously in pain, appealed to human sympathy as any animal might. This proved to me that drawing general conclusions about Olanchanos and owls was an unproductive undertaking.

The *alcaraván* (Double-striped Thick-knee), a common savanna resident, has a mournful nocturnal cry cherished by farmers and urbanites alike. *Doña* Edita laments the inexplicable disappearance of the birds around her place in La Venta, while *doña* Clara and *doña* Juana in Juticalpa both think they make good "watchbirds" around the house. The early twentieth-century poet Froylán Turcios, a native of Juticalpa, penned a brief, well-known piece called "Los Alcaravanes" that evokes the essence of the bird and its habitat. The *alcaraván* in his poem embodies the spirit of the "llanura inmensa," the immense open plain over which it flies lazily in the sun and wind. The birds huddle together in the cruel cold nights of winter on these same plains, while during summer they break the nocturnal silence of the *llano* with their calls.[7]

The *pucuyo* (Pauraque) is familiar to almost all, and its "pu-cu-yo" call is an integral part of the Honduran night. A related bird, the Common Potoo, is known only to experienced nocturnal hunters like the Urbinas, who call it the *pájaro estaca* ("stick bird") because it is camouflaged to resemble a limb. The Common Potoo is called *pájaro búho* ("owl bird") by the few in El Boquerón who have seen it.

The nocturnal calls of unknown marsh birds often inspire fear. Jesús Aguilar Paz mentions the *Zaracoaco de la Ñanga*, presumably a type of rail or bittern, calling in the mangrove swamps of southern Honduras. Like the *Estiquirín* spirit of the interior, this bird is invoked by exasperated parents to threaten misbehaving small children.[8] In central Olancho, the commonest rail is the *cocoleca* (Gray-necked Wood-Rail), a reclusive resident of the bottomlands, valued for its meat and not feared at all.

Many birds associated with the night are feared or revered all over the world, but as people come to know the flesh-and-blood species, they learn to sympathize. Owls are also those that stare intently from side-by-side eyes, wise and fascinating. In Olancho, of all nocturnal birds, only the Barn Owl can be said to have been singled out for destruction by human beings. Nevertheless, because one so often finds it nesting in belfries, one suspects that its habitat is not threatened. Other owls, and night birds in general, seem to suffer most from that most common of ills, habitat destruction. Danger from pesticide magnification in food webs, though not proven, is probably another threat in many areas. Deliberate killing is probably not as large a threat to owls as to diurnal raptors (see chapter 8). Indeed, the bad luck attributed to killing an *estiquirín* may even help to protect it.

Golden-cheeked Warblers and Mountain Pine Forests

The highland pine forest may seem an unlikely margin, for it is the dominant habitat across the hills and mountains of Honduras.[9] Pine is the national tree, and pine forests are cherished resources for Honduran culture and economy. Unlike the deep, dense, and stagnant *montaña,* the *serranía* is arid, open, and breezy, hot at midday but usually refreshed by mountain breezes. Honduran pine forest air is similar to the "sea air" one reads about in nineteenth-century English novels: so favorable that it used to be prescribed as medicine for ailing residents of Tegucigalpa. Today, more than ever, *tegucigalpeños* who can do so flee their city's polluted environment on weekend trips to old mining towns like Santa Lucía up in the healthful mountains. Those with more income desert the city altogether and buy lots landscaped into the cool, clean pine forest in new subdivisions with names like Brisas del Ocotal or Pinares del Rancho ("Pine Breezes," "Pine Ranch").

To small farmers, too much pine forest can be a curse rather than a blessing. Almost all pine forests are useless for agriculture. Thus, despite the abundance of *serranías* across the highlands, they remain impoverished landscapes, useful for logging, for pine timber and oak firewood extraction, and for their lush grass understory. Cattle proliferate in these pine pastures, and in reality many *serranías* are as much cattle pastures as woods.

The majority of Honduran pine forests are composed of only one species, most commonly *Pinus oocarpa.* Their biodiversity, even in older stands, is low in comparison to that of adjacent dry or humid broadleaf forests. The pine forests are neither seriously endangered as an ecosystem nor overly important to biodiversity and thus form the margins of conservation as well as farming culture.

What urban Hondurans know as pine woods are pale shadows of the old-growth stands that were once much more common. Today, giant pines can still be found on the high, wet fringes of montane rain forests like the Montaña de Babilonia and Montaña de Botaderos, protected or too remote for loggers. The groves of pines in these zones of transition to broadleaf forest are known as *pinabetales,* as distinguished from the lower *ocotal.* The former involves a high altitude species, generally *Pinus maximinoi,* while *ocote* usually refers to *Pinus oocarpa.* In Olancho, there are at least five other species of pine as well. The avifauna of Babilonia's high *pinabetal* includes characteristic pine forest birds such as certain wood-warblers, and because of its proximity to *montaña* it also favors visiting deep forest species such as Crested Guans (and spider monkeys).

In the lower, warmer, and drier *ocotales,* the avifauna is highly distinct from that of both the plains and the *montaña.* Local people in these pine-oak woodlands recognize and understand the natural histories of distinctive birds such as the *pecho rojo* (Green Parakeet) and *pájaro azul* (Eastern Bluebird), not to mention the loudest and most common bird, the *chaco de robledal* (Acorn Woodpecker). Few characteristic *ocotal* birds have folkloric traditions attached to them in Olancho (the *estiquirín* is an exception), but this may be simply due to the relative paucity of recognized species. The *serranía's* avifauna is dominated by "generic" *mosqueros, cucaracheros, arroceros,* and a great number of *chipes.*

Among the *chipes* of Agalta are many species of migrant wood-warblers and vireos. The most important of these, in conservationist terms, is the Golden-cheeked Warbler, federally designated an endangered species in the United States, with a breeding habitat restricted to the Edwards Plateau in Texas. Its wintering range includes Chiapas, Guatemala, and Honduras, with a handful of reports from El Salvador and Nicaragua (the southern limit of montane pine woods). In January and February, 1995, Daniel Thompson, a biologist from Austin, Texas, searched for Golden-cheeked Warblers in Guatemala and Honduras, because the existing records published in the literature were of thirty- to sixty-year-old collection sites. Where he rediscovered the warblers, including one historical and one new site in Honduras, they were gleaning for insects on *Quercus* (oaks), an important component of the pine forests. The pine forests containing the endangered warblers varied from 10 percent to 75 percent canopy cover.[10]

Thompson's work was followed by an in-depth survey of historical sites and possible new locations by John Rappole and his research team, who worked in Honduras from late 1995 to early 1996. In addition to confirming the Golden-cheeked Warbler's present-day occupation of wintering grounds recorded sixty years ago in the outlying *serranías* of Parque Nacional La Tigra (the Montaña de San Juancito north of Tegucigalpa, and other areas), they found small groups and pairs of the birds scattered across the country. While Thompson's sightings had been confined to the high altitude forests from 1,400 to 2,000 meters, Rappole's team found Golden-cheeked Warblers as low as 1,000 meters.[11]

I once believed that I had glimpsed a Golden-cheeked Warbler in the *serranía,* along the trail to the La Chorrera waterfall in the Montaña de Babilonia in 1991, but later convinced myself this couldn't be so. The 1,100-meter elevation was too low; it was quite far from the bird's known wintering range in the mountains of central and western Honduras; and besides, what would be my chances of seeing such an incredibly scarce bird, just along the trail I knew best, within the tens of thousands of square kilometers of pine forest that cover Honduras?

On October 20, 1995, during a hike with Peace Corps trainees on this same trail, at approximately 1,100 meters above sea level, a few of us birding laggards were surveying a mixed foraging flock of warblers at 10:30 in the morning. We calmly noted migrant Yellow-throated and Townsend's warblers as well as the permanent resident Hepatic Tanager. To our great amazement, a male Golden-cheeked Warbler, gleaning an epiphyte-draped oak, was also a part of the flock. We had to distinguish carefully between this species and the similar Townsend's, Hermit, and Black-throated Green warblers, all of which had been recorded in the area. Like the individuals Daniel Thompson had observed, this one restricted itself to the few oaks in the vicinity. The rest of the forest consisted of pines with trunks up to a foot in diameter. All bore deep fire scars, and the understory contained lush grass with some brambles interspersed.

Dr. Rappole's team, acting on my tip, visited the same trail a few months later and recorded a couple of individuals. In all, the ornithological studies found several dozen Golden-cheeked Warblers in Honduras, indicating that the country is an important wintering ground. To conservationists, the *serranía* acquired a special value with this revelation. How does the pine forest as a margin affect the species' status in Honduras?

In Texas, the old-growth junipers used by Golden-cheeked Warblers are bulldozed into piles to make room for ranches and for new subdivisions of booming cities like Austin. By law, almost every human disturbance has to be monitored for potential detrimental effects on the warblers, often fostering negative relationships between the state and private landholders. The scenario of landowners destroying all their juniper before looking for nesting Golden-cheeked Warblers can easily be imagined when the alternatives are zoning restrictions on private lands with nests.

The Golden-cheeked Warbler seems to be safer on its wintering grounds. No one has reason to harbor resentment against it. In Honduras, the majority of pine forest land is owned by the state *(tierra nacional),* even if fenced and managed as private rangeland. Logging concessions generally do selective cuts that have little effect on twisted and economically useless oaks. This is not to suggest that the forests are doing fine. They have been thinned considerably by human use and by nonhuman pests in the last half century. However, tropical pines are amazingly resilient and quick to regrow, and in areas of low population density like Olancho, they still seem endless.

The Golden-cheeked Warbler, like all Neotropical migrants, is an integral part of the local avifauna, situated within the local cultural landscape just like a native toucan, quetzal, or bellbird. The irony is that this endangered Middle American/Texan bird is unknown to local people among the myriad *chipes.* Like Neotropical migrants in general, the Golden-cheeked Warbler is a marginal concern, a poor competitor with the macaw, *zorzal,* or *guardabarrancos* for popular affection. I find it hard to envision the *reinita cachetidorada* (our translation of Golden-cheeked Warbler) becoming the centerpiece of a conservation project in a region with close to five hundred other bird species.

Though the Golden-cheeked Warbler is invisible in Honduran culture, its habitat is not, and here may lie the key to the species' future conservation. Pine forests, after all, have been passed over as worthless by farmers. Unlike in the *montaña,* their soils cannot support agriculture, so they are not subject to the kind of landscape transformation affecting the broadleaf forests. The Golden-cheeked Warbler thrives in a habitat that has been altered for centuries, even millennia, by humans. Every square meter has been burned, grazed, cut over, hunted in, and gathered in.

And yet, where it separates rich agricultural plains from montane rain forests, it remains a marginal landscape, highly appreciated and not obliterated to satisfy basic needs.

Francisco Urbina and the rest of the management team for the Parque Nacional Sierra de Agalta in Gualaco have supported local villages in the management of their pine forests, which comprise the park's "buffer zone." In the past, pine forests were left to the state to manage, and local people had little stake in the protection even of their own watersheds. Using the unifying concept of the "microwatershed" combined with the Parque Nacional Sierra de Agalta, communities are beginning to take control of what is first and foremost their resource, not that of loggers and ranchers from outside. Warblers cannot help but benefit from this, since the protected *serranía* recovers rapidly.

Even Hurricane Mitch could not eradicate Golden-cheeked Warblers from Agalta. In late October, 1998, gales pounded the high sierra for several days, destroying great swaths of pine forest and weeding out the rain forest. In the approaches to the Montaña de Babilonia, windward pine forests were smashed, and only a few oaks remained standing. Leeward slopes were untouched. The area where Golden-cheeked Warblers had wintered a few years before became an open pasture, and a year later Neotropical migrants were nowhere to be seen. Nevertheless, in September, 1999, we found a pair of Golden-cheeked Warblers in a patch of pine woods surrounded by cloud forest on a nearby ridge at 1,600 meters.

The earth has no natural margins. Places are remote and marginalized because human societies make them that way. Pine forests have been marginal to local people in large part because they are useless for agriculture. They are too often overlooked by conservationists and biologists because their biodiversity is low. But, as night and day are inseparable, so the pines and other "unimportant" margins interlock with the rich plains and rain forests.

It is deceptive to represent the margins as safe places for avifauna. Protecting the Middle American pine forests to the best of human ability will not guarantee the Golden-cheeked Warbler's future. The species depends as well on human decisions made in Texas, and on nonhuman conditions at which we can only guess. The *cacao* holds on in the margins, but its problems go beyond loss of habitat. If agricultural chemicals or logging are at fault, then no place, no matter how remote, can protect it.

Conservationists should grasp a region's geography as a whole before deciding where to focus efforts. In Honduras, conservation legislation and action began in the 1970s and picked up force in the 1980s. Almost all terrestrial protected areas were evergreen broadleaf humid forests: cloud forests, midlevel montane rain forests, and lowland rain forests. Pine forests, tropical dry forest, and thorn forest, not to mention non-forest ecosystems such as native grass savannas, have usually been considered important only where they buffer "virgin" evergreen broadleaf forest. Many biologists and conservationists have been entranced by the old-growth rain forest, seeing everything else as second best. As already noted, some dismiss any land showing human disturbance as "trashed" or "degraded." But this is mostly a matter of perspective. There are pre-columbian ruins and half-buried pine trunks deep inside what is today old-growth rain forest in Olancho. Honduras's only endemic bird species, the Honduran Emerald, was discovered to live in the thorn forest, not the cloud forest.

Bit by bit, other habitats are coming into their own, not as second best after virgin rain forest but as unique and important wherever they occur and whatever their appearance. The people who live in or near them are key to their preservation. To these people, such woods and prairies are not marginal or remote at all but are part of their home landscapes, at the center of their world. What is remote remains a matter of perspective. When conservationists can think of everywhere as home, we can celebrate and investigate rather than denigrate the margins.

Chapter 8

People and Avifauna of
Montane Rain Forests

Olanchanos refer to both the rain forest and cloud forest landscapes as *montañas*. Historically, *montañas* were infrequently visited, mysterious worlds in which only indigenous people and Ladino hunters and gatherers felt comfortable, while the remainder of the plains and *serranía* population stayed away. The *montañas* were refuges for rebellious and shy Pech and Tawahka. Where navigable rivers ran nearby, the vast forests yielded mahogany logs and other rain forest products for the international market.

In the twentieth century, as social and environmental situations in Honduras forced massive migrations, the *montañas* became frontiers attractive to settlers, who found them moderately productive for agriculture. Cattle ranchers looking for cheap and "barren" land stripped many *montañas* bare, and lumbering outfits accelerated extractive mahogany harvesting through new roads linking regions like Olancho to the coastal ports. All classes became heavily involved in shade coffee growing, which in Olancho is the principal economic function of the highland *montaña*.

In local parlance, *montaña* can mean any landscape of humid broadleaf evergreen forest, whether on the plains or in the hills, whether a coffee farm or an old-growth forest. However, there is a specific vocabulary for forest that local people perceive as untouched by humans, and they contrast it strongly to the humanized *montañas*. Ancient forests are known as *pura montaña*, pure and unadulterated forest. Other interchangeable local terms for it are *montaña cruda* (raw forest), *montaña espesa* (thick forest), and *montaña virgen* (virgin forest).

The *montañas* are shrinking fast, a fact of which almost everyone is aware, but for which adequate solutions are lacking. Even though most *pura montaña* is now within protected areas, and legally off limits to human use, agricultural and pastoral expansion continues. By the end of the millennium, most of the local population was aware of the importance of the *montañas* in the Sierra de Agalta for water production, slope stability, fauna and flora, and other material benefits. Hurricane Mitch ravaged slopes near Catacamas that had no forest on them, scoring them with massive landslides that buried many victims. Cloud forest slopes nearby were barely affected. This put an exclamation point on local environmentalists' warnings about deforestation. A limited withdrawal from the *montaña* began, and it seemed to loom threateningly over its would-be destroyers.

Despite the hurricane, the rain forest frontiers of Olancho will continue to be irresistible to people who need to transform them into more useful landscapes. Their birds, or at least those that cannot adapt quickly to human disturbance, will go the way of the forests. As long as the Honduran economy continues to labor under massive debt payments and to depend on the whims of international markets and development banks, its decades-long recession will continue. Until the forests are gone, local people will always have the frontier as an income alternative, and Honduran society will have a safety valve.

On paper, most of the old-growth rain forests of eastern Honduras are locked up in reserves that may aid to seal the frontier from human disturbance. Who will do this sealing is a somewhat fuzzy issue, however. Most conservation projects are based in Tegucigalpa, not Juticalpa or Catacamas (where they maintain regional offices), and they are funded not by local in-kind contributions but by international funds such as taxpayer dollars. Easy come, easy go: the dependence of a system of protected areas on international welfare rather than on locally extracted revenue (e.g., most wealthy residents in Olancho go untaxed) creates a wasps' nest of problems, including unsustainability. And even though international projects work with local Ladino as well as Pech and Tawahka communities, the *terratenientes,* often shadowy but always immensely powerful agents of deforestation, are almost completely ignored.

In the Cordillera de Agalta, unlike along the lowland rain forest frontier, *terratenientes* have a limited presence, because steep and cold mountain land is unattractive for cattle. Small farmers are on the slopes largely because the plains are taken up by large haciendas. Many coffee farms in Agalta (particularly on the north slope) are impossible to reach by road, so they remain the property of the poor, who still depend on beasts of burden. Agalta is a landscape of land-starved *campesinos* who, despite their thirst for resources, are usually willing to aid in protecting the *pura montaña* if they are brought into the management process and designated the protectors of their own watersheds and extractive buffer zones. The Parque Nacional Sierra de Agalta has operated since 1987 with minimal budget, personnel, and infrastructure, yet greater progress has been made there than in larger rain forest reserves that have had hundreds of thousands of dollars poured into them. How can this be?

On minuscule salaries, conservationists like Francisco Urbina gain respect in local communities, getting to know each and every family that depends on the *montaña* for its livelihood. Local people in some villages have come to feel as responsible for protection as they have been made to feel for destruction, and they are no longer waiting for outsiders to arrive and do the work. As Francisco often puts it, they *are* the park.

On the north side of the Sierra de Agalta, in the Montaña de Babilonia, deforestation is far less than on the south side. Unlike on the slopes above Catacamas, no permanent villages have become established. Density of population on the plains is still low, and in-migration is slight. Mountain slopes are the territory of villages like La Venta, and few outsiders are present. Those farmers who spend time in the Montaña de Babilonia neither hate nor fear it (reasons that some conservationists mention for unrepentant deforestation); instead they regard it as an inexhaustible source of wealth, a never-ending cornucopia of flora and fauna. Though not their everyday landscape, the *montaña* is part of home to them. They spend two to four months of every year there and are sustained by hunting and gathering while involved with their beanfields and coffee farms.

Each village has a unique relationship to its *montaña,* and village by village, conservation solutions exist. Conservationists don't have to wait until the foreign debt is paid or Honduras stops depending on the whims of the international market. Nor do they need to cordon off the forest and surround it with armed guards. The *montaña* and its birds can be protected by its residents and neighbors, and outside conservation projects need to recognize and support this. Just because clearcuts are everywhere does not mean that farmers hate the forest or desire to re-move it all. The *montaña* remains an enchanted and wonder-filled land-scape in Olanchano culture, and these old values can be sustained. Local rain forest conservation, to a certain extent, can base itself in cultural ap-preciation of *montaña* even while economic conditions across Honduras worsen with every decade. Eventually, it is hoped that land reform, lower birth and in-migration rates, and a better job market will lure settlers away from the *pura montaña* altogether, but in the meantime the conflict of human needs and biodiversity preservation is an urgent problem that many Olanchanos and outsiders are trying to solve through noncon-frontational means.

Seven Names for the Bellbird

In La Avispa, people call the bellbird *pájaro cafetero* because it calls when the coffee cherries are ripening. The Pech of El Carbón know it as *pimentero,* because they hear it when the *pimienta gorda* (allspice) berries are maturing. In La Venta and the Montaña de Babilonia, it is known as the *calandria* ("lark"); in nearby Pie del Cerro the *templador* ("bell tuner"), and in San Esteban the *campanero* ("bell ringer"). Local conser-vationists employ *pájaro campana,* a translation of the English name bell-bird. Six in Spanish and one in English: few birds in Olancho have de-served such an array of evocative names, and none is as closely entangled with human awareness of seasons in the *montaña.* Yet to those who know the forest little, the bellbird is at most a vague presence without a name. Knowledge of the bellbird marks one as a student in the ways of the montane rain forest.[1]

My initial encounter with the Three-wattled Bellbird came in August, 1991, during my first trip into the Parque Nacional Sierra de Agalta, on a trail that clambers from the twin waterfalls of La Chorrera at 1,100 me-ters above sea level to the highest point in the range and in all of Olan-cho, the 2,354-meter peak dubbed La Picucha. After a couple of days on top, I was descending the final slope toward the waterfalls on the return hike when I heard the loudest, most arresting bird sounds of my experi-ence. The stentorian calls drowned out a male howler monkey, which paused in his roaring nearby.

Across from me, on a high branch, a male bellbird sat near two females. He was creamy-headed with a light brown body, and three fleshy appendages dangled from his face. The females were smaller, silent, and olive-green. As he called, the male swiveled this way and that, "throwing" his voice ventriloquially in different directions into the forest and sky. To call with such force, he opened his mouth seemingly to unhinge it, and after blaring two or three sonorous, faintly bell-like notes ("like a screeching bell," I wrote in my notes), he emitted a banjo-like twang. After a few minutes the birds flew off, and the quiet of the *montaña* resounded deafeningly. The calls of Slate-colored Solitaires could be heard again — flutelike notes from dark side ravines. Then the howlers resumed their usual racket.

Central Olancho is close to the edge of the Three-wattled Bellbird's range, which stretches from Honduras to Panama. But before 1991, Olancho records consisted only of a series of eleven skins that collector Cecil Underwood took from El Boquerón in 1937. As yet it is not proven that the bellbird nests in Honduras, but it certainly migrates there outside the breeding season.[2]

Not only on the La Picucha trail can one hear bellbirds. In different seasons and in varying concentrations, they visit *montañas* up and down the spine of the Cordillera de Agalta, from Cerro Agua Buena above the Ladino village of El Boquerón to Cerro del Diablo, a mountain sacred to the Pech of Santa María del Carbón. In June, 1994, Francisco Urbina and Robert Gallardo taped bellbirds on a trail that crosses the range in the Montaña de Malacate between Dulce Nombre de Culmí and San Esteban. The more than forty calling birds in the vicinity included some with hoarse, raspy, incomplete songs, which the recorders thought were immature males.

Despite my serendipitous first encounter, bellbirds are notoriously difficult to observe, because they generally sit in the canopy out of sight and "throw their voices." Even among local people, not all those who go to the *montaña* are familiar with these birds, especially if they go only for the December-to-February coffee harvest, when the birds may be absent. But those who have heard these birds never forget.

People who live on the edges of the Valle de Agalta below the Montaña de Babilonia are aware of the bellbird's tendency to come down from the high *montaña* to the coffee zone during certain seasons. Bellbirds even show up occasionally on the edges of the plains. In 1994, Francisco Urbina recorded one in a grove of pines not far from his house.

In La Avispa — an area so drastically deforested during the last four decades that it is no longer known as the Montaña de La Avispa — the *pájaro cafetero,* formerly abundant enough to be considered a portent, is now quite scarce. When one individual shows up these days, it is a noteworthy event.

Francisco considers the bellbird one of his personal favorites. He has given it a prominent place in Parque Nacional Sierra de Agalta promotional materials such as slide shows, signs, and shirts, as well as the park's logo. These give the bird a high profile in places like Gualaco, where many townspeople unfamiliar with the *montaña* were not previously acquainted with it. Gualaqueños can be heard to exclaim that they strongly desire to hike to La Picucha to see the views, the elfin forest, and the bellbirds. A schoolteacher from San Esteban once told me that two of his goals in life were to hike to the top of the Sierra de Agalta and to glimpse a bellbird.

The bellbird has been an integral part of the La Picucha hike ever since the trail was first constructed. Previously, Olanchanos who did not farm or hunt in the *montaña* rarely had opportunities or reasons to visit their cloud forests. When the La Picucha trail was opened in the mid-1980s to access a now-defunct radio tower on the summit, it was initially reported as a treacherous hike where one might be devoured by a jaguar or fall in a hole, an allusion to the mossy tangles of roots in the dwarf forests of the summit. But after 1991, representatives of the Parque Nacional Sierra de Agalta began to stir up interest in the trail by showing slides in Gualaco to audiences of up to four hundred. La Picucha and its wonders added to their pride in what the town possessed. They began to feel it belonged to them, that it was their *patrimonio* (municipal patrimony) and that it deserved protection.

The bellbird, in becoming a symbol, helped to bring this most remote of *montañas* into the everyday popular consciousness on the plains. But another bird, although equally exotic to some, has failed to capture the rural Olanchano public imagination in the same way.

Quetzals and Other Altitudinal Migrants

The *quetzal* has but one local name in central Olancho, though it is a familiar bird of the *montaña.* While outsiders may think of it as mysterious, exotic, rare, or endangered, local farmers know it to be a common bird that nests in dead snags in their coffee farms, or wherever else it encounters its favorite food, *aguacatillos* (wild avocados).[3]

Until the mid-1990s, when the Resplendent Quetzal began to appear in environmentalist promotional materials for the Parque Nacional La Muralla, many *juticalpenses* and other urban Olanchanos were unaware that it occurred in their department. They associated the bird with the central or western highlands, where human populations are often adjacent to quetzal habitat.

Luz Bonta recounts an episode in Tegucigalpa when her father got into an argument with an acquaintance who insisted that there were no *quetzales* at all in Honduras. These birds existed only in Guatemala; how could Honduras, which didn't even have any forests left, contain quetzals? To give the man credit, the latter country has enshrined the quetzal as a national symbolic icon, while Honduras has preferred the *zorzal* (Clay-colored Robin) and the *guara* (Scarlet Macaw). Nevertheless, its more than thirty separate cloud forests containing nesting habitat for quetzals make Honduras an important refuge for this species, which ranges from southeastern Mexico to Panama.

Quetzals are common in the high *montañas* of Olancho, but only in the past few generations has human activity advanced upslope to penetrate their nesting grounds. In Guatemala, and in the Lenca highlands of western Honduras, people and quetzals have shared the same forests for far longer. Centuries-old Lenca towns like Guajiquiro, La Paz, at 2,000 meters, border quetzal habitat. The birds nest in woods at the edge of town.

In Olancho, quetzals nest in *pura montaña* and coffee farms between April and June, occasionally raising a second brood from September to November.[4] After nesting, family groups disperse to fruiting *aguacatillo* trees downslope. By January, they have moved from their nesting grounds between 2,000 and 1,200 meters above sea level to gallery forests between 1,100 and 400 meters. To those familiar with Resplendent Quetzals, the latter elevation may seem excessively low, but it reflects the abrupt topography of the Boquerón canyon. Birds nesting on Cerro Agua Buena drop down into the bottomland along the Río de Olancho between El Boquerón village and La Avispa. Casual observers there often confuse them with other trogon (*coa*) species, because the males lack their tail plumes.[5]

Honduran quetzals turn up not only at record low elevations but in another unconventional place as well: the *serranía* pine forest. In the early 1990s, Eric Nielsen, a Peace Corps volunteer, reported them from the pine forest buffer zone of La Muralla; Pilar Thorn, a member of the biology faculty at the Universidad Nacional Autónoma de Honduras, has observed them in pines near the Parque Nacional Cusuco in northwestern Honduras; and Elmer Maradiaga tells me that they come down from the Montaña de Comunayaca into the pines around his house.

The tendency for quetzals to show up in peoples' backyards can be seen as problematic for their survival, but it can also force conservationists to think beyond polygonal strategies of "locking them up" in rain forest or cloud forest reserves. The quetzal helps us to think beyond the deep forest and to appreciate its place in the human landscape too. This can be an opportunity as well as a threat.

Some conservation planning models transform local people's *pura montaña* into an untouchable core zone ("nucleus"), assigning "buffer zone" status to the human-affected *montaña* and *serranía,* while consigning the plains to "degraded" environmental status. But altitudinally migrant species such as quetzals defy such models, "refusing" to be locked up. Many other birds also bring the *montaña* to the plains and the plains to the *montaña.* Trogons, cousins to the *quetzal,* make altitudinal migrations familiar to observant local people. The Violaceous Trogon is commonly seen in El Boquerón and La Avispa all year round, because it courts and nests in the bottomlands. During the dry season, it is joined not only by the quetzal but by another visitor from on high, the *coa de montaña* or *cacahuata* (Collared Trogon).

The toucans are widely associated with altitudinal migration. The three types of *pico navaja* ("knife bill") are among the most appreciated and remarked upon birds of the *montaña,* but they are also important seasonal residents of plains bottomlands and occasionally roam the pine forests.

Local people know that in addition to the many forest birds that come down from *el alto* ("the highlands"), there are also birds that go up (*suben*) from *el bajo* ("the lowlands"). In seasonal coffee villages like Planes de Babilonia and Agua Buena, plains birds begin to take up residence as the *pura montaña* is thinned and opened. Scrub and beanfield openings in the *montaña* harbor familiar birds like Groove-billed Anis,

Great-tailed Grackles, and Melodious Blackbirds, while House Wrens take up residence in and around houses with sufficient open space, and *zorzales* claim dooryard gardens.

The message of the quetzal to rain forest conservationists in Olancho is in its altitudinal migrations. Long known to farmers, and now to outsiders as well, seasonal movements call attention to the fact that neither the quetzals nor many other birds are safe if the rain forest alone is protected. Quetzals, trogons, toucans, and others need protection wherever they are found. Another meaning of altitudinal migrations is that such birds knit different landscapes together, forcing conservationists to reconsider management schemes that attempt to keep birds and people apart.

"Me Voy Para la Montaña"

In the Montaña de Babilonia, a *champa* is the locus of home, a temporary abode that may be used by anyone when its owners are not present. One's *champa* is connected to one's permanent home on the plains or in the *serranía* by a grueling trail that may rise a thousand meters in only two kilometers as it follows the steepest grades along the knife-edge ridges, avoiding slippery and treacherous gully walls. Such trails are of two types—passable or impassable by pack animals. The difference between the two is substantial when one considers the difficulty of carrying hundred-pound sacks of beans or coffee down on one's back. Pack trails allow a family to bring up more supplies more quickly and to transport crops out more effectively. As yet, the road accessible to pickup trucks, a third category of entryway that changes the economy drastically, has not yet been introduced to the Montaña de Babilonia beyond its border of high *serranía,* due mostly to the presence of the Parque Nacional Sierra de Agalta.

There is great significance wrapped up in the simple phrase "Me voy para la montaña." To a plains dweller it evokes an experience out of the ordinary. It speaks of getting away from the suffocating heat, of generating income, and of bringing back desperately needed meat. One's trip to the *montaña* may be for a day of weeding or for a longer stay during field preparation, sowing, or harvest. Many people maintain small plots of coffee for cash income but also grow beans that will feed them no matter how well their coffee sells. Most years, the rains of *invierno* (winter) start in June, and one plants one's *frijolar* (beanfield) soon thereafter, returning once or twice to weed, and then to harvest (*arrancar*) in August. This first crop cycle is known as *la primera. La postrera,* the second growing season, usually begins in November, and the crop is harvestable by February. Meanwhile, coffee flowers at the beginning of winter, and cherries ripen by December. Families relocate to the *montaña* around Christmas, picking the ripe and almost-ripe berries (often with hired help) in three rounds or *cortes.* The coffee harvest, known locally as *La Cosecha,* lasts until mid-February. Many small farmers hope to recoup their losses and repay the loans they took out over the preceding year, feed and pay their pickers (if they employ any), and still generate enough cash income to live on for a while. In bad years (e.g., most of the 1990s), one may not break even.

The *Cosecha* period from December to February is when the cold fronts arrive from the temperate zone. These *nortes* bring days of rain and chill detrimental to cattle, one reason why the Montaña de Babilonia's coffee belt is little threatened by expansion of pastures. By March, the precipitation has ended, and on the plains many trees lose their leaves, intermittent streams dry up, and the dusty, breathless summer sets in. Pastures are set alight to encourage new grass and to clear out ticks and other pests; *milpa* (cornfield) stubble is also burned. During some burning seasons, the pall of smoke becomes so thick over Honduras that airports close, respiratory diseases become widespread, and drivers have to turn on their headlights at noon. At this time, field preparation in the *montaña* may include opening a new plot (*descombrando*), or *limpiando* ("cleaning") meaning clearing out the *guamiles* (fallow scrub) with machetes, axes, and chainsaws. After a brief period to dry, the *descombro* (clearcut) is torched. Meanwhile, passersby toss burning brands in the *serranías,* which, igniting easily, scorch out most of the new herbaceous and woody growth.

Walking from the Valle de Agalta to one's *champa* in the *montaña* may take four hours or more. On some occasions, one steams up at four in the morning and returns to the plains by nightfall. At other times, one might move up the family, the skinny dogs, the radio, the maize for tortillas, the salt, sugar, and lard, the old muskets and shot, the machetes and sharpener, and perhaps a few pack animals. These and a few other necessities are enough to establish home in the *champa* for a week of bean harvest or two months of *Cosecha*. The rhythm of life for men is farm work in the morning, hunting in the afternoon and perhaps at night. Women arise at three in the morning to make tortillas for the family and for hired *mozos* (laborers) and, after recovering from this arduous labor, carry out a great number of other tasks throughout the course of the day. Children also work hard in the *montaña*, making the hours count helping the adults. Whatever *carne de monte* (bush meat) can be procured—*tepescuintle, mono, guatuza, quequeo,* or even *jagüilla* (paca, monkey, Central American agouti, collared and white-lipped peccary)—augments the slim diet of beans, tortillas, and coffee (unless one has toted up a few laying hens).

Upon reclaiming one's *champa* for a long stay, the first order of business is to clean it up, smoke out the bugs, snakes, and other undesirables, sweep and repair the clay stove, and go into the forest to get *tapuca* palm leaves with which to pad the slat beds and repair the roofs. Other farmers may dwell more comfortably under tin roofs, less traditional but more practical barriers against pests and precipitation. Vegetation in the immediate vicinity of the house and on the nearby trails needs to be trimmed back with machetes. For these activities, one can normally make do with whatever is at hand, but there is still constant back-and-forth with the plains, so one is not cut off completely. During the *primera* and *postrera*, excess beans need to be carried down to the plains to be dried, because up in the *montaña* they mold quickly. For this and for purposes of protecting the property, at least one family member often remains down below.

Coffee cherries need to be picked, washed, depulped, and partially dried before being bagged and taken as quickly as possible to the plains, where a *coyote* (middleman) will buy them at reasonably low prices, drive them to Juticalpa or another town, and resell them to a processing plant with capacity to dry the coffee to the necessary percentage of moisture required by exporters. During the *Cosecha*, villages like the Planes de Babilonia are alive from dawn to dusk with mule trains coming and going, with the shouting of their drivers, and with thousands of blood-sucking ticks of varying sizes and colors swarming in the neat rows of coffee bushes. In the coffee forest, the songs and calls of birds intermingle with those of the pickers; whether farmers or hired hands, people are glad to be there (despite the scourge of ticks), glad to be earning cash income, and not a little high on the air and the abundant fresh coffee.

Due to each grower's different crop and shade management strategies, vegetation varies widely from one coffee farm to the next. The resultant landscape is a mosaic of coffee plots, beanfields, and *guamiles* on the least favorable land, interspersed with patches of *pura montaña*. *Platanares* and *chateras* (groves of edible Musaceae) provide further subsistence food. Around the older *champas,* small dooryard gardens contain trees bearing edible fruit.

The vegetative cover in this humanized *montaña* is in rapid flux, a fact that may surprise the outside visitor from one year to the next. In December, for example, inside a wall of trees that marks the *pura montaña* and the edge of the Parque Nacional Sierra de Agalta nucleus, one might notice a few small understory palms tentatively chopped down. During the following May, one encounters a smoldering field of ash, then a thicket in December. The following year it is a patch of ash again, then a beanfield with a profusion of delicious beans. This off-and-on cycle continues for a couple of years, and bean yields may hold steady; but most often they drop, so the field is "abandoned" to grow up into what the outsider calls "second-growth rain forest."

To someone working for the Parque Nacional Sierra de Agalta, the original *descombro* (clearcut) was a setback, but the seemingly abandoned secondary forest is recategorized as part of the nucleus. Imagine the surprise of the rain forest conservationist-in-training upon finding second-growth rain forest suddenly reduced to ash again five or ten years later! The message is that the *montaña,* when shorn of its *pura* designation, does not lose its owners.[6]

All this does not signify that the farmer actually dislikes the forest. One cannot reliably pin the blame for Neotropical deforestation on those who wield the axes and chainsaws without seeing the invisible socioeconomic forces behind them, at both the local and global scales. One cannot assume that because people cut down the forest, they hate it, or that because they hate it, they cut it down. Francisco Urbina feels that most local farmers neither dislike the *pura montaña* nor wish it gone. Rather, they regard it with awe and great respect, and many are as interested as the visiting ecotrekker in going out to explore it, which they do during hunting and gathering forays.

The outsider may have a difficult time understanding how anyone can feel great pride in having destroyed a forest to plant beans but still marvel at the magnificence of the *pura montaña* yet to be destroyed. After the farmer has verbally agreed with the conservationist's assessment of the forest as a resource that is valuable when left standing, and after he has agreed that the birds are certainly beautiful and the "biodiversidad" may hold great treasures, then the conservationist feels swindled when the farmer has not discontinued fire-fallow agriculture on the basis of words, management plans, and paper laws. As every conservationist is reminded again and again, even though farmers know that the State considers their actions illegal, they continue out of a need that outsiders can understand only with difficulty: "We don't want to, but we must." Fire-fallow rain forest agriculture has been around for millennia; the Parque Nacional Sierra de Agalta became law in 1987.

Raptors as Symbols of Tropical Forest Destruction?

Raptors often seem to prove the point made by outsiders that children in Honduras (and elsewhere in the Neotropics) are weaned on slingshots to become farmers who shoot every hawk, owl, and eagle in sight. Indeed, of all birds, diurnal raptors appear to be the most threatened by human depredation in Olancho. Nevertheless, not all raptors are threatened by all people at all times. Attitudes and practices vary by person, by locality, and by species. It is worthwhile to look at human appreciation and persecution of raptors in the rain forest and beyond to understand that generalizations about how and why men kill them cannot be extended to sweeping proscriptions on the separation of people and tropical nature.

Diurnal raptors probably suffer from human depredation as much in the rain forests as on the plains. But though the birds sometimes become stew ingredients, farmers do not consider them game species. Hawks, eagles, kites, and falcons are pests, and the frontiersman's decision to shoot one is often a calculation based on whether he can afford the ammunition. On the plains, raptors may be destroyed because they are believed to be predators of domestic fowl, but in the *montaña* they are just good targets. However, not all relationships between local people and raptors are destructive and devoid of ornithophilic sentiment. The *tijer-*

illa (Swallow-tailed Kite), an inhabitant of *montaña* edges and *serranía,* is cherished for its graceful, acrobatic aerial maneuvers. The sublime White Hawk or *gavilán garza* ("egret hawk"), evincing little fear of humans, is admired and usually left alone. Because the diet of the *cangrejero* or Common Black-Hawk is known to be crabs, not chickens, it is generally left alone.

Though there are more than thirty species of diurnal raptors in central Olancho, local taxonomies do not contain nearly as many names. Kites, hawks, and falcons are lumped as *gavilanes.* Among the falcons, four are quite familiar: the *cacao* (Red-throated Caracara), *tera* or *quebrantahuesos* (Crested Caracara), *guaco* (Laughing Falcon), and *clis-clis* (American Kestrel). Only the latter can be found in the *montaña.* These falcons are considered to be beneficial or at least harmless. The *clis-clis* takes small prey and the *tera,* like the vultures, is a sanitary agent, cleaning carcasses. The *guaco* is widely regarded as a portent of death but is rarely harmed. Two forest-falcons, both *montaña* dwellers, as well as the Bat Falcon, are easily confused with small hawks and collectively referred to as *gavilancillos.*

The Osprey is familiar as the *águila pesquera* or *gavilán pescador* and is known to fish along rivers and occasionally at cattle ponds. It is not considered a threat to domestic animals and is probably left alone more than it is molested.

The group of persecuted raptors, including several *montaña* residents, are the hawks and kites known as *gavilanes polleros* or *ratoneros* ("chicken hawks" or "mousers"). The Black-shouldered Kite is the most notorious predator and is easily recognized by its stationary hovering over open fields. Many other raptors, including all Buteos, are labeled as chicken killers, whether or not they are—even the Ornate Hawk-Eagle that Esteban Urbina mistook for a large *gavilán pollero.* The most likely candidates, however, are the two most common small hawks around dwelling places, the Gray Hawk of the plains and the Roadside Hawk of the *serranía* and *montaña.* However, the scarcer Hook-billed Kite, Double-toothed Kite, Plumbeous Kite, Broad-winged Hawk (a migrant), Red-tailed Hawk, Crane Hawk, White-tailed Hawk, and Short-tailed Hawk are also targets.

Mischievous chicken hawks play distinctive roles in Honduran traditional culture. In an old imitative dance called El Gavilán (a close relative of the game described in chapter 3), the dancers played a hawk, a chicken, and her chick.[7] The hawk tried to steal the chick, but the chicken repulsed him. At the end, the hawk prevailed.

La Gallina con Pollos, a children's game, is still played in the Olancho countryside.[8] This version is Mario Ardón Mejía's quote from another author who described it in the 1950s from an unnamed Honduran location.

The chicken with chicks

The children formed a long line, each hugging the next's waist. These were the chicks. Nobody was allowed to let go. The two principal players were the chicken, at the head of the line, who had to be strong and defend her chicks, and the hawk, who tried to steal the chicks. The following dialogue ensued:

Hawk: "Is this rice for me?"
Hen: "What if my chicks eat it?"
Hawk: Then I'll catch one."
Hen: "The moon rises here" (pointing to the sky).
Hawk: "The sun rises here" (pointing in the opposite direction).
Hen: "Then we clash."

A desperate fight ensued between hawk and hen. The chicks tried with all their might not to let go, following the sinuous movements of the line. The hawk caught them one by one, eventually ending the game. Much hilarity was caused by the attempts not to get caught.

Another game, La Paloma y El Gavilán, involved a hawk trying to catch a dove that was trespassing in his beanfield. The idea was that whoever became the dove had to escape the hawk by being let inside a ring of children, or outside, while the hawk was trapped inside.[9]

Though chicken hawks and by extension all diurnal raptors are tagged with a certain fiendish character in Honduran culture, there is another characteristic of hawks that is captured by large raptors of the *montaña* such as the Common Black-Hawk, Great Black-Hawk, hawk-eagles, and Harpy Eagle. To many farmers I have interviewed, these evoke elegance, power, and freedom, and even sympathy with a fellow predator. This is made evident by their invocation in toponyms: in Olancho, there is a village of Gavilanes, a Cerro de los Gavilanes, a hamlet of El Aguila ("The Eagle"), a Cerro del Aguila, and a Quebrada del Aguila.

Hunters of Birds

If a farmer in the *montaña* does not take potshots at a hawk, perhaps he is saving his bullets for more palatable prey. After a morning of work, the farmer finds diversion and food for the family in afternoon and nighttime excursions around the coffee *montaña* and sometimes deep into the *pura montaña*. This type of subsistence hunting is often (though not always) based on an intricate knowledge of each animal's trails, its preferred habitat, its food sources, its calls and cries. In the role of hunter, the local farmer takes on the *montaña* not as an obstacle to be cleared but as a landscape to be read and explored.

One cannot overstate the difficulty of hunting in *pura montaña*. In addition to the steep and slippery terrain, the many armed plants, poisonous snakes, wasps, and ants, the prey itself can hide and escape in labyrinthine thickets or in the soaring, interlocking canopy. Hunting forays are often exercises in frustration. To deal with the intricate difficulties of navigating the *montaña*, hunters develop complex mental maps of slope, vegetation, streams, canopy height, and percentage of cover. With enough experience, one "feels" the landscape, "knows" the terrain, and is able to read a multitude of signs to be successful.

The white-tailed deer of the nearby *serranía* is at the top of the hierarchy of desirable animals in the Montaña de Babilonia. The other highly valued game species are the *tepescuintle* (paca), *pava* (Crested Guan), and *chancho de monte* (*quequeo* and *jagüilla*) (collared and white-lipped peccary). These four *montaña* denizens are delicious and yield abundant meat. Farther down the hierarchy are the *guatuza* (agouti), the three monkeys, and an assortment of rarer fauna such as the *tilopo* (red brocket deer), *paujín* (Great Curassow), and *gongolona chinga* (Great Tinamou). According to José Mendoza of El Boquerón, the effort expended in hunting small but succulent *chingas* (tinamous), doves, *gallos de monte* (wood-partridges), and others is usually not worth it, so these are killed only if they are encountered ("Al hallar, los cazan"). As long as Crested Guans, pacas, and agoutis are common, hunters see little cause to go after doves, tinamou, or partridges, which tend to have more feathers than meat. At the other end of the scale, the common, tasty, and enormous *danto* (Baird's tapir) is rarely sought out either, because unless an entire village makes it a feast, few can afford the amount of salt needed to preserve it.

Other animals are hunted to sell as pets, for their skins, or simply for fun; but most of these — like the *tigre* (jaguar), *tigrillos* (ocelot and margay), and *perezosos* (two- and three-toed sloths) are quite difficult to find. Among birds, the Keel-billed Toucan, White-crowned Parrot, and occasionally the *jilguero* (Slate-colored Solitaire) as well as certain species of doves are captured as ornaments for the house, as gifts, or for sale. In the Montaña de Babilonia, hunters stigmatize the cooking and eating of nongame birds, but in other parts of Olancho and Honduras, birds such as parrots, jays, and woodpeckers are minor protein sources.

The *pava* (Crested Guan), as large as a domestic turkey, is an easy and rewarding prey. Guans associate in flocks of five to fifteen and are commonly found at their roosts, in fruiting trees, or in other feeding spots. They are large and ungainly, trundling along the high branches to escape, rather than flying. Like monkeys, they flee the coffee *montaña* during the *Cosecha,* retreating into the *pura montaña* fastness to avoid falling into the stewpot. From March onward they begin to return to the fringes. *Pavas* are among the most appreciated and admired birds in Olancho, as reflected in a plethora of villages, hills, and streams that bear their name.

Two cousins of the *pava,* the *pavilla* (Highland Guan) and *paujín* (also *paujíl* or *pajuíl,* Great Curassow), are hunted in the *pura montaña,* while the *chachalaca* (either Plain or Gray-headed Chachalaca) is taken from scrub and low forest throughout the region. Occasionally, the curassow is captured to be sold as a pet on the plains, while the *pavilla* may be kept around dwellings in the *montaña.* The *pavilla* is most common in the highest *montañas* where hunters rarely go but also practices altitudinal migrations that bring it down into the coffee belt. Highland Guans are best known by their upsliding whistles and crepuscular wing-beating, trunk-running displays. The *chachalaca,* also known as *madre de gallina* ("mother of chickens"), is favored for taming and mixing with domestic fowl on the plains. In the wild, it lives in boisterous groups that begin a racket in the early morning hours; talkative people are dubbed *chachalacas.* The calling of chachalacas is said to forecast rainfall. Jesús Aguilar Paz notes that duetting birds say "no hay cacao, no hay cacao" ("there is no cacao") and respond "se buscará, se buscará" (literally "it will be looked for").[10]

The other large game bird of the *montaña* is the *gongolona* (Great Tinamou), which inhabits deep forest. It is usually solitary, and reputedly very succulent, but extremely wary. The *chinga* (Little Tinamou) and *chinga de montaña* (Slaty-breasted Tinamou) are smaller and more common. The former is abundant almost everywhere in pine forests and montane scrub, while the latter replaces it in the *pura montaña*. The frequent, mournful whistles of the *chinga de montaña* makes it relatively easy to detect, but it is highly secretive, keeping to the dense undergrowth. Local people believe that *chingas* are tailless pigeons.[11]

The gallinaceous birds are small and difficult to hunt. The most abundant of these is the *mascarita* or *codorniz* (Crested Bobwhite); its two-note call is heard in open fields. In the *serranías*, another *mascarita*, the Ocellated Quail, is scarce and difficult to observe. In the *montaña*, a rare find is the solitary *gallito de monte* (Buffy-crowned Wood-Partridge). The *polla de monte* (Spotted Wood-Quail) runs in sizable coveys and is as boisterous as the *chachalaca*. Experienced hunters recognize instantly the calls of each type of gallinaceous bird.

A riddle recorded by Pompilio Ortega captures the *perdiz,* in its generic sense of partridge or quail.[12]

> I am completely humble
> and I fight with no one
> but I can scare the bravest one,
> even though I never even think of hurting him.

The allusion is to the *perdiz*'s tendency to explode from its cover.

Local people are far more knowledgeable about game birds than about birds in general. If the largest, most coveted species have already gone the way of their *montañas,* people lament their passing. Regarding Cerro Agua Buena, José Mendoza brags to anyone who will listen that this *montaña,* though small, holds all the important species. In the Montaña de Babilonia, local hunters have noticed population decreases among very few species, but they are well aware of what is happening in other areas. They also know that only the *pura montaña* is adequate refuge for the biggest and most important game species. Since farmers in

Babilonia depend on wild species to feed them during the *Cosecha,* they favor protection of the old-growth forest.

For the time being, Francisco Urbina, as park manager of the Sierra de Agalta, is lenient on subsistence hunting of meat species in the Montaña de Babilonia, in exchange for promises that local people will discontinue killing nonfood species. He believes that the need for "bush meat" is a valid use of the *montaña* and that, if expansion of clearcuts can be stopped, game species will continue to have enough habitat. Some day, he hopes that all hunting can be controlled and licensed, and that white-tailed deer reserves can be managed in the pine forests, taking pressure off the *montaña* altogether. He and most local people who use the *montaña* are unequivocal in their condemnation of urban hunting club groups who show up with semi-automatic rifles and expensive dogs, taking out more fauna as trophies in a week than an entire village might eat in a year. The hunting clubs, through their carnage, encourage villages to stand up and claim what is theirs, an important step in sharing management of the national park with the government.

🌿 *Enchantment*

In a society desperate for resources, pragmatic arguments for protecting old-growth rain forest are easy to accept at face value but extremely difficult to implement. For me, it has been enthralling to learn that despite the destruction of forest with little hope of short-term generation, *pura montaña* casts as strong a spell on Olanchanos as it does on outsiders. Not only ecotourists, Peace Corps volunteers, and conservation scientists feel the ineffable nature of Honduran old-growth forest — Olanchanos feel it as well. In the final analysis, I suspect that this "enchanted" quality sensed by outsiders and local people alike serves to unify conservation agendas. Birds, of course, play their part.

In the old days, recounts Nicolás Mayorquín of Juticalpa, hunters sought the *jilguero* (Slate-colored Solitaire) to sell as a cage bird. A dark thrush of deep ravines in the high *montaña,* the *jilguero* emits a series of ethereal notes and is said to be a ventriloquist, misleading its pursuers, luring them from the path, and losing them in the forest. In the Montaña de Babilonia, as in many other Honduran *montañas,* the lost hunter is said to arrive at a beautiful lake in the middle of the *pura montaña,* ringed by fruit trees, and sometimes inhabited by forest sprites or a lost Indian tribe. If he drinks the water or pockets any fruit, he will never escape or will wander back to his village an amnesiac or insane.[13]

A hidden, enchanted lake is said to be located in every highland *montaña* I have visited, even in small forests crisscrossed by trails. In the Montaña de Babilonia, hunters tell of a lost city that can be glimpsed from a ridge but never reached. Throughout Olancho, grinding stones and other precolumbian artifacts have been uncovered in *pura montaña*, indicating to local people that the *antepasados* (ancestors) once lived there. In some places, especially on limestone mountains such as Cerro Agua Buena, small lakes do exist, at least seasonally.

Conservationists in Honduras often consider stories about lakes deep in the *montaña* as traditional explanations for the abundant water that the cloud forest "sponge" stores and releases slowly into the streams, which run cold and deep even when the plains are bone dry at the height of summer. But it is clear from the dense symbolism of *jilgueros*, fruit trees, and other features that Honduran folklore has deeper currents than the explanation of a natural phenomenon. At times, it seems to me that these might be echoes of Edenic narratives: indigenous peoples may once have understood Catholic teachings in terms of the local landscape, situating Paradise and its fruit trees within the most mysterious of forests known to them (in contrast, the Mesoamerican afterlife was accessible through caves). On the other hand, the toponym Babilonia points to local perception of *montaña cruda* as a site of perdition and sin (the origin of the place name is unknown — it may stem from missionary presence in the region dating back to the late 1600s).

The *montaña* is one among many mysterious and enchanted landscapes in a land with a traditional geography enshrouding almost every spring, hill, cave, gorge, pool, solitary old tree, marsh, and woods with some degree of supernatural significance. Along with the bewitched (*embrujado* or *encantado*) nature of many landscape features, religiously significant places are also common. Local appearances of the Virgin Mary in caves and forests, though not officially recognized by the Catholic Church, are not infrequent. Some forests, and most other landscapes, are haunted by precolumbian ruins, and *pichingos* (clay or stone figurines) are encountered in trackless *montaña*, adding to its mysteries. Phenomena such as swamp gas and ball lightning, ringing rocks, moaning caves, and rains of fishes are other manifestations of enchanted geography.[14]

The Montaña de Babilonia holds fauna such as jaguar and tapir that can no longer be found in the "outside world" of the plains. And there are others. The *Sisimite,* a huge and hairy anthropoid creature known throughout Mesoamerica, is commonly believed to subsist only in the remotest reaches of the forest, where people never go. *El Silencio,* known in other parts of Honduras as *El Gritón* ("The Silent One," "The Shouter"), was described to Francisco and me as a very tall and thin humanoid sometimes heard from across narrow valleys (farmers communicate across ravines by high-pitched "ays" and other sounds that carry well). As long as one does not answer, the beast is not to be feared. Our informant was unsure of the consequences of shouting back at *El Silencio.*

The *Sipe,* said still to be common in Olancho's forests, is described as a tiny human no more than a foot or two tall. *Sipes* live in packs in the deep *montaña,* expertly keeping out of sight of people. They eat wood ash and are therefore sometimes glimpsed at the edge of clearcuts. On seeing people, they flee into the welcoming gloom of the *montaña cruda.* Once in a while, they are captured when they venture boldly into kitchens to eat the ash from wood fires.

Unnamed birds, heard but almost never seen, contribute to the great element of mystery that local people attach to the *pura montaña.* The calls of antbirds and other understory species—hollow series of hoots—have evolved to reverberate in the catacomb-like sound spaces of deep forest. Red-capped Manakins snap their wings like whips. Forest owls growl and scream. Large woodcreepers produce sad, down-sliding whistles, loud, arresting "laughs," and whinnies. The invisible Nightingale Wren's hesitant music haunts the ravines with pure notes and echoes.

Francisco Urbina and I have become quite familiar with the avifauna of the *montaña,* and the number of calls we can't recognize has diminished. However, we never feel that it has yielded all its avifaunal mysteries. For example, we have detected the presence of a brown and gray Olivaceous Woodcreeper, as well as an "orange-bellied" trogon. Ornithologically, not much can be said about the birds without at least photos and preferably skins, so they remain as possible individual mutations, unknown color morphs, or perhaps new races. More frustrating have been Francisco's two outstanding records that cannot be added to the list of Honduran bird species. Without photo or tape, neither his record of the Sooty-faced Finch (endemic to Panama and Costa Rica) nor the Brown Thrasher (to my knowledge never recorded to migrate to Central America) would endure the scrutiny of professional ornithology even though in both instances he observed birds that were identical to these species for several minutes at close range.

The rain forest, more than any other place, never becomes wholly ex-plicable or familiar to anyone. This points to common ground between local and outside knowledge, between conservation geography and farmer folklore. The rumor of the mysterious that murmurs through the "new and noteworthy" journal articles and shouts from the topo-nyms and stories is the perfect translation of *montaña* to "rain forest" and rain forest to *montaña*. On the far side of the clearcut, farmers and con-servationists feel many of the same emotions. The forest calls to us and gathers us together.

Landscape Dialogues

The landscape speaks to all who listen. Bellbirds still call from the trees around El Murmullo, a village nestled in the Sierra de Agalta above Catacamas. Murmullo, "Murmuring," is the sound that the nearby river makes as its white waters tumble over limestone boulders. Just up the road is Las Delicias, "The Delights." Both communities were founded not many decades ago by migrants who came to the *montaña* seeking better lives. While transforming the old-growth rain forest to shaded coffee farms, they were listening intently to their surroundings, reveling in the landscape. After Mitch's hurricane rains slumped the mountain down on top of several families in 1998, those who remained mourned their dead, but they didn't hate the *montaña* for what had happened, here or at a dozen other Agalta landslide tombs. The *montaña* had spoken forcefully, demanding respect. They began to retreat from the steepest, most delicate slopes. The murmur went on through the tolling of bells.

Birds and people are likewise in constant communication. Different types of people communicate with birds in different ways. Some are obsessed with birds, many are ornithophilic, others are oblivious, and a few are hostile. But opinions can change surprisingly fast. Conservation projects should seek diversity in communication, fostering exchange between wealthy ranchers and poor farmers, ornithologists and hunters, loggers and children, mixing them together in village meetings and workshops, and eventually encouraging them to share work responsibilities. A conservation hierarchy cannot do this, because it will tend to separate identities and compartmentalize interest groups and issues. A conservation network, on the other hand, can function to blur identities and transport interests and needs from one sector to another, relying on faith in common human traits such as language that are capable of creating consensus.

Another Name for the Bellbird

In this book I present and discuss relationships between people and birds in Olancho. I emphasize local knowledge, traditions, and behavior, because most outsiders are either unaware of ornithophilia or do not sufficiently appreciate its depth and complexity in countries such as Honduras. I mention six Spanish names and one English name for the bellbird, signifying the heterogeneous nature of human relationships to birds, varying from person to person, family to family, village to village, and culture to culture. But what of *Procnias tricarunculata,* the name by which the Three-wattled Bellbird is situated in ornithology? What does natural science offer, if it is not the only acceptable authority for conservation?

Conservation geography benefits greatly from the wisdom of ornithology, which transcends political boundaries and local concerns to reveal facets of avian worlds that not even the most knowledgeable local people can imagine. Without ornithological insights, avian conservation projects can become fragmented and misguided, and in the worst cases fail altogether to address the needs of birds. Ornithologists should be participants in landscape conservation, and their expertise should contribute to decisions regarding the preservation of birds. They should be in the same meetings with local farmers, ranchers, small town conservationists, big city environmentalists, politicians, social scientists, other natural scientists. The challenge of a geographical and transdisciplinary conservation project is to foster dialogues and collaboration to protect the landscape for a multiplicity of uses, from celebrating birds to watershed protection, ecotourism to subsistence hunting. The consensus building that may help to bring about the reversal of habitat destruction and biodiversity loss can occur only when distinct knowledges — traditional, geographical, and ornithological, for example — are translated, exchanged, and mutually respected.

Conservation is a crucial human endeavor that encourages the fostering of smooth relationships with the earth, given that modern humanity controls and simplifies (and often destroys) the complex webs of life in which we are participants. Avian conservation is founded in a belief that birds need human stewards. Enough birds have become extinct recently to prove that we need serious checks on our actions. If necessary, birds need to be cordoned off from people to be kept safe. *However, it is wrong to employ a "birds versus people" strategy or paradigm everywhere that species are threatened.* Sensitivity to human culture is paramount. Dichotomization of Nature and Culture is not only unrealistic and unenforceable but also a mark of flawed science. The separation of people and nature cannot be enforced in highly biodiverse and fluid frontier regions such as Olancho, and conservationists in Neotropical countries should not attempt to erect a wall along the deforestation front. To find historical analogues to present-day situations, those who become frustrated because the tropical rain forest and its avifauna are not being "saved" fast enough need look no farther than the United States, where the destruction of old-growth forest continues to this day; or one can thumb through the archipelago-like range maps in European field guides.

Sustainable Solutions Need Local Focus

The present-day horror that conservationists feel when they think about Neotropical biodiversity loss has to do with the vast scale of destruction combined with awareness of what will be lost. However, even if we know too well what is being lost and where, it is not politically possible to intervene in regions with dire socioeconomic inequities and impose sustainable conservation solutions from above. Successful — that is, sustainable — conservation solutions are not those modeled on the United States and western Europe, nor are they blueprints hatched in Tegucigalpa. They may combine elements of outside inspiration, but primordially they must arise from the landscapes they purport to protect. They must mesh with local, ongoing, non-capital-dependent strategies of adaptation to the land; if they involve large areas (like whole mountain ranges) they must be constructed piece by piece, village by village.

Unfortunately, before rapid destruction of Neotropical biodiversity can be slowed across entire regions, unjust socioeconomic conditions have to change. In Central America, just the opposite is happening: weak economies are becoming more export-oriented while consumption becomes more dependent on imports. Multinational corporations are becoming ever more powerful players in energy generation, road building, and plantation agriculture, to name three practices that destroy Neotropical landscapes quickly and drastically. Despite structural adjustment (austerity measures) imposed on Honduras by the International Monetary Fund, the external debt wracked up in large part during the militarization phase of the Cold War 1980s is still crippling. Indeed, even Hurricane Mitch, the most powerful storm to hit the Western Hemisphere in recorded history, was not enough to convince international financial groups to forgive Honduras's debt. The Honduran health, education, and military budgets have been decimated as the country struggles to pay its debts (while borrowing more) and still have enough left over for the government to function. Privatization, that panacea of neoliberal economic orthodoxy, is failing — privatized state companies seem to have little interest in serving the public, and their fees, for the vast majority, are prohibitively expensive.

This dismal milieu is the context for a hemisphere-wide free trade zone of the near future, the so-called Free Trade Area of the Americas (FTAA), in which Honduras as one of the poorest countries will be least equipped to partake. As Honduras becomes more impoverished, only through force can decimation of biodiversity be controlled, because it has become obvious to many middle-class and poor Hondurans that multinational corporations (especially the banana companies and the mining companies) are rewarded for destruction of the environment. Why should the person in the street behave any differently? At the same time, environmentalists are being assassinated in Olancho and across the country when they try to mobilize public support for local protection of resources (whether they are protesting against local *terratenientes,* government interests, or multinational involvement). Nevertheless, at time of writing there is in Honduras a massive societal will to protect the environment, but it does not yet engulf the spheres of politics and economics (despite frequent lip service). Due to this, sustainable conservation must be done with little fanfare and minuscule budget, and with connection neither to persons and organizations widely seen as corrupt and self-serving nor to groups seen as distant and arrogant. Or, if such connections are unavoidable, they should be minimized and should never represent controlling interests.

Conservation solutions in Honduras in the new millennium have to be localized, because at the local scale there is a certain degree of control over the landscape and a knowledge of who the key players are. Local people and concerned outsiders need to continue to put their heads together to invent solutions appropriate to the landscapes and sensitive to needs of diverse groups. The first thing they need to recognize and enshrine as "success" is what is already being done and what is already known. The human landscape is not a blank slate; conservation is always already happening in some way, and new projects that ignore or otherwise do not recognize this may be reinventing the wheel. Think of the Resplendent Quetzal—a project that sought to "rescue" it in Olancho would be successful only inasmuch as it first identified and rewarded shade coffee growers who let the birds nest on their farms without harming them. By "reward" I mean, for example, incentives to grow and export organic, bird-friendly coffee.

Conservationists focusing on the Neotropics should not think solely in terms of the virgin rain forest, nor consign other terrestrial habitats to "degraded" status (with the possible exception of strip mines and banana, pineapple, and oil palm plantations). One of my objectives in this book is to help readers understand that in complex terrain like Central America, old-growth rain forest is but one of a staggering number of habitats, and that this would be true even without the presence of humans. Archie Carr's *Outline for a Classification of Animal Habitats in Honduras,* published in 1950, remains the finest such written description of this landscape diversity. Carr, who spent more than five years roaming Honduras, describes and illustrates over thirty terrestrial habitats, from steppe and savanna to pine woods, thorn forest, rain forest, and cloud forest. The old-growth rain forest is under siege, but it is not the only area where endangered and threatened species are found. In Olancho, the Red-throated Caracara is a denizen of dry forests and pine forests. The Honduran Emerald, the country's only endemic bird, is restricted to thorn forest. The endangered Golden-cheeked Warbler is found in pine-oak forests. These habitats are not results of tropical rain forest destruction. They are natural formations resulting from slope, geology, soils, microclimates, and other factors. Like the rain forests, they have been altered and shaped by humans for millennia.

The rain forest frontier in eastern Honduras is not a crisp division between open land and forest, a line running as far as the eye can see. Instead, the frontier is a fractalized landscape characterized by degrees

of modern human disturbance. What looks green and "virgin" on a satellite photo may already be slated for transformation to fields; without
that knowledge, planners for protected areas have frequently designated
as parts of the "nucleus" lands that have already been bought and sold
and are, so to speak, on the chopping block. As guides for conservation
planning, two-dimensional maps of forest cover can be misleading: the
most accurate "maps" are illustrated textual accounts of local relations
with the forest, indicating environmental history, present degrees of
disturbance, and future trends. GIS and GPS technology can contribute
to conservation planning but should never take the place of home-by-
home, village-by-village qualitative analyses of human-forest interaction, in which local people (mestizo and indigenous, long-time resident
and recent migrant alike) are numbered among the planners.

Conservation Geography in Action

Conservation solutions are always contextual—what works in
Olancho may not work in other regions. Solutions for La Venta may
have little luck in El Boquerón. Experimentation is of the essence—
conservation should be strategic and malleable more often than rigid and
plan-driven. Following are themes and possibilities for conservation in
Olancho that are both geographical and practical and may serve to
inspire work in other regions.

LOCAL PEOPLE
The people provide the key to bird conservation. This simple fact should
never be forgotten by outsiders, nor should "local people–driven" become an empty phrase to impress funding agencies. Local people should
be appreciated in all their complexity, neither scorned nor romanticized.
They should always be among the paid experts on management teams
for large protected areas such as national parks.

LANDSCAPE
To geographers, "landscape" suggests people and nature coexisting in
the same places at the same times. The term "pine forest" seems to mean
that people are outsiders and can only go "into" it. By contrast, "pine forest landscape" signifies pines, other plants and animals, soils and rocks,

slope and climate, and people. Conservation solutions should be applied to human landscapes, not to "natural ecosystems" that make human presence seem like unnatural interference.

In Olancho, *serranía* means essentially "pine forest landscape"—trees, terrain, and whatever and whoever dwells therein. *Montaña* is a similar term for trees, terrain, and inhabitants. Local landscape terms should be used generously by outsiders — saying *serranía* is far better than referring to "el bosque de pino"; *la montaña* speaks volumes, while "pluviselva" and "bosque húmedo" have little or no meaning to most people.

EDUCATION

This is an ongoing process within local society, not an event that can happen only when outsiders are present. Environmental education characterizes everyday interaction within and between families, friends, villages, urban neighborhoods, and foreign visitors alike. Environmental education may indeed come about when conservationists hold workshops and field courses — but only when they learn from their "students" and vice versa.

Bird education as part of a conservation project should build on local knowledge, when this is considered by participants to be useful or at least not prejudicial to bird populations. Bird workshops should contain a mixture of local and scientific knowledge. If local people feel that what they know is important and is respected by outside experts, some may become more deeply involved in conservation, as the example of Francisco Urbina demonstrates.

Education is always a mode of action, not solely a preparatory stage. Since 1997, I have participated in three bird count workshops in Gualaco, modeled loosely on the U.S. Christmas Bird Count and International Migratory Bird Day but with substantial variations. Participants range from teachers and farmers to Peace Corps volunteers and youth groups. For one or two intense days, participants study birds already somewhat familiar to them and are also introduced to "unknown" species. They learn about field guides and ornithology. After classroom discussions and talks, participants practice in the field preparatory to the day-long count.

The count day itself begins at 4:00 A.M. Half the groups disperse to various points of the Valle de Gualaco and Valle de Agalta, count bird species and numbers on hikes of ten to twenty kilometers, and return to base at dusk (sometimes long after). Other groups, who miss the preliminary training days, go on treks to the Sierra de Agalta. They take two days to get to their counting sites and use the count day itself to return (downhill) to the trailhead. After the day's counting is concluded, all groups gather for supper and swap birding stories. Compilers put together the data for presentation the following morning. Between 120 and 200 species are usually recorded, and numbers of each species are noted as well. (The lack of more than two or three expert birders, combined with the difficulty of the terrain, prohibit spectacularly high numbers such as those garnered by count groups in other parts of Central America. Under ideal conditions, around 300 species would probably be counted).

To conclude, the groups discuss the highlights, the problems, and suggestions for improving the activity. As counts become annual events, the data begin to take on long-term significance for conservation. In addition to generating new and exciting information about local birds, the counts have inspired participants (teachers and extensionists, for example) to incorporate birds into their everyday work activities.

GENDER AND AGE

This should be a concern in all conservation projects, especially because so often it has been ignored. In most cases, women manage money better than men, and they are also usually in charge of the household. They need to become integral to the functioning of conservation networks.

Children should be looked on not as blank slates but as those with the most intricate knowledge of the avian landscape. They should become leaders of conservation initiatives and train their parents. In Olancho, this is a pragmatic solution, because children are far more likely to be literate than their elders.

At the other end of the spectrum, the knowledge about birds locked in the heads of Olancho's oldest citizens is rapidly being lost. Folklore collecting and oral history projects are always invaluable endeavors, and knowledge about the environment should be a major focus in the preservation of the past.

PLANNING

Conservation projects should be planned by outsiders and local people together. "Outsiders" means not only foreign conservationists and biologists but also Hondurans who do not inhabit the rural landscape. The examples of Juticalpa and of the *terratenientes* showed how distinct urban and wealthy Hondurans are from rural dwellers, and this is common across Latin America.

Planning should involve human needs and the needs of the environment together and should not be seen as an excuse to effect one on the pretext of caring about the other. Microwatershed (*microcuenca*) protection is a fine example of an integrated project that is beneficial to the landscape and all its components. Sanctioned by law and custom, communities across Honduras are delimiting and managing their watersheds, protecting vegetative cover and restricting human use, with resultant benefits to flora and fauna.

Planning needs to be dynamic, strategic, and ongoing. Bulky management plans that are ends in themselves take too much time and money to prepare — every protected area in Honduras has at least one, and some have several, stacked on shelves and gathering dust. Today's projects need to have alternative strategies built into them to allow for contingencies; if they are rigid and predefined for a five-year span, for example, they may become impossible to implement due to rapidly fluctuating socioeconomic and political conditions. Brief operative plans should suffice as toolkits for action but should not smother human initiative and ingenuity. Project management teams should possess background studies as resources but should not necessarily spend valuable time synthesizing this information in lengthy documents.[1]

LEARNING TO READ THE LANDSCAPE

Each of the preceding chapters considered distinct spaces and diverse problems. Conservation projects in the planning stage need to identify such spatial regions and concerns. Societal anchoring points should be treated as highly important, even if they possess low biodiversity. Juticalpa, for example, as a central place in the decision-making hierarchy and a key node in cultural networks, is the place where local people from around Olancho meet and exchange information and where political decisions are made. Juticalpa is also a filter of the outside, where the wider world meets Olancho. Because they will not change the nature of central places and cannot ignore them, conservation projects need to lean on these places to their benefit, like epiphytes on a tree. Olancho decision makers cluster in Juticalpa and take environmental messages to the national congress. Radio stations based here are received in every corner of the department. There are regional offices of government agencies, international projects, and NGOs, all with considerable say in landscape management. How successful can a conservation project be if it bypasses Juticalpa, concentrating on the countryside and based in Tegucigalpa? Yet many do just this.

Another spatial anchor in Olancho is the rural domestic landscape. I stress the village and its *pajaral* because conservation comes about first and foremost through the decisions and practices of villagers. The *pajaral* is a home territory over which disenfranchised people have control. In a wider sense, the *pajaral* as home extends from the plains to the *montaña*. Conservation should start at home.

Human space is intricately textured, and outsiders need to become sensitive to differences such as those between a smallholder landscape and a *terrateniente* landscape, because these are as important for success as knowing how to differentiate types of forest. To use a common geographic phrase, conservationists need to learn how to read the landscape. They need to investigate how and why it is managed the way it is, what emotions it inspires in its residents, and how change is "built in." In conservation actions, local people also learn other ways of reading: the small farmer with the eyes of a rancher, the rancher with the eyes of a birder.

PROJECTS

"Conservation" signifies much more than special efforts on the part of a management team. Conservation projects are necessary, however, to focus the efforts—for example, on particular areas and species at risk. Projects may not need to be justified in terms of economic development using financial incentives: in Honduras, many people consider birds to be important because they are part of local and national heritage (*patrimonio*). Whether the Honduran Emerald is saved or extinguished will not make a difference to economic development, but that does not mean that the emerald is "insignificant." Nevertheless, local people can easily be manipulated by interested parties who feel threatened, with the result that the protection of birds can be made to appear a frivolous "luxury" demanded solely by outsiders. However, as I have shown, any idea that local people believe "nature" is unnecessary if it does not provide economic benefits is far from reality. Indeed, where they do mouth this opinion, I often detect the presence of an outsider hostile to environmentalists (there are many of these, particularly within development projects focused on high-yield and fast-results "sustainable" agriculture). I suspect this is the case not only in Olancho but also across Latin America.

Projects need not have names or publicity. I have observed numerous projects and have participated in some that are preceded by great reputations and publicity, glossy pamphlets, and numerous meetings but become bogged down at the stage of achieving concrete results. Projects obsessed by form (reports, meetings, publications, vehicles, offices, politics, appearances) may appear slick, especially when one visits them for a day or reads about them from afar, but this does not mean that they are received well (or at all) in their target landscapes. Even though well-planned, well-funded, and well-executed programs may indeed be as effective as they are impressive, they are not the only way. Ad hoc groups of people may form for a purpose and then dissolve, having achieved their goals even if no one else noticed and they wrote no final report. Lasting friendships and private initiatives, like those described in this book, can lead to "undocumented" conservation.

MONEY

The money trap is currently dooming conservation initiatives across Honduras. Now that money is available (conservation having become mainstream for many development initiatives, especially those funded by the World Bank and USAID), numerous projects stake their futures on secure budgets and high salaries rather than on volunteerism and dedication to the cause. Being strapped for funds — the norm for conservation in Olancho — should never be reason for inaction. Some of the most important and genuinely sustainable projects are extensive conversations, which don't cost anything. Talk is free. What of the mobility that is necessary for many projects, a need that big agencies and NGOs meet through use of expensive donated vehicles? It is perfectly possible to use bicycles and public buses; walking or riding beasts of burden can be solutions in other situations. When I worked on the management team of the Parque Nacional Sierra de Agalta, we felt freer and achieved a lot more when we stopped depending on rides from government agencies and NGOs to reach remote areas. If rides were forthcoming, we would not refuse them; but otherwise, as Peace Corps volunteers and as private activists, we learned to get to where we wanted to go using any means at our disposal. The alternative, in the case of government agencies such as COHDEFOR, was to wait hours and even days for the local boss to assign us a vehicle; often, the vehicle would nevertheless be diverted to other errands.

Funding should come from local sources if at all possible. Can landowners take on the expense of protecting their birds? Can local farmers pay for bus fare to arrive at a meeting? Encouraging people to pay even symbolic amounts is better than giving "free rides" and creating dependence. When rumors of huge funds are abroad, people with pecuniary interests take note while those who don't wish to be perceived as corrupt give well-funded projects a wide berth. Though generating jobs in conservation is an important goal, attracting people who are involved solely for the money can become a serious political problem.

Funds for program operation should be raised first at the local level, for it is here that the project should have highest visibility. Even though direct dependence on foreign aid is common in rural landscapes across Latin America, this does not mean that local businesses, churches, civil groups, and private citizens will not be willing to give monetary or in-kind donations. In many cases, NGOs simply forget to ask them. Local offices of government agencies involved in natural resource management should be enlisted for in-kind contributions to private projects. The more local money circulates in a project, the more it will take on relevance; many will see it as something in which they have a stake rather than as a foreign implant.

MOUTHS

Subsistence hunting for food or other basic needs should not be prohibited or condemned out of hand without knowledge of who is hunting what, and why. In many cases, animal and bird populations can recover or be reintroduced if habitat is protected. Hunters who become managers of fauna on public as well as private land are preferable to "poachers." Wildlife management involves give and take with local sustenance requirements. In Olancho, utilization of common species such as the paca and agouti, both abundant in many areas, can be traded off for protection of threatened biota such as cats, raptors, and monkeys.

The need to eat should be taken extremely seriously. Land cannot be taken away from poor farmers who have no other place to go. Conservation projects that attempt this will not only lose credibility at the local and regional level; they may put their participants in physical danger.

GUNS

Frontier regions in Central America became rife with automatic weapons in the post–Cold War era. In Olancho, many poor as well as wealthy families define their strength by the AK-47 assault rifles that they possess. Guns are often said to settle disputes definitively, though in reality guns feed long-running family vendettas. Because of this, conservation in a heavily armed region like the Cordillera de Agalta cannot help but be conciliatory and peaceful. Nongovernment conservation projects should divorce themselves from association with the use of force and seek at all times to keep their personnel far from danger. Research stations being burned down and extensionists being threatened are signs to back off. In any case, when conservationists are murdered it is often because they have opposed powerful and corrupt interests, not peasant farmers.

TALK

When visiting a village, action-oriented conservationists can become frustrated by ethnographic researchers like me, who linger over a strong cup of coffee and a good conversation. According to some, nothing is being achieved by sitting around and chatting. My belief, on the other hand, is that in many cases it is extremely important to spend many hours in open discussion on people's porches. It is important to savor conversations with and among local people — to enjoy conversing, rather than looking upon it as a requirement or a bore. Finding out about the meanings that landscapes have for local people is part of the process of becoming entangled with the local world. If this is not important to a conservation project, then it will be unsuccessful. Conservationists who are unable to build trust (*confianza*), the glue of Central American social relations, will be perceived as objects to be exploited for access to privileges and funds.

Talk circulates. Once talking becomes part of conservationist practice, one attempts meaningful conversations with all local residents, house by house (not only in public meetings). More important, local people continue to discuss with each other issues that have been raised, achieving a multiplier effect. When "everyone is talking," it can become socially acceptable to undertake bird conservation actions where it might previously have been regarded as odd behavior. Mostly through talk, with José Mendoza as catalyst, burning of fields and unnecessary killing of birds on Cerro Agua Buena became unpopular among its coffee farmers. Constant discussion there focuses on whether this should continue to be the case; as long as the consensus is yes, those who go against the grain will be censured by their peers. In most cases this censure is far more effective than punishment imposed from above.

LEGISLATION

The fact that laws are difficult to enforce in frontier regions does not mean they should be ignored by conservationists. Just the opposite: all relevant environmental clauses should be learned by heart by local people and outsiders. Laws, even if not easily applicable, should have at least a theoretical presence. Many impoverished people are unaware of the power that laws may afford them — for example, to protect their watersheds from powerful usurpers such as timber and hydroelectric companies. In Olancho, despite its reputation for lawlessness, an overwhelming majority clamors for law enforcement that will allow people to live in dignity and will permit the environment to recover.

LANGUAGE

The words that conservationists know are often inappropriate to local situations. Why use generic ecosystem terms when talking with farmers? "Bosque húmedo subtropical" is a poor substitute for *serranía*. Why employ "bosque lluvioso tropical" when *montaña* says it better? Rural Olanchanos who have not been exposed to outside environmentalists or foresters use *bosque* in the limited sense of a grove of trees. Talking with them about the forest as *el bosque* is unproductive. Conservation takes place in the local landscape, not in the university or the office, so it makes most sense to draw from the local lexicon wherever possible and to avoid employing generic words from elsewhere. If the local vocabulary does not suffice, for example in the naming of obscure antbirds and ovenbirds, then appropriate translations should make sense in cultural context.

Language is a serious problem in bird conservation, because almost all available field guides are in English, making them the exclusive provenance of educated outsiders who possess a specialized knowledge, thus

alienating many local people. Serious efforts should be made to dissem-
inate materials in the local primary or secondary language. In Honduras,
for example, a field guide to Honduran birds, in Spanish, would be an
excellent project. In the meantime, we make do with spliced-together
photocopies of various guides from other countries, crossing out foreign
names and inserting local ones.

🐦 When a conservation network functions to transport interests between sectors of the human population, landscape dialogues are en-
livened and enriched. Awareness expands; new perspectives take hold as
common interests materialize. Who would have thought there would be
so many established local names for the rarely seen Three-wattled Bellbird, all within a limited area of a single province in Honduras? How can
conservationists have missed or dismissed for so long the importance to
birds of the smallholder landscape and the dooryard garden? Who could
have imagined that "ordinary" *serranía* would serve as a haven for the
Golden-cheeked Warbler? Or that large landowners would have flocks
of six hundred Black-bellied Whistling-Ducks and would hold the key to
local conservation of a thorn forest species like the Honduran Emerald?
The potential for consensus, mutual respect, and effective long-term
conservation of biodiversity multiplies with every round of landscape
dialogue.

Appendix
Birds Recorded in Central Olancho, 1937–2002

This list contains the 476 bird species recorded to date from the area covered in this book. The area is shown in figure 2 and amounts to approximately three thousand square kilometers (excluding the southern Valle de Azacualpa sector). Please note that as little as 5 percent of the total area has actually been surveyed in detail; however, all the major habitats have been visited. The bird list is distilled from more detailed inventories and lists, some unpublished (see Bonta in bibliography), which contain altitudes, habitats, sites, and other data. Also included are the records Burt Monroe described for Olancho in *A Distributional Survey of the Birds of Honduras* (1968), based on collections of species made in 1937 (C. F. Underwood, El Boquerón and Catacamas); 1948 (A. Twomey and R. Hawkins, San Esteban and environs); and 1962–63 (J. and R. Graber, Sierra de Agalta at Vallecito, San José de Río Tinto). Fifteen species have not been recorded between 1991 and 2002; several of these may be extirpated from the region. The total number of fully confirmed bird species for Honduras is 701 (Bonta and Anderson, 2003).

Latin and English names, as well as taxonomic sequence, follow the American Ornithologists' Union *Check-list of North American Birds,* seventh edition, in its online version (http://www.aou.org/aou/birdlist.html). This is kept current as the "List of the 2,030 bird species (with scientific and English names) known from the A.O.U. Check-list area," incorporating changes made in supplements 42 and 43 to the *Check-list,* as published in the *Auk* 117: 847–58 (2000) and 119: 897–906 (2002). The AOU *Check-list* varies slightly in taxonomic sequence and nomenclature from the two most useful field guides for the eastern Honduran region (Howell and Webb 1995, Ridgely and Gwynne 1989). Because neither guide alone contains plates of all possible species in eastern Honduras, avid birdwatchers may want to carry both guides in Olancho, and a North American guide is useful for plates of Neotropical migrants.

Though I have documented many local names in Olancho, this project is by no means complete. In the text I make infrequent mention of non-Olanchano local names; those have not been incorporated here. Readers familiar with other parts of Honduras and Central America will find that many of the names in this list apply to different birds elsewhere (e.g., *jilguero, guardabarrancos*) or vary widely in their onomatopoeic interpretations.

The terms *chipe* and *arrocero* are applied so widely and loosely that they do not appear here; other names that are noted to designate a family should be understood to mean any member of that family without distinction.

For sake of clarity, the Spanish names we have borrowed from nonlocal sources or invented when local names do not exist are not included here. Nonlocal and invented names are explained in the glossary.

TINAMIFORMES

Tinamidae   *Palomas Chingas;*
Gallos Chingos

Tinamus major	*gongolona*	Tinamou, Great
Crypturellus soui	*chinga; paloma chinga*	Tinamou, Little
Crypturellus boucardi	*chinga de montaña*	Tinamou, Slaty-breasted

PODICIPEDIFORMES

Podicipedidae

Tachybaptus dominicus	*pato zambullidor; yaguaza*	Grebe, Least
Podilymbus podiceps		Grebe, Pied-billed

PELECANIFORMES

Pelecanidae

Pelecanus occidentalis	*pelícano*	Pelican, Brown

Phalacrocoracidae

Phalacrocorax brasilianus		Cormorant, Neotropic

Anhingidae

Anhinga anhinga	*pato aguja*	Anhinga

CICONIIFORMES

Ardeidae

Tigrisoma mexicanum	*afoque; ahoque*	Tiger-Heron, Bare-throated
Ardea herodias	*afoque; ahoque; garzón moreno*	Heron, Great Blue
Ardea alba	*garzón*	Egret, Great
Egretta thula	*garcita*	Egret, Snowy
Egretta caerulea	*garcita morena ; garza morena; morencita*	Heron, Little Blue
Egretta tricolor	*garza*	Heron, Tricolored
Bubulcus ibis	*bueyera; garcita bueyera*	Egret, Cattle
Butorides virescens	*ahoquillo*	Heron, Green
Agamia agami		Heron, Agami
Nyctanassa violacea	*bujaja*	Night-Heron, Yellow-crowned

Threskiornithidae

Eudocimus albus		Ibis, White
Platalea ajaja	*espátula*	Spoonbill, Roseate

Ciconiidae

Mycteria americana	*cigüeña*	Stork, Wood

Cathartidae   *Zopes, Cutes, Buitres,*
Viudas

Coragyps atratus	*zopilote; zope; cabeza pelada*	Vulture, Black
Cathartes aura	*tincute; cute*	Vulture, Turkey
Sarcoramphus papa	*rey zope; zopilote rey*	Vulture, King

ANSERIFORMES
Anatidae

Dendrocygna autumnalis	*pichiche; piche*	Duck, Black-bellied Whistling-
Cairina moschata	*pato; pato negro; pato real;*	Duck, Muscovy
	pato de monte; pato grande	
Anas discors	*yaguaza*	Teal, Blue-winged
Nomonyx dominicana	*patito*	Duck, Masked

FALCONIFORMES
Accipitridae

Pandion haliaetus	*águila pescador; águila pesquera;*	Osprey
	gavilán pescador	
Leptodon cayanensis	*gavilán*	Kite, Gray-headed
Chondrohierax uncinatus	*gavilán*	Kite, Hook-billed
Elanoides forficatus	*gavilán tijereta; tijereta*	Kite, Swallow-tailed
Elanus leucurus	*gavilán pollero; ratonero*	Kite, White-tailed
Harpagus bidentatus	*gavilán*	Kite, Double-toothed
Accipiter striatus	*gavilán*	Hawk, Sharp-shinned
Accipiter bicolor	*gavilán*	Hawk, Bicolored
Geranospiza caerulescens	*gavilán*	Hawk, Crane
Leucopternis albicollis	*gavilán blanco; gavilán garza*	Hawk, White
Asturina nitida	*gavilán*	Hawk, Gray
Buteogallus anthracinus	*cangrejero*	Hawk, Common Black-
Buteogallus urubitinga	*gavilán negro*	Hawk, Great Black-
Buteo magnirostris	*gavilán*	Hawk, Roadside
Buteo platypterus	*gavilán*	Hawk, Broad-winged
Buteo brachyurus	*gavilán*	Hawk, Short-tailed
Buteo albicaudatus	*gavilán*	Hawk, White-tailed
Buteo albonotatus	*gavilán*	Hawk, Zone-tailed
Buteo jamaicensis	*gavilán de serranía*	Hawk, Red-tailed
Spizastur melanoleucus	*aguiluche; cazamicos*	Hawk-Eagle, Black-and-white
Spizaetus tyrannus	*aguiluche; cazamicos;*	Hawk-Eagle, Black
	pascua florida	
Spizaetus ornatus	*aguiluche; cazamicos*	Hawk-Eagle, Ornate

Falconidae

Micrastur ruficollis	*gavilancillo*	Forest-Falcon, Barred
Micrastur semitorquatus	*gavilancillo*	Forest-Falcon, Collared
Ibycter americanus	*cacao; cacatao; racacao; talcacao*	Caracara, Red-throated
Caracara cheriway	*tera; quebrantahuesos*	Caracara, Crested
Herpetotheres cachinnans	*guaco*	Falcon, Laughing
Falco sparverius	*clis-clis; lis-lis*	Kestrel, American
Falco columbarius		Merlin
Falco femoralis		Falcon, Aplomado

Falconidae continued

Falco rufigularis	*gavilancillo*	Falcon, Bat
Falco deiroleucus		Falcon, Orange-breasted

GALLIFORMES
Cracidae

Ortalis cinereiceps	*chacha; chachalaca*	Chachalaca, Gray-headed
Penelope purpurascens	*pava*	Guan, Crested
Penelopina nigra	*pavilla*	Guan, Highland
Crax rubra	*pajuíl; paujíl; paujín*	Curassow, Great

Odontophoridae

Colinus cristatus	*codorniz; mascarita*	Bobwhite, Crested
Dendrortyx leucophrys	*gallito de monte; polla de monte*	Wood-Partridge, Buffy-crowned
Odontophorus melanotis		Wood-Quail, Black-eared
Odontophorus guttatus	*gallito de monte; polla de monte*	Wood-Quail, Spotted
Dactylortyx thoracicus conoveri	*codorniz*	Quail, Singing
Cyrtonyx ocellatus	*codorniz*	Quail, Ocellated

GRUIFORMES
Rallidae

Laterallus ruber		Crake, Ruddy
Aramides cajanea	*cocolea; cocoleca*	Rail, Gray-necked Wood-
Amaurolimnas concolor		Crake, Uniform
Porphyrio martinica	*polla de agua*	Gallinule, Purple
Gallinula chloropus	*polla de agua*	Moorhen, Common
Fulica americana	*polla de agua*	Coot, American

Heliornithidae

Heliornis fulica		Sungrebe

Eurypygidae

Eurypygia helias		Sunbittern

CHARADRIIFORMES
Burhinidae

Burhinus bistriatus	*alcaraván*	Thick-knee, Double-striped

Charadriidae

Charadrius collaris		Plover, Collared
Charadrius vociferus		Killdeer

Recurvirostridae

Himantopus mexicanus		Stilt, Black-necked

Jacanidae

Jacana spinosa	*pico de oro*	Jacana, Northern

Scolopacidae   **Pespitas; Pispitas**

Tringa flavipes		Yellowlegs, Lesser
Tringa solitaria		Sandpiper, Solitary

Actitis macularia		Sandpiper, Spotted
Calidris pusilla		Sandpiper, Semipalmated
Calidris mauri		Sandpiper, Western
Calidris minutilla		Sandpiper, Least
Gallinago delicata		Snipe, Wilson's

Laridae

Larus atricilla	*gaviota*	Gull, Laughing
Chlidonias niger		Tern, Black

COLUMBIFORMES
Columbidae

Columba livia	*paloma de Castilla*	Dove, Rock
Columba cayennensis	*paloma azulona; turca azulona*	Pigeon, Pale-vented
Columba speciosa		Pigeon, Scaled
Columba flavirostris	*paloma azulona; pico rojo; turca azulona*	Pigeon, Red-billed
Columba fasciata	*paloma azulona; paloma de montaña*	Pigeon, Band-tailed
Columba nigrirostris	*paloma de montaña; tres pesos; Voy para Tocoa*	Pigeon, Short-billed
Zenaida asiatica	*ala blanca; frijolera; sabanera*	Dove, White-winged
Zenaida macroura	*sabanera*	Dove, Mourning
Columbina inca	*sabanera; turquita*	Dove, Inca
Columbina passerina	*sabanera; turquita*	Dove, Common Ground-
Columbina talpacoti	*Santa Cruz; tortolita*	Dove, Ruddy Ground-
Claravis pretiosa	*sabanera; turquita*	Dove, Blue Ground-
Leptotila verreauxi	*barranquera; barranqueña; paloma barranquera; paloma bruja; la bruja; viuda*	Dove, White-tipped
Leptotila rufaxilla	*turca chelona*	Dove, Gray-fronted
Leptotila cassini	*turca chelona*	Dove, Gray-chested
Geotrygon albifacies	*turca chelona*	Quail-Dove, White-faced
Geotrygon montana	*turca chelona*	Quail-Dove, Ruddy

PSITTACIFORMES
Psittacidae

Aratinga holochlora	*barba roja; ocotero; pecho rojo*	Parakeet, Green
Aratinga nana	*chocoyito; chocoyo*	Parakeet, Olive-throated
Ara ambigua	*guara; guara verde*	Macaw, Great Green
Ara macao	*guara; guara roja*	Macaw, Scarlet
Bolborhynchus lineola	*periquito de montaña*	Parakeet, Barred
Brotogeris jugularis	*periquito*	Parakeet, Orange-chinned
Pionopsitta haematotis	*lora*	Parrot, Brown-hooded
Pionus senilis	*lora come-maíz; lora de montaña; loro negro; pico blanco*	Parrot, White-crowned

Psittacidae *continued*

Amazona albifrons	*fueteté; guayabero; hueteté; lora naranjera;*	Parrot, White-fronted
Amazona autumnalis	*Cristobal; frijol; licoy; pico rojo; picoy*	Parrot, Red-lored
Amazona farinosa	*lora*	Parrot, Mealy

CUCULIFORMES
Cuculidae

Coccyzus erythropthalmus		Cuckoo, Black-billed
Coccyzus americanus		Cuckoo, Yellow-billed
Piaya cayana	*pájaro león*	Cuckoo, Squirrel
Tapera naevia	*pájaro pichete*	Cuckoo, Striped
Dromococcyx phasianellus		Cuckoo, Pheasant
Geococcyx velox	*alma de perro*	Roadrunner, Lesser
Crotophaga sulcirostris	*tijuíl; tijúl; tíjul; tijulio; Tío Julio*	Ani, Groove-billed

STRIGIFORMES
Tytonidae

Tyto alba	*lechuza; lechuza de campanario; lechuza de sangre; lechuza mantequera*	Owl, Barn

Strigidae

Otus trichopsis	*orejita*	Owl, Whiskered Screech-
Otus guatemalae	*orejita*	Owl, Vermiculated Screech-
Lophostrix cristata	*búho*	Owl, Crested
Pulsatrix perspicillata	*búho*	Owl, Spectacled
Bubo virginianus	*estiquirín*	Owl, Great Horned
Glaucidium gnoma	*picapiedras*	Owl, Northern Pygmy-
Glaucidium brasilianum	*picapiedras; gallina del diablo (not used in Olancho)*	Owl, Ferruginous Pygmy-
Ciccaba virgata	*búho; tecolote; tocolote*	Owl, Mottled
Ciccaba nigrilineata	*búho*	Owl, Black-and-white
Strix fulvescens	*búho*	Owl, Fulvous

CAPRIMULGIFORMES
Caprimulgidae

Chordeiles acutipennis		Nighthawk, Lesser
Chordeiles minor		Nighthawk, Common
Nyctidromus albicollis	*pucuyo*	Pauraque, Common
Caprimulgus vociferus		Whip-poor-will

Nyctibiidae

Nyctibius grandis		Potoo, Great
Nyctibius jamaicensis	*pájaro estaca*	Potoo, Northern

APODIFORMES

Apodidae   Golondrinas voladoras

Cypseloides cryptus — Swift, White-chinned

Streptoprocne rutila — Swift, Chestnut-collared

Streptoprocne zonaris — golondrina de cueva; golondrina de monte; golondrina de montaña — Swift, White-collared

Chaetura pelagica — Swift, Chimney

Chaetura vauxi — Swift, Vaux's

Panyptila cayennensis — golondrina tijerilla — Swift, Lesser Swallow-tailed

Panyptila sanctihieronymi — golondrina tijerilla — Swift, Great Swallow-tailed

Trochilidae   Gorriones; Picaflores; Chupaflores; Colibríes; Gorriones abeja (tiny species)

Threnetes ruckeri — Barbthroat, Band-tailed

Phaethornis longirostris — Hermit, Long-billed

Phaethornis striigularis — Hermit, Stripe-throated

Phaeochroa cuvierii — Hummingbird, Scaly-breasted

Campylopterus curvipennis — Sabrewing, Wedge-tailed

Campylopterus hemileucurus — La corbata — Sabrewing, Violet

Florisuga mellivora — Jacobin, White-necked

Colibri delphinae — Violet-ear, Brown

Colibri thalassinus — Violet-ear, Green

Anthracothorax prevostii — Mango, Green-breasted

Klais guimeti — Hummingbird, Violet-headed

Abeillia abeillei — Hummingbird, Emerald-chinned

Lophornis helenae — Coquette, Black-crested

Chlorostilbon canivetii — Emerald, Canivet's

Thalurania colombica — Woodnymph, Violet-crowned

Hylocharis eliciae — Goldentail, Blue-throated

Hylocharis leucotis — Hummingbird, White-eared

Amazilia candida — Emerald, White-bellied

Amazilia luciae — Emerald, Honduran

Amazilia cyanocephala — Hummingbird, Azure-crowned

Amazilia beryllina — Hummingbird, Berylline

Amazilia cyanura — Hummingbird, Blue-tailed

Amazilia tzacatl — Hummingbird, Rufous-tailed

Amazilia rutila — Hummingbird, Cinnamon

Eupherusa eximia — Hummingbird, Stripe-tailed

Trochilidae continued

Lampornis sybillae		Mountain-gem, Green-breasted
Lampornis amethystinus		Hummingbird, Amethyst-throated
Lamprolaima rhami		Hummingbird, Garnet-throated
Eugenes fulgens		Hummingbird, Magnificent
Heliothryx barroti		Fairy, Purple-crowned
Heliomaster longirostris		Starthroat, Long-billed
Heliomaster constantii		Starthroat, Plain-capped
Tilmatura dupontii		Hummingbird, Sparkling-tailed
Archilochus colubris		Hummingbird, Ruby-throated

TROGONIFORMES
Trogonidae

Trogon violaceus	coa	Trogon, Violaceous
Trogon elegans	coa	Trogon, Elegant
Trogon collaris	*cacahuata; coa de montaña*	Trogon, Collared
Trogon massena	coa	Trogon, Slaty-tailed
Pharomachrus mocinno	quetzal	Quetzal, Resplendent

CORACIIFORMES
Momotidae

Hylomanes momotula		Motmot, Tody
Momotus momota	*taragón*	Motmot, Blue-crowned
Electron carinatum	*taragón*	Motmot, Keel-billed
Electron platyrhynchum	*taragón*	Motmot, Broad-billed
Eumomota superciliosa	*guardabarrancos; rompebarrancos; taragón*	Motmot, Turquoise-browed

Alcedinidae **Martines Pescadores; Pájaros Pesqueros**

Ceryle torquata		Kingfisher, Ringed
Ceryle alcyon		Kingfisher, Belted
Chloroceryle amazona		Kingfisher, Amazon
Chloroceryle americana		Kingfisher, Green

PICIFORMES
Bucconidae

Notharchus macrorhynchus		Puffbird, White-necked
Malacoptila panamensis		Puffbird, White-whiskered

Galbulidae

Galbula ruficauda		Jacamar, Rufous-tailed

Ramphastidae

Aulacorhynchus prasinus — *pico navaja; tucanillo; tucán verde* — Toucanet, Emerald

Pteroglossus torquatus — *tilís* — Aracari, Collared

Selenidera spectabilis — *tucanillo* — Toucanet, Yellow-eared

Ramphastos sulfuratus — *pico navaja; tucán* — Toucan, Keel-billed

Ramphastos swainsonii — *Dios-te-dé* — Toucan, Chestnut-mandibled

Picidae — **Chacos; Checos; Carpinteros**

Picumnus olivaceus — Piculet, Olivaceous

Melanerpes formicivorus — *chaco de robledal* — Woodpecker, Acorn

Melanerpes pucherani — *chaco* — Woodpecker, Black-cheeked

Melanerpes aurifrons — *chaco; checo; cheje* — Woodpecker, Golden-fronted

Sphyrapicus varius — Sapsucker, Yellow-bellied

Picoides villosus — *chaco* — Woodpecker, Hairy

Veniliornis fumigatus — Woodpecker, Smoky-brown

Piculus rubiginosus — *chaco naranjero* — Woodpecker, Golden-olive

Colaptes auratus — *chaco* — Flicker, Northern

Celeus castaneus — Woodpecker, Chestnut-colored

Dryocopus lineatus — *carpintero; monte zumba; pito real* — Woodpecker, Lineated

Campephilus guatemalensis — *carpintero; monte zumba; pito real* — Woodpecker, Pale-billed

PASSERIFORMES

Furnariidae

Automolus ochrolaemus — Foliage-gleaner, Buff-throated

Automolus rubiginosus — Foliage-gleaner, Ruddy

Xenops minutus — Xenops, Plain

Sclerurus mexicanus — Leaftosser, Tawny-throated

Sclerurus guatemalensis — Leaftosser, Scaly-throated

Dendrocolaptidae — **Carpinteros; Trepapalos; Trepatroncos**

Dendrocincla anabatina — Woodcreeper, Tawny-winged

Dendrocincla homochroa — Woodcreeper, Ruddy

Sittasomus griseicapillus — Woodcreeper, Olivaceous

Deconychura longicauda — Woodcreeper, Long-tailed

Glyphorhynchus spirurus — Woodcreeper, Wedge-billed

Xiphocolaptes promeropirhynchus — Woodcreeper, Strong-billed

Dendrocolaptes sanctithomae — Woodcreeper, Northern Barred-

Dendrocolaptes picumnus — Woodcreeper, Black-banded

Dendrocolaptidae *continued*

Xiphorhynchus susurrans	Woodcreeper, Cocoa
Xiphorhynchus flavigaster	Woodcreeper, Ivory-billed
Xiphorhynchus erythropygius	Woodcreeper, Spotted
Lepidocolaptes souleyetii	Woodcreeper, Streak-headed
Lepidocolaptes affinis	Woodcreeper, Spot-crowned

Thamnophilidae

Thamnophilus doliatus	Antshrike, Barred
Dysithamnus mentalis	Antvireo, Plain
Myrmotherula fulviventris	Antwren, Checker-throated
Myrmotherula axillaris	Antwren, White-flanked
Myrmotherula schisticolor	Antwren, Slaty
Microrhopias quixensis	Antwren, Dot-winged
Cercomacra tyrannina	Antbird, Dusky
Myrmeciza exsul	Antbird, Chestnut-backed
Hylophylax naevioides	Antbird, Spotted
Gymnopithys leucaspis	Antbird, Bicolored
Phaenostictus mcleannani	Antbird, Ocellated

Formicariidae

Formicarius analis	*gallito de montaña*	Antthrush, Black-faced
Grallaria guatimalensis		Antpitta, Scaled

Tyrannidae — *Cazamoscas; Cazamosquitos; Moscaderos; Mosqueritos; Mosqueros; Mosquiteros; Papamoscas*

Camptostoma imberbe		Tyrannulet, Northern Beardless
Elaenia flavogaster		Elaenia, Yellow-bellied
Elaenia frantzii		Elaenia, Mountain
Mionectes oleagineus		Flycatcher, Ochre-bellied
Leptopogon amaurocephalus		Flycatcher, Sepia-capped
Zimmerius vilissimus		Tyrannulet, Paltry
Oncostoma cinereigulare		Bentbill, Northern
Poccilotriccus sylvia		Flycatcher, Slate-headed Tody-
Todirostrum cinereum		Flycatcher, Common Tody-
Rhynchocyclus brevirostris		Flatbill, Eye-ringed
Tolmomyias sulphurescens		Flycatcher, Yellow-olive
Platyrinchus cancrominus		Spadebill, Stub-tailed
Platyrinchus coronatus		Spadebill, Golden-crowned
Onychorhynchus coronatus	*rínzon*	Flycatcher, Royal
Terenotriccus erythrurus		Flycatcher, Ruddy-tailed
Myiobius sulphureipygius		Flycatcher, Sulphur-rumped
Mitrephanes phaeocercus	*mosquerito*	Flycatcher, Tufted
Contopus cooperi		Flycatcher, Olive-sided

Contopus pertinax	*mosquerito*	Pewee, Greater
Contopus sordidulus	*mosquerito*	Pewee, Western Wood-
Contopus virens	*mosquerito*	Pewee, Eastern Wood-
Contopus cinereus	*mosquerito*	Pewee, Tropical
Empidonax flaviventris	*mosquerito*	Flycatcher, Yellow-bellied
Empidonax virescens		Flycatcher, Acadian
Empidonax traillii	*mosquerito*	Flycatcher, Willow
Empidonax albigularis		Flycatcher, White-throated
Empidonax minimus		Flycatcher, Least
Empidonax hammondii		Flycatcher, Hammond's
Empidonax flavescens	*mosquerito*	Flycatcher, Yellowish
Empidonax fulvifrons		Flycatcher, Buff-breasted
Sayornis nigricans	*zórzalo*	Phoebe, Black
Attila spadiceus		Attila, Bright-rumped
Rhytipterna holerythra		Mourner, Rufous
Myiarchus tuberculifer		Flycatcher, Dusky-capped
Myiarchus crinitus	*mosquero*	Flycatcher, Great Crested
Myiarchus tyrannulus	*mosquero*	Flycatcher, Brown-crested
Pitangus sulphuratus	*bicho; bicho feo; Christofue; dicho feo; fuiste al río; nicho; nicho feo*	Kiskadee, Great
Megarhynchus pitangua	*Dicho feo*	Flycatcher, Boat-billed
Myiozetetes similis	*bicho; bicho feo; Christofue; dicho feo; fuiste al río; nicho; nicho feo; Luisito*	Flycatcher, Social
Myiodynastes maculatus		Flycatcher, Streaked
Myiodynastes luteiventris	*mosquero*	Flycatcher, Sulphur-bellied
Legatus leucophaius		Flycatcher, Piratic
Tyrannus melancholicus	*tijereta*	Kingbird, Tropical
Tyrannus tyrannus		Kingbird, Eastern
Tyrannus forficatus	*tijerilla*	Flycatcher, Scissor-tailed
Tyrannus savana	*tijerilla*	Flycatcher, Fork-tailed
Schiffornis turdinus		Schiffornis, Thrush-like
Piprites griseiceps		Piprites, Gray-headed
Laniocera rufescens		Mourner, Speckled
Pachyramphus major		Becard, Gray-collared
Pachyramphus aglaiae		Becard, Rose-throated
Tityra semifasciata	*torreja*	Tityra, Masked
Tityra inquisitor	*torreja*	Tityra, Black-crowned

Cotingidae

Cotinga amabilis		Cotinga, Lovely
Procnias tricarunculata	*calandria; pájaro cafetero; pájaro campana; pimentero; campanero; templador*	Bellbird, Three-wattled

Pipridae

Manacus candei — Manakin, White-collared
Corapipo altera — Manakin, White-ruffed
Pipra mentalis — tronador — Manakin, Red-capped

Vireonidae

Vireo griseus — Vireo, White-eyed
Vireo flavifrons — Vireo, Yellow-throated
Vireo plumbeus — Vireo, Plumbeous
Vireo solitarius — Vireo, Blue-headed
Vireo gilvus — Vireo, Warbling
Vireo leucophrys — Vireo, Brown-capped
Vireo philadelphicus — Vireo, Philadelphia
Vireo olivaceus — Vireo, Red-eyed
Vireo flavoviridis — Vireo, Yellow-green
Hylophilus ochraceiceps — Greenlet, Tawny-crowned
Hylophilus decurtatus — Greenlet, Lesser
Vireolanius pulchellus — Vireo, Green Shrike-
Cyclarhis gujanensis — Peppershrike, Rufous-browed

Corvidae

Cyanocitta stelleri — Jay, Steller's
Cyanocorax yncas — Jay, Green
Cyanocorax morio — pía — Jay, Brown
Cyanocorax melanocyaneus — serenqueque — Jay, Bushy-crested
Cyanolyca cucullata — Jay, Azure-hooded
Aphelocoma unicolor — Jay, Unicolored
Corvus corax — cuervo — Raven, Common

Hirundinidae — **Golondrinas**

Progne chalybea — golondrina casera — Martin, Gray-breasted
Tachycineta albilinea — golondrina — Swallow, Mangrove
Tachycineta thalassina — golondrina — Swallow, Violet-green
Stelgidopteryx serripennis — golondrina casera — Swallow, Northern Rough-winged
Stelgidopteryx ruficollis — golondrina casera — Swallow, Southern Rough-winged
Riparia riparia — golondrina — Swallow, Bank
Hirundo rustica — golondrina — Swallow, Barn

Certhiidae

Certhia americana — Creeper, Brown

Troglodytidae — **Cucharacheros**

Campylorhynchus zonatus — Wren, Band-backed
Thryothorus maculipectus — cucarachero — Wren, Spot-breasted
Thryothorus rufalbus — cucarachero — Wren, Rufous-and-white
Thryothorus modestus — cucarachero — Wren, Plain

Troglodytes aedon	*cucarachero casero*	Wren, House
Troglodytes rufociliatus	*cucarachero*	Wren, Rufous-browed
Henicorhina leucosticta	*cucarachero de montaña*	Wren, White-breasted Wood-
Henicorhina leucophrys	*cucarachero de montaña*	Wren, Gray-breasted Wood-
Microcerculus philomela		Wren, Nightingale

Cinclidae

Cinclus mexicanus		Dipper, American

Sylviidae

Ramphocaenus melanurus		Gnatwren, Long-billed
Polioptila caerulea		Gnatcatcher, Blue-gray
Polioptila albiloris		Gnatcatcher, White-lored
Polioptila plumbea		Gnatcatcher, Tropical

Turdidae

Sialia sialis	*pájaro azul*	Bluebird, Eastern
Myadestes unicolor	*jilguero*	Solitaire, Slate-colored
Catharus aurantiirostris	*zorzal*	Thrush, Orange-billed Nightingale-
Catharus frantzii	*zorzal*	Thrush, Ruddy-capped Nightingale-
Catharus mexicanus	*zorzal*	Thrush, Black-headed Nightingale-
Catharus minimus		Thrush, Gray-cheeked
Catharus ustulatus		Thrush, Swainson's
Hylocichla mustelina	*zorzal*	Thrush, Wood
Turdus plebejus	*zorzal*	Robin, Mountain
Turdus grayi	*zorzal*	Robin, Clay-colored
Turdus assimilis	*zorzal de montaña*	Robin, White-throated

Mimidae

Dumetella carolinensis		Catbird, Gray
Melanotis hypoleucus		Mockingbird, Blue-and-white

Bombycillidae

Bombycilla cedrorum		Waxwing, Cedar

Peucedramidae

Peucedramus taeniatus		Warbler, Olive

Parulidae

Vermivora pinus		Warbler, Blue-winged
Vermivora chrysoptera		Warbler, Golden-winged
Vermivora peregrina		Warbler, Tennessee
Vermivora ruficapilla		Warbler, Nashville
Parula superciliosa		Warbler, Crescent-chested
Parula pitiayumi		Parula, Tropical
Dendroica petechia		Warbler, Yellow
Dendroica pensylvanica		Warbler, Chestnut-sided
Dendroica magnolia		Warbler, Magnolia

Parulidae continued

Dendroica caerulescens		Warbler, Black-throated Blue
Dendroica chrysoparia		Warbler, Golden-cheeked
Dendroica virens		Warbler, Black-throated Green-
Dendroica townsendi		Warbler, Townsend's
Dendroica occidentalis		Warbler, Hermit
Dendroica fusca		Warbler, Blackburnian
Dendroica dominica		Warbler, Yellow-throated
Dendroica graciae		Warbler, Grace's
Dendroica castanea		Warbler, Bay-breasted
Dendroica cerulea		Warbler, Cerulean
Mniotilta varia		Warbler, Black-and-white
Setophaga ruticilla		Redstart, American
Protonotaria citrea		Warbler, Prothonotary
Helmitheros vermivorus		Warbler, Worm-eating
Seiurus aurocapillus		Ovenbird
Seiurus noveboracensis	*pespita*	Waterthrush, Northern
Seiurus motacilla	*pespita*	Waterthrush, Louisiana
Oporornis formosus		Warbler, Kentucky
Oporornis philadelphia		Warbler, Mourning
Oporornis tolmiei		Warbler, MacGillivray's
Geothlypis trichas		Yellowthroat, Common
Geothlypis semiflava		Yellowthroat, Olive-crowned
Geothlypis poliocephala		Yellowthroat, Gray-crowned
Wilsonia citrina		Warbler, Hooded
Wilsonia pusilla		Warbler, Wilson's
Wilsonia canadensis		Warbler, Canada
Myioborus pictus		Redstart, Painted
Myioborus miniatus		Redstart, Slate-throated
Basileuterus culicivorus		Warbler, Golden-crowned
Basileuterus rufifrons		Warbler, Rufous-capped
Basileuterus belli		Warbler, Golden-browed
Phaeothlypis fulvicauda		Warbler, Buff-rumped
Icteria virens		Chat, Yellow-breasted

Coerebidae

Coereba flaveola		Bananaquit

Thraupidae

Chlorospingus ophthalmicus		Tanager, Common Bush
Eucometis penicillata		Tanager, Gray-headed
Lanio leucothorax		Tanager, White-throated Shrike-
Tachyphonus luctuosus		Tanager, White-shouldered

Habia rubica		Tanager, Red-crowned Ant-
Habia fuscicauda		Tanager, Red-throated Ant-
Piranga flava		Tanager, Hepatic
Piranga rubra		Tanager, Summer
Piranga olivacea		Tanager, Scarlet
Piranga bidentata		Tanager, Flame-colored
Piranga leucoptera		Tanager, White-winged
Ramphoceluss sanguinolentus	*soldadito*	Tanager, Crimson-collared
Ramphocelus passerinii		Tanager, Passerini's
Thraupis episcopus	*azulejo; viuda; viudita*	Tanager, Blue-gray
Thraupis abbas		Tanager, Yellow-winged
Euphonia affinis		Euphonia, Scrub
Euphonia hirundinacea		Euphonia, Yellow-throated
Euphonia elegantissima		Euphonia, Elegant
Euphonia gouldi		Euphonia, Olive-backed
Euphonia minuta		Euphonia, White-vented
Chlorophonia occipitalis		Chlorophonia, Blue-crowned
Tangara lavinia		Tanager, Rufous-winged
Tangara larvata		Tanager, Golden-hooded

Emberizidae

Volatinia jacarina	*saltarín*	Grassquit, Blue-black
Sporophila americana	*semillero*	Seedeater, Variable
Sporophila torqueola	*collarín; semillero*	Seedeater, White-collared
Sporophila minuta		Seedeater, Ruddy-breasted
Oryzoborus funereus		Finch, Thick-billed Seed-
Amaurospiza concolor		Seedeater, Blue
Tiaris olivacea		Grassquit, Yellow-faced
Diglossa baritula		Flowerpiercer, Cinnamon-bellied
Atlapetes albinucha		Finch, White-naped Brush-
Buarremon brunneinuchus		Finch, Chestnut-capped Brush-
Arremonops chloronotus twomeyi		Sparrow, Green-backed
Arremonops conirostris		Sparrow, Black-striped
Melozone leucotis		Sparrow, White-eared Ground-
Aimophila rufescens	*arrocero; pispa*	Sparrow, Rusty
Spizella passerina	*arrocero*	Sparrow, Chipping

Cardinalidae

Saltator coerulescens		Saltator, Grayish
Saltator maximus		Saltator, Buff-throated
Saltator atriceps	*chorcha corralera; chorcha loca*	Saltator, Black-headed

Cardinalidae continued

Caryothraustes poliogaster		Grosbeak, Black-faced
Pheucticus ludovicianus		Grosbeak, Rose-breasted
Cyanocompsa cyanoides		Grosbeak, Blue-black
Cyanocompsa parellina		Bunting, Blue
Passerina caerulea		Grosbeak, Blue
Passerina cyanea		Bunting, Indigo

Icteridae

Sturnella magna	chira; chirunchira	Meadowlark, Eastern
Dives dives	huachíl; huachín; huachír	Blackbird, Melodious
Quiscalus mexicanus	clarín; clarinero; zanate	Grackle, Great-tailed
Molothrus aeneus	tordito	Cowbird, Bronzed
Molothrus oryzivora		Cowbird, Giant
Icterus prosthemelas	chorcha	Oriole, Black-cowled
Icterus wagleri	chorcha	Oriole, Black-vented
Icterus spurius	chorcha	Oriole, Orchard
Icterus chrysater	chorcha	Oriole, Yellow-backed
Icterus mesomelas	chorcha	Oriole, Yellow-tailed
Icterus pustulatus	chorcha	Oriole, Streak-backed
Icterus pectoralis	chorcha	Oriole, Spot-breasted
Icterus gularis	chorcha	Oriole, Altamira
Icterus galbula	chorcha	Oriole, Baltimore
Amblycercus holosericeus	pico blanco	Cacique, Yellow-billed
Psarocolius wagleri	oropéndula; urrupa	Oropendola, Chestnut-headed
Psarocolius montezuma	oropéndula	Oropendola, Montezuma

Fringillidae

Loxia curvirostra		Crossbill, Red
Carduelis notata		Siskin, Black-headed
Carduelis psaltria		Goldfinch, Lesser

Passeridae

Passer domesticus		Sparrow, House

Notes

Chapter 1. Ornithophilia

1. "Neotropics" refers to a biogeographical realm broadly defined as the New World Tropics, including the Caribbean islands, most of Mexico, all of Central America, and South America excluding its southernmost, temperate zone.

2. Honduras has seven motmot species, more than any other country. In addition to the two common species mentioned here, there are also the Rufous, Keel-billed, Broad-billed, and Tody motmots of the rain forest understory and the Blue-throated Motmot of the high cloud forest. All ten species of the Momotidae family are restricted to the Neotropics.

3. Three sources for Honduran bird toponyms are notable: the 1:50,000-scale topographic maps produced by the Instituto Geográfico Nacional, which cover the entire country; Jesús Aguilar Paz, *Toponimias y regionalismos indígenas de Honduras* (1970); Alberto Membreño, *Toponimias indígenas de Centroamérica (Honduras, El Salvador, Guatemala y Nicaragua)* (1994 [1901]). Membreño, who was a philologist, is also a useful source for "Honduranisms," including the significance and origin of several bird names: see, for example, *Hondureñismos: Vocabulario de los provincialismos de Honduras* (1895). Aguilar Paz, whose work I cite repeatedly in this book, was a geographer (among many other things) who created the first detailed map of Honduras, compiled from his own notes on numerous journeys across the republic in the 1910s and 20s. His posthumously published *Tradiciones y leyendas de Honduras* (1989), which is the best collection available of Honduran folklore, contains sections about birds and other fauna; his *El refranero hondureño* (1981) also contains popular sayings inspired by birds, such as "pava que mucho canta, no tiene manteca" ("a guan that sings frequently has little fat"; no. 20, p. 11).

   Honduras, much like other countries in Latin America, takes nationalistic pride in its folklore, and a fair number of collections exist. Though none are dedicated exclusively to the avifauna, most incorporate a few stories, riddles, songs, and other material involving birds. Pompilio Ortega, from whom I draw in this book, published the very popular *Patrios lares* in 1946; the second edition (1951) includes new material. Mario Ardón Mejía recorded children's traditions in *Folklore lúdico infantíl hondureño* (1986); Jesús Muñoz Tábora collected folklore for didactic application in *Folklore y educación en Honduras* (1983); Antonio Osorio Orellana published *Nuestro pueblo y su folklore, II Libro* (1994). Recently, the multivolume *Literatura oral de la Zona Sur,* sponsored by the Honduran Secretaría de Cultura y las Artes, has included several excellent systematic collections of folklore from southern Honduras that seem to be exact transcriptions of oral accounts. Karen

Ramos and Melissa Valenzuela have collected and published five volumes as of 1997; I have examined volumes 3, 4, and 5: *Por cuentas aquí en Nacaome, Por cuentas aquí en Sabanagrande,* and *Por cuentas aquí en Texiguat.* All contain bird folklore.

In Honduran literary prose and poetry, bird images are often evoked. An author especially relevant to Olancho is the poet Froylán Turcios. His *Tierra maternal: Olancho* (1990 [1911]) includes poems such as "Los Alcaravanes" ("The Double-striped Thick-knees") and "Pájaros del crepúsculo" ("Birds of the dusk"). Rafael Heliodoro Valle, a Honduran journalist and folklorist who resided in Mexico, compiled *Semblanza de Honduras* (ca. 1947), a multi-author collection of excerpts from geographical accounts of his native country. Page 84 contains "Familia multicolor," an excerpt from an account by Visitación Padilla, who was famous for her early twentieth-century work in women's rights. On the same page is "Zorzales de San Pedro Sula," a poem by Manuel Escoto. A similar collection of geographically inspired patriotic works is the poetic anthology *Exaltación de Honduras,* edited by Oscar Acosta and Pompeyo del Valle (1971). More than any other available work, this collection helps one appreciate the Honduran sense of place among the urban middle class. The section "Bestiario" contains a few bird poems.

Systematic accounts of Honduran birds have been the almost exclusive provenance of outsiders, but a few published works written by Hondurans exist. For example, sections on birds are found in most of the teacher-compiled series of departmental *Monografías* produced in the 1920s and 1930s. The only Honduran works specifically about birds of which I am aware are Luis Landa's *Aves regionales de Honduras* (1970); Sergio Midence's *Aves silvestres de Honduras* (1985) and *Conociendo y coloreando 10 de nuestras aves* (1985); Arturo Sosa, *Aves del manglar* (1999). Landa was a teacher; his forty-seven-page book has been useful to Hondurans because it includes treatment of ornithology and taxonomy as well as "Poesías relacionadas con la vida de las aves." Midence is a biologist and conservationist whose works on birds were produced under the auspices of the now defunct Asociación Hondureña de Ecología, as part of an attempt to popularize birds, especially in schools. Sosa is a wildlife photographer.

Chapter 2. Historical and Geographical Background

1. There is a rather sparse literature dealing specifically with human-bird relationships. The most thorough accounts have been produced by ethnographers and other anthropologists as well as folklorists and oral historians. Within the field of ethnozoology, E. S. Hunn's *Tzeltal Folk Zoology: The Classification of Discontinuities in Nature* (1977) contains perhaps the most detailed and rigorous study for the contemporary Middle American region. A more specific Middle American structural analysis is E. Hunt's *The Transformation of the Hummingbird: Cultural Roots of a Zinacantecan Mythical Poem* (1977). Data about birds often appear in Middle American archaeo-

logy, both in analyses of icons and in excavation of sites: N. Hamblin's *Animal Use by the Cozumel Maya* (1984) is particularly helpful.

Folklore collections from around the world contain stories of birds. Geographies usually do not, but there are a handful of ethnological works that deal in full or in part with humans and birds. Of these, R. K. Nelson's intricate and sensitive account of an Athapaskan group's relationships with birds (and the landscape in general) in *Make Prayers to the Raven: A Koyukon View of the Northern Forest* (1983) is outstanding; I. S. Majnep and R. Bulmer's *Birds of My Kalem Country* (1977) is an excellent account of quotidian relationships with birds in New Guinea. Other notable place- or species-centered works are J. Hobbs's *Bedouin Life in the Egyptian Wilderness* (1989); R. Doughty's *The Mockingbird* (1988); and W. J. Phillipps's *The Book of the Huia* (1963). The "acoustemology" of S. Feld in New Guinea weaves bird song into studies of the constitution of place among the Kaluli: see "Waterfalls of Song: An Acoustemology of Place Resounding in Bosavi, Papua New Guinea" (1996).

Folklore and historical compendia on birds include E. Armstrong, *The Folklore of Birds* (1958) and *The Life and Lore of Birds in Nature, Art, Myth and Literature* (1975); J. H. Gurney, *Early Annals of Ornithology* (1921); E. Ingersoll, *Birds in Legend, Fable and Folklore* (1968); J. W. Krutch and P. S. Eriksson, *A Treasury of Bird-Lore* (1962); T. Pearse, *Birds of the Early Explorers in the Northern Pacific* (1968); B. Rowland, *Birds with Human Souls: A Guide to Bird Symbolism* (1978); A. W. Schorger, *The Passenger Pigeon: Its Natural History and Extinction* (1955) and *The Wild Turkey: Its History and Domestication* (1966); and M. C. Walker, *Bird Legend and Life* (1908).

2. F. López de Gómara, *Historia general de las Indias* (1966 [1552]).

3. A. de León Pinelo, *El paraíso en el Nuevo Mundo, tomo II* (1943 [1656]).

4. In the *Florentine Codex: General History of the Things of New Spain,* edited and translated by C. E. Dibble and A. J. O. Anderson, (1950–69 [1579]), one can appreciate the language of the original Nahuatl and its direct translation to English; in *Historia general de las cosas de la Nueva España* (1946), one reads the accounts as they were made comprehensible to Spanish speakers by Sahagún. In the Dibble and Anderson translation from the Nahuatl, one needs to be aware that certain avian species may have been misidentified or have been renamed and/or reassigned taxonomically since the 1960s; in the quoted text, I have changed "blue cotinga" to its current "lovely cotinga."

5. Bird names are those that appear in translation. Trogonorus = trogon; troupial = Montezuma's Oropendola (*zaquan*); blue cotinga = Lovely Cotinga (*tziuhtli*).

6. William Wells, *Explorations and Adventures in Honduras, Comprising Sketches of Travel in the Gold Regions of Olancho, and A Review of the History and General Resources of Central America* (1857).

7. Linda Newson, *The Cost Of Conquest: Indian Decline under Spanish Rule in Honduras* (1986; in translation by Jorge Federico Travieso as *El costo de la*

conquista, 1992) is an elaborately documented account, part of a multi-disciplinary literature that documents the decline of New World indigenous populations after 1492. In Honduras, early conquistadors apparently encountered a wide-open land, well maintained and easy to move about in. A century later, much of the country had grown back to scrub and forest.

8. Gonzalo Fernández de Oviedo, "De otras cosas e particularidades de Honduras, e de las minas ricas de oro y plata que en aquella tierra hay," chapter 11 (pp. 392–94) of book 13 of part 2, or book 32 overall, of the *Historia general y natural de las Indias* (1959 [1535–57]). Oviedo resided in León, Nicaragua, in the 1520s and had close contact with conquistadors who established a *ciudad* called Villa Hermosa in Olancho. His descriptions of eagles may have come from witnesses in that area.

9. "Onduras e Igueras: Relación de la Provincia de Honduras y Higueras [sic] por el obispo D. Cristobal de Pedraza, Obispo de Honduras," pp. 385–434 in *Relaciones de Yucatán,* vol. 11: *Colección de documentos inéditos relativos al descubrimiento, conquista y organización de las antiguas posesiones españoles de ultramar, segunda serie*). Pedraza became Honduras's first resident bishop.

10. See *Journals and Other Documents on the Life and Voyages of Christopher Columbus,* ed. and trans. S. E. Morison (1963 [1492–1502]). It is easy to understand the importance of birds on the first voyage, when Columbus, like all good mariners of the time, spurred his crew onward using birds as sure signs of land. What he did not know was that they had run into the great southward ocean-going migrations. Eventually, however, certain birds never seen far from land did point them toward the Bahamas.

11. P. Martyr d'Anghiera, *Decadas del Nuevo Mundo, por Pedro Martir de Angleria, primer cronista de Indias* (1964 [1524]).

12. The book is also available in Spanish and French. Chapman has also written on the Lenca.

13. Sources are from my dissertation, Mapping Enredos of Complex Spaces (2001), which contains a lengthy section on Olancho's colonial history (chap. 3, "Cultural Histories").

14. W. V. Wells, in *Explorations and Adventures in Honduras* (1857), transcribes a list of goods received by a Boston shipping company from the Honduran north coast ports of Trujillo and Omoa. During four voyages in 1855–56, more than ten thousand deer skins came out of Trujillo (chap. 29, pp. 558–67).

   Johannessen's *Savannas of Interior Honduras* (1963) is the best historical geography of cattle ranching and of the plains in general; Wells offers unparalleled (though heavily racially biased) portraits of Olanchano culture and nature in the mid-nineteenth century. E. G. Squier's *Notes on Central America* (1855) has detailed descriptions of extractive processes such as mahogany cutting.

15. J. A. Sarmiento, *Historia de Olancho* (1990).

Chapter 3. Women, Children, and Birds

1. J. E. Brady, G. Hasemann, and J. H. Fogerty, "Harvest of skulls and bones," *Archaeology* 48(3): 36–40 (1995).

Chapter 4. Counterpoint of *Zorzal* and *Zopilote* in Juticalpa

1. See references to Archivo Histórico del Municipio de Juticalpa in the bibliography.
2. In W. V. Wells, "Adventures in the gold fields of Central America" (1856).
3. See P. Ortega, "También los zopes tienen rey," in *Patrios lares* (1st ed., 1946), 53; "Los zopes tienen rey," (2nd ed., 1951), 64–65.
4. P. Francisco Mateos, ed., *Obras de P. Bernabé Cobo de la Compañía de Jesús* (1956 [1653]). There are short paragraphs or "chapters" on Peruvian birds in book 8 of the *Historia* (more than sixty types of birds in fifty-nine chapters, pp. 313–31).
5. F. Hernández, *Historia natural de la Nueva España,* vol. 2 (1957).
6. Aguilar Paz, *Toponimias y regionalismos indígenas de Honduras,* 11: "Si hablamos de medicinas, sin ambajes ni pamplinas, recordemos del TIJUL y también del ZOPILOTE y su pariente el TINCUTE, que en caldo y en cataplasmas dicen que curan el asma."
7. Muñoz Tábora, *Folklore y educación,* 51.
8. Ibid., 83.
9. "El Zopilote," in Ardón Mejía, *Folklore lúdico infantil,* 79. The author is quoting "Alvarado," a folklorist who wrote the account in 1959.
10. I interviewed Clara Luz Rojas in June, 1998, eliciting spontaneous written responses to my mentions of several common species.
11. Ortega, *Patrios lares* (2nd ed.), 166–68.
12. Ortega is probably equating a Central American species of *Turdus* with the American Robin, which does not migrate to Honduras.

Chapter 5. Large Private Landowners as Conservationists

1. I have also written about large landowners as conservationists in "Jealous Conservationists: *Terratenientes* and Wildlife Conservation in Olancho, Honduras," in M. Steinberg and P. Hudson, eds., *Cultural and Physical Expositions: Geographic Studies in the Southern United States and Latin America* (2002). Though I employ the same conversations, in this book I have retranslated the passages less literally, in an attempt to capture better the flow and meaning of the *terratenientes'* words.
2. There is some local confusion about the *tres pesos.* Elmer Maradiaga believes it is a type of wren, but his neighbors are probably referring to the Short-billed Pigeon. Another possible confusion is with the Striped Cuckoo.
3. The Honduran Emerald is globally threatened. See N. J. Collar et al., *Threatened Birds of the Americas: The ICBP/IUCN Red Data Book,* 3rd ed. (1992).
4. Steve N. G. Howell and Sophie Webb have covered the Honduran Emerald

in three publications: "Notes on the Honduran emerald," *Wilson Bulletin* 101(4): 642–43 (1989); "New and noteworthy bird records from Guatemala and Honduras," *Bulletin of the British Ornithologists' Club* 112: 42–49 (1991); and *A Guide to the Birds of Mexico and Northern Central America* (1995). The 1989 article described their collecting trip in May and early June, 1988, to sites in the upper valley of the Río Aguán. They give the first and only published natural historical account of the bird and its habitat, including associated tree and bird species, behavior of the emeralds, and state of the habitat.

Photographs and Sophie Webb's sketches of the emerald and its habitat are deposited in the American Museum of Natural History in New York. A watercolor of two emeralds faces the title page of Burt Monroe's 1968 monograph, *A Distributional Survey of the Birds of Honduras.*

In 1999, the Honduran postal service (HONDUCOR) published a stamp of the Honduran Emerald in its series "Aves de Honduras en Peligro de Extincción," funded by Banco Sogerin and available for purchase at their central Tegucigalpa facility. The panel containing the Honduran Emerald and nineteen other species can be viewed at http://www.birdtheme.org/image/hon080799a.jpg ("Theme Birds on Stamps" website; link active March, 2002).

5. T. G. Yuncker collected along the North Coast and in the Valle de Aguán between June and August, 1938. His first publication based on this trip was "Notes on a semi-arid region in the Aguan River Valley, Republic of Honduras," *Torreya* 1939(5): 133–39. In 1940, he published "Flora of the Aguan Valley and the coastal regions near La Ceiba Honduras," pp. 243–346 in *Botanical Series, Field Museum of Natural History* 9(4) (Publication 466). He wrote a brief geographical account followed by a species inventory that includes several plants new to botany. Finally, in 1945, Yuncker mentioned the thorn forest in "The vegetation of Honduras: A brief review," pp. 55–56 of *Plants and Plant Science in Latin America* (ed. F. Verdoorn).

6. See B. Monroe, *Notes on the Avian Genus* Arremonops *with Description of a New Subspecies from Honduras, Occasional Papers of the Museum of Zoology* 28 (1963). See his "Analysis of the avifauna" and "Derivation of the Honduran avifauna," pp. 390–407 in *Distributional Survey,* especially 404–405, where he considers the lack of distinctive thorn forest species: "The arid Aguán, Agalta and Olancho valleys . . . do not support any endemic forms in the arid scrub-thorn forest habitat (except perhaps *Arremonops chloronotus twomeyi*)."

7. In addition to the authors mentioned in the text, thorn forests have been discussed by others, including several botanists. Antonio Molina gives a detailed floral list of an entire dry forest valley in "Vegetación del Valle de Comayagua," *Ceiba* 18(1–2): 47–69 (1974). Many arid forest plants are described briefly, and some are pictured, in Cyril Hardy Nelson's two-volume *Plantas comunes de Honduras* (1986). Paul Standley's "The woody plants of

Siguatepeque, Honduras," *Journal of the Arnold Arboretum* 11: 15–46 (1930) includes a brief description of the Comayagua thorn forest (19–20) as well as accounts of its species. In *Snakes of Honduras* (1985), Wilson and Meyer use the Holdridge Life Zone classification system in a brief description of the "Tropical Arid Forest" (13–14). In "Notes on the physiography of Honduras" (*Geographical Review* 16: 403–13 [1926]), a standard source for later accounts, geographer Nels Bengtson describes the geomorphology of Honduran terrace plains where "the desert type of vegetation prevails, several cacti of tree size being the predominant forms" (412). Another geographer, Karl Helbig, in his *Areas y paisajes del noreste de Honduras* (1965), briefly details the *espinal* of the Valle de Agalta (74–75) as well as the *carbonal* of the Valle de Olancho (61–62). Archie Carr, in his seminal 1950 monograph "Outline for a Classification of Animal Habitats in Honduras" (*Bulletin of the American Museum of Natural History* 94: 563–94 [1950]), affords an important place to the arid habitats.

8. The intricately detailed hypothesis, based on the distribution patterns of terrestrial amphibians and reptiles, was put forth by Jay Savage in 1966 in "The origins and history of the Central American herpetofauna," *Copeia* 1966(4): 719–66; it was supported in the same volume by L. C. Stuart's "The environment of the Central American cold-blooded vertebrate fauna" (684–99) and William Duellman's "The Central American herpetofauna: An ecological perspective" (700–19). On page 755, Savage presents a useful map (fig. 23) showing lowland dispersal routes of the herpetofauna during the Pleistocene.

9. The importance of the Mexican thorn forests is described by Alwyn Gentry in "Diversity and floristic composition of neotropical dry forests," chapter 7 in S. Bullock et al., eds., *Seasonally Dry Tropical Forests* (1995). W. H. Portig's 1965 "Central American rainfall," in *Geographical Review* 65(1): 68–90, is a good source for approaching an understanding of the complexity of local and regional climate regimes in Honduras.

10. Johannessen did, however, conclude that savannas in Honduras are human creations, even if many of the constituent grasses are native. He failed to cite Archie Carr's work on the thorn forest. Probably no one but Carr and Yuncker ever celebrated the thorn forest's biological importance, and only in the past few years has it become possible for the Honduran conservation movement to contemplate saving remnants of thorn forest. Proposals for protected areas have surfaced for the Aguán, but I am unaware if at present any actual conservation projects have been undertaken.

11. A program funded by the World Bank has recently (post-2000) focused attention on Honduran Emerald populations in the Valle de Aguán and to a lesser extent the Valle de Agalta. Studies have been carried out to determine population sizes and threats; the impetus for the attention was the imminent construction of a new highway. Both Pilar Thorn (Universidad Nacional

Autónoma de Honduras) and Francisco Urbina were involved in the survey effort. At time of writing I am unaware of any concrete plans for state protection of the Honduran Emerald following this exciting study. According to Francisco Urbina, the survey team discovered emeralds in the Valle de Agalta at locations other than the Sabana La Lima.

12. The following quotes are from both Uniberto and Lesbia Madrid.

Chapter 6. *Pajarales* in Human Landscapes

1. Ortega, *Patrios lares* (2nd ed.), 159–60.
2. The Great Green Macaw appears never to have ranged west of the Moskitia lowland rain forests—Olancho was probably the extreme northwestern edge of its range in Middle America. Archie Carr reported Great Green Macaws along the road between Juticalpa and Catacamas in the 1950s (Monroe, *Distributional Survey,* 138); nevertheless, I have not found anyone who remembers the bird occurring in central Olancho, indicating that it was probably scarce even then. M. Marcus, in "Notes on the great green macaw (*Ara ambigua*) in Honduras," *Ceiba* 25: 151–55 (1984), reported the species to be common in the Moskitia; D. Anderson (Avian diversity in the Río Plátano Biosphere Reserve, Honduras: The influence of indigenous agricultural practices [1998]) encountered it frequently.

The uncertain historical status of the Great Green Macaw in Olancho has been eclipsed by the disappearance of the Scarlet Macaw. But a curious pair of anecdotes indicates yet another race or population of macaws belonging to the realm of cryptozoology: "Toward the coast the beautiful green species is said to exist, much more elegant than his rainbow cousin; but both of these pale before the superb blue macaw, one of the rarest birds of the country. I heard of some domesticated in the town of Manto [Olancho], but could never get sight of one. They are said to avoid the other members of the macaw family, and affect the vicinity of the Lean coast, between Truxillo and Omoa" (Wells, *Explorations and Adventures,* 398).

Thus wrote traveler William Wells in 1857. One can easily dismiss the "blue macaw" as a yarn Olanchanos fabricated for Wells's benefit, though his hearsay information on the Great Green Macaw was correct, even if ornithologists could not accept its definitive presence in the country until Mickey Marcus collected a specimen in October, 1980 (M. Marcus, "Additions to the avifauna of Honduras," *Auk* 100: 621–29, [1983]). In the late 1920s, professional colonizing agent Hugo Komor traveled through Olancho to determine places to settle European immigrant farmers. He writes: "El Guacamayo Rojo y Azul (Crysots Diademata y Crysots Hondurensis), este último sobrepasa en riqueza de plumaje a cualquiera otra clase de los que se encuentran en los otros países de América Latina" (*Apuntes de viaje,* in *La tierra del nuevo hogar* [1930], 43). This raises more questions (whence the scientific name?) than it answers.

3. J. Coyne and W. Critchfield, "Identity and terpene composition of Honduran pines attacked by the bark beetle *Dendroctonus frontalis* (Scolytidae)," *Turrialba* 24(3): 327–31 (1974), cited by J. Perry in *The Pines of Mexico and Central America* (1990), 210.

4. Aguilar Paz, *Tradiciones y leyendas,* 216.

5. See "Alma de perro o tanuno," in Aguilar Paz, *Tradiciones y leyendas,* 112.

6. See "La tubuca y el león," in Osorio Orellana, *Nuestro pueblo y su folklore,* 55. To my knowledge, *tubuca* is not used in Olancho.

7. Formerly, while most rural people were nominally Catholic, many had only occasional contact with the Church and its doctrines. At most, the visit of a priest or someone else capable of saying a mass was an infrequent event. By contrast, non-Catholic churches can be built anywhere, require little formal training or infrastructure, and can be attended every day of the year. There are numerous reasons why many Hondurans are turning to non-Catholic religions. Although there is animosity between Protestants and Catholics at the level of Church and private rhetoric, practitioners of myriad new faiths, among themselves and with Catholics, usually seem to get along quite well.

8. There are no terms in La Venta to distinguish the three common varieties of almost identical *dicho feo.* One of Francisco Urbina's favorite ways to impress skeptical friends who inquire as to his motives for engaging in the rather strange hobby of birdwatching is to comment that there is a lot they don't know—just look at the *dicho feo.* Did you know it is actually three? There is a small and raucous one, that's the "social." People are taken aback: isn't the small one the young of the bigger one? Its close cousin, the Great Kiskadee, is the "real" *dicho feo,* and is noticeably larger. The Boat-billed, largest of the three, has a distinct call, like a creaking door, and is mostly commonly found in the *vegas.* Francisco proves his point by showing plates in bird guides to the questioner. If still skeptical, the friend can be won over by an entire page filled with *dicho feo* look-alikes from across Latin America.

9. See the description in D. Anderson et al., "New and noteworthy bird records from Honduras" (1998). The other new find in which I participated involved the White-eared Ground-Sparrow (see chap. 3), a resident of coffee farms. It is significant that both new species inhabit the *human* landscape. Meanwhile, David Anderson has located several new Honduran species in the rain forests of the Río Plátano Biosphere Reserve, a zone extremely rich in avifauna and still relatively poorly known. See also D. Anderson (2001). Robert Gallardo, a butterfly farmer and bird tour leader based in La Ceiba (and at one time a Peace Corps volunteer in Gualaco), has also added several new species to the Honduras list from his travels on the North Coast and the Moskitia. Recent finds include the Stygian Owl and South Polar Skua (from "Honduras This Week Online": R. Gallardo, "Rare encounter with Stygian Owl," 9-10-2001, http://www.marrder.com/htw/special/environment/90.htm).

Chapter 7. Owls, *Cacaos,* and Golden-cheeked Warblers

1. The name *cacao* for the Red-throated Caracara is onomatopoeic: variations include *talcacao, racacao,* and *cacatao.*

2. Monroe's 1968 *Distributional Survey* (87–88) summarized the state of ornithological knowledge on the species, and nothing has been published since then. Eighteen Red-throated Caracara specimens have been collected in Honduras from the department of Yoro, from Olancho, from eastern Francisco Morazán, and from far eastern El Paraíso. All were taken between 1932 and 1955 and are from either dry plains or pine forest, with the exception of Arenal in El Paraíso, which is lowland rain forest. These twentieth-century records are from the north-central and northeastern highlands of the country, with the exception, again, of Arenal. Two published reports from 1860 and 1870 are from northwestern Honduras, near Lago Yojoa and San Pedro Sula.

   Monroe called the bird an "uncommon resident of rain forests," though we know now that it occurs in dry forest and pine forest as well. Robert Ridgely and John Gwynne, Jr., in *A Guide to the Birds of Panama, with Costa Rica, Nicaragua and Honduras* (1989), describe it as having become extremely scarce everywhere north and west of the Panama Canal; they write that no recent reports have come from anywhere north of Costa Rica in its former range, which reached as far as Chiapas: "A study attempting to address the reasons for its spectacular, and unexpected, decline is badly needed; there seems to be no evidence of an equivalent decline in South America" (107). In South America the species ranges as far south as Peru and southern Brazil.

   In D. Stotz et al., *Neotropical Birds: Ecology and Conservation* (1996), we can gain a contemporary perspective on the state of knowledge about the *cacao* as it appears in the book's detailed tables. These authors note that it is "declining in parts of range; causes unknown"; conservation priority for the species is given as medium; research priority, medium (147). The ecological requirements of the species as a whole are summarized thus: high sensitivity (to human disturbance); foraging stratum is the canopy; center of abundance is the Lower Tropical Zone (0–500 meters above sea level); relative abundance is fairly common/patchily distributed; the species occurs from sea level to 1,400 meters; and habitats are tropical lowland evergreen forest and montane evergreen forest (146). Its range is broken down by country: a former breeding species in Mexico and still (presumably barring hard evidence that it has been extirpated) a breeding species in Guatemala, Honduras, Nicaragua, Costa Rica, and Panama as well as most tropical countries of South America (302).

3. The area lies in the *municipios* of San Esteban, Gualaco, Guata, and Jano. Broken by occasional *montañas,* the *serranías* extend westward into northwestern Olancho, Yoro, and northern Francisco Morazán, where *cacaos* have also been collected.

4. Monroe, *Distributional Survey,* 87.
5. Antonio de Herrera, *Historia general de los hechos de los Castellanos en las Islas y Tierra-Firme del Mar Oceano* (1991 [1601–15]).
6. See Aguilar Paz, *Tradiciones y leyendas,* 218: "El *Picapiedrales* o Gallina del diablo, otro de los pájaros melancólicos, variedad de coa, que cincela la estatua de su desconocido ideal y que en las noches de luna pone notas tristes de Pierrot desencantado." Aguilar Paz is not confusing this owl with the *coa* or trogon but pointing out that it is a "folkloric cousin": their calls are similar and easily confused.
7. Turcios, *Tierra maternal,* 27.
8. Aguilar Paz, *Tradiciones y leyendas,* 218.
9. W. M. Denevan's 1961 "The upland pine forests of Nicaragua: A study in cultural plant geography" is one of the best sources for understanding the human geography of pines in Central America and is especially applicable to Olancho.
10. D. Thompson, Observations of Golden-cheeked Warblers Wintering in Guatemala and Honduras (1995).
11. J. H. Rappole, Golden-cheeked Warbler Winter Habitat Delineation. Final report to the National Biological Service (1996); Rappole, "Winter ecology of the endangered Golden-cheeked warbler," *Condor* 101 (4): 762–70 (1999).

Chapter 8. People and Avifauna of Montane Rain Forests

1. D. Snow's *The Cotingas, Bellbirds, Umbrellabirds and Other Species* (1982) is a standard reference work for the family Cotingidae.
2. Monroe, *Distributional Survey,* 250: ten males and possibly a female, between August 22 and October 25, at or near El Boquerón. The only other published record for Honduras is of a single female that T. R. Howell collected in Arenal, El Paraíso, on January 13, 1955. In 2002, both Francisco Urbina and I confirmed the Three-wattled Bellbird from separate locations along the northern border of Olancho with Colón, in the heretofore ornithologically unknown Montaña de Botaderos rain forest south of the Valle de Aguán. Bellbirds were common in both sites (in May and in August); we presume that the species, like so many others, reaches its northern range limit in the Botaderos mountains. It has not, to our knowledge, been recorded on the north side of the Valle de Aguán.
3. One of the classic texts about quetzals is V. W. von Hagen's 1945 *Jungle in the Clouds,* a well-written and adventurous account of how he procured quetzals for zoos from cloud forests in Yoro department, Honduras.
4. Personal communication with Pilar Thorn. During the early 1990s, she and Peace Corps volunteer Austin Stokes undertook a bird inventory of Parque Nacional La Muralla in northwestern Olancho, where quetzals are common and easy to observe. They have nested next to the visitors' center on the cloud forest's edge at 1,400 meters.
5. A fine natural history of the Resplendent Quetzal can be found in Alexander

Skutch's *Birds of Tropical America* (1983), 143–61. D. Stotz et al. (*Neotropical Birds,* 188–89) list this species, *Pharomachrus mocinno,* as a member of a genus of five, but the other four quetzals (without elaborate plumes) are found only in South America. They cite it as ranging as low as 900 meters.

6. This chapter was written before the recent usurpation of the Planes de Babilonia by an outside hydroelectric project (Proyecto Babilonia) that villagers from the Valle de Agalta had been fighting since 1997. Despite almost total rejection of a hydroelectric project by local coffee farmers and national park employees, and widespread, internationally condemned human rights abuses perpetrated by project employees against local protestors, construction continues at the time of writing. Though it is unclear whether the farms will disappear under reservoir waters, the treatment of local coffee farmers has been so harsh as to suggest that their activities will at the very least be seriously curtailed. Ironically, though the interests funding the hydro project have not hesitated to go as far as assassinating a protestor, they paint themselves as environmentally friendly and claim that the Proyecto Babilonia will actually do a better job at protecting the drainage basin of the Río Babilonia than the villagers ever could.

7. "10. El Gavilán" in "Danzas Criollas de Imitación," in Muñoz Tábora, *Folklore y educación,* 82. The dance was described from eastern El Paraíso department.

8. "3.2.6 La Gallina con Pollos — JL," in Ardón Mejía, *Folklore lúdico infantil,* 70.

9. "3.2.18 La Paloma y el Gavilán — JC(1)1," in Ardón Mejía, *Folklore lúdico infantil,* 83.

10. Aguilar Paz, *Tradiciones y leyendas,* 216.

11. In other areas, people call tinamous *gallos chingos,* "tailless roosters." José Mendoza uses *gallo* or *gallito* for the very rarely seen but frequently heard Black-faced Antthrush and Scaled Antpitta.

12. Ortega, *Patrios lares* (1st ed.), 22.

13. Aguilar Paz's *Tradiciones y leyendas de Honduras* contains several such stories.

14. *Tradiciones y leyendas* contains stories about all these.

Chapter 9. Landscape Dialogues

1. These suggestions are inspired by my own experiences and the observations of James Barborak and Manuel Rey Figueroa.

Glossary of Spanish Terms

Scientific names of plants are from Cyril Hardy Nelson's *Plantas comunes de Honduras* (1986). Latin and English names of mammals are those used by Fiona Reid in *A Field Guide to the Mammals of Central America and Southeast Mexico* (1997). Latin names of birds do not appear here but can be found in the appendix preceding the notes.

Achiote Annatto, *Bixa orellana* (Bixaceae)
Aguacate Any large-fruited wild avocado, *Persea* sp., of the *montaña;* also refers to the domestic avocado
Aguacatillo Wild avocado with small fruit (Lauraceae, several genera)
Aguila Eagle
Aguila pescador "Fishing eagle": Osprey
Aguiluche Any large hawk or hawk-eagle
Ajoque May mean Bare-throated Tiger-Heron, Green Heron, or other similar species
Alcaraván Double-striped Thick-knee
Alma de perro "Soul of a dog": Lesser Roadrunner
Alto, El The highlands: *serranía* and *montaña*
Ambientalismo Environmentalism
Ambientalista Environmentalist
Antepasados (Precolumbian) "ancient ones" or "ancestors"
Arboleda Area with trees; woodlot
Arrancar To harvest beans (literally, "to rip up")
Arrocero "Rice eater": any sparrowlike bird; often the abundant Rusty Sparrow
Azulona Red-billed Pigeon
Bajar To come down from the *montaña*
Bajareque Wattle-and-daub construction
Bajo, El The plains: *valle*
Barba roja "Red beard": Green Parakeet
Barranco Bank, gully
Barranquera, barranqueña White-tipped Dove
Beneficio Coffee processing plant
Bicho feo See *Dicho feo*
Bombón Cochlospermum vitifolium (Cochlospermaceae)
Bosque Locally: a small area of trees; otherwise: woods or forest
Brisas Breezes
Bruja, la "The witch": White-tipped Dove
Bueyera Cattle Egret
Búho Owl

Bujaja Night-heron spp. or Boat-billed Heron (onomatopoeic)

Burusco Vine tangle, hedgerow, or other thick patch of vegetation

Cabeza pelada "Bald head": Black Vulture

Cabildo Municipal building

Cacahuata Collared Trogon (onomatopoeic)

Cacao (plant) *Theobroma cacao* (Esterculiaceae)

Cacao Red-throated Caracara (onomatopoeic)

Café caturra Variety of coffee

Café de palo "Coffee [brewed] from the bush": as opposed to coffee processed
   in a factory

Café indio Any "traditional" (i.e., non–Green Revolution) coffee variety: low-
   yielding, low-input, long-living

Cafetal Plot of coffee

Calandria "Lark": Three-wattled Bellbird

Camarón Crayfish (not shrimp)

Campesino, -a Country dweller; poor farmer (not pejorative)

Campo The countryside

Canecha Freshwater crab

Cangrejero "Crab eater": Common Black-Hawk

Cañón Gorge or canyon

Capulín "Cherry": in this book, probably refers to a species of *Saurauia*
   (Saurauiaceae)

Carbonal Thick stand of *Mimosa tenuiflora* (Leguminosae), or *carbón*

Carne de monte "Bush meat": wild game

Carnezuelo *Acacia hindsi* (Leguminosae)

Carpintero Any woodpecker, especially with a crest

Carpintero grande Large crested woodpecker (Pale-billed or Lineated)

Casco de burro "Burro's hoof": type of arboreal wasp nest

Caserío Hamlet

Caulote *Guazuma ulmifolia* (Esterculiaceae)

Cazamicos "Monkey hunter": any eagle that preys on monkeys

Ceiba *Ceiba pentandra* (Bombacaceae)

Chachalaca Plain or Gray-headed Chachalaca (onomatopoeic)

Chaco Any small woodpecker, but especially the Golden-fronted
   (onomatopoeic)

Chaco de robledal "Oak grove woodpecker": Acorn Woodpecker

Chaco naranjero "Orange eater": Golden-olive Woodpecker

Champa Building comprising (at least) a thatch roof and its supports

Chancho de monte "Bush pig": collared or white-lipped peccary (*Tayassu tajacu;*
   Dicotyles pecari)

Charcha Dewlap

Chata *Musa sapientum* var. *rubra* (Musaceae)

Checo See *Chaco*

Cheje See *Chaco*

Glossary (191

Chelona Abbreviation of *turca chelona,* meaning any of several species of rain forest doves

Chile *Capsicum* pepper; *chile dulce* is the "sweet," green pepper

Chile picante Hot *Capsicum* pepper, of several varieties

Chinche Rheduviid (assassin bug)

Chincho *Zanthoxylum culantrillo* (Rutaceae)

Chinga "Tailless": any tinamou; Little Tinamou

Chinga de montaña Slaty-breasted Tinamou

Chipe Any small "chipping" bird, such as a wood-warbler

Chira Eastern Meadowlark (onomatopoeic)

Chirunchira Eastern Meadowlark

Chocoyito Olive-throated Parakeet

Chocoyo Olive-throated Parakeet

Chompipe Domestic turkey

Chorcha Oriole

Chorcha cajetera Unknown type of oriole

Chorcha corralera Black-headed Saltator

Chorcha loca "Crazy oriole": Black-headed Saltator

Chupaflor "Flower sucker": Hummingbird

Cigüeña Wood Stork

Ciruelo *Spondias purpurea* (Anacardiaceae), hog plum; *ciruela* is the fruit

Clarinero "Bugler": male Great-tailed Grackle, also *clarín.*

Clinuda See *Guatuza*

Clis-clis American Kestrel (onomatopoeic)

Coa Trogon (onomatopoeic)

Coa de montaña Collared Trogon

Coco Coconut palm, *Cocos nucifera* (Palmae)

Cocolea Gray-necked Wood-Rail (onomatopoeic)

Cocoleca Gray-necked Wood-Rail

Codorniz Quail or bobwhite

Colibrí Hummingbird (rarely used in the *campo*)

Collarín "Little collar": White-collared Seedeater

Comedero Feeding spot, such as a fruiting tree

Comelenguas "Tongue-eater": a supernatural animal, often portrayed with wings

Come-maíz "Maize eater": White-crowned Parrot

Correcaminos Roadrunner (rarely used locally)

Corte "Cut"; one of usually several pickings of coffee

Cosecha, la Coffee harvest

Coyol *Acrocomia mexicana,* a spiny palm used for wine, among other things

Coyote Middleman; also refers to the mammal

Cristobal Red-lored Parrot (onomatopoeic)

Cucarachero "Cockroach eater": any wren; in towns, usually refers to House Wren

Cucarachero casero House Wren

Culantro Culantro de pata: *Eryngium foetidum* (Umbeliferae), a pungent
  native herb
Culto Protestant church service
Cusuco Nine-banded armadillo, *Dasypus novemcinctus*
Cute "Buzzard"
Cuyamel Warm-water fish highly valued for its meat (and a threatened species)
Danto Baird's Tapir, *Tapirus bairdii*
Descombro Clearcut—the opening stage of fire-fallow (swidden, slash-and-
  burn) agriculture
Dicho feo Social Flycatcher or Great Kiskadee, and sometimes Boat-billed
  Flycatcher (onomatopoeic)
Don, doña Title of respect for adults
Embrujado Bewitched
Encantado Enchanted
Encinal, encino Woods
Encino Narrow-leaved *Quercus,* oak
Esmeralda hondureña Honduran Emerald (not a traditional local name)
Espantapájaros Scarecrow
Espátula Roseate Spoonbill
Espinal Thorn scrub, thicket, or forest
Espino blanco *Acacia farnesiana* (Leguminosae)
Espino verde *Prosopis julifera* (Leguminosae)
Estanquera Owner of an *estanco* (drinking establishment)
Estiquirín Great Horned Owl; a spirit in the form of a Great Horned Owl
  (onomatopoeic)
Fajina Greenbelt
Filo Ridge
Finca Farm
Frijól Bean, *Phaseolus vulgaris* (Papilionaceae): most local varieties are red
Frijolar Beanfield
Frijolera "Bean eater": White-winged Dove
Fruta de culebra "Snake fruit": *Casearia williamsiana* (Flacourtiaceae)
Fueteté White-fronted Parrot (onomatopoeic); also *hueteté*
Fuiste al río "You went to the river": Social Flycatcher or Great Kiskadee
Gallina del Diablo "Devil's chicken": Ferruginous Pygmy-owl; see *picapiedras*
Gallito "Little rooster" (in reference to several birds); bromeliad
Gallo de monte Partridge or wood-quail
Ganadero Rancher
Garcita Small heron or egret
Garcita bueyera Cattle Egret
Garcita morena Little Blue Heron
Garza Any heron or egret
Garzón moreno Great Blue Heron
Gato de monte "Bush cat": gray fox, *Urocyon cinereoargenteus*

Gavilán Hawk

Gavilán cangrejero "Crab-eating hawk": Common Black-Hawk

Gavilancillo "Little hawk": a forest-falcon or similar raptor

Gavilán de serranía "Piney woods hawk": Red-tailed Hawk

Gavilán garza "Egret hawk": White Hawk

Gavilán pescador "Fishing hawk": Osprey

Gavilán pollero "Chicken hawk": White-tailed Kite; occasionally refers to other species

Gaviota (Laughing) gull

Golondrina Swallow, martin, or swift

Gongolona Great Tinamou; *gongolona* possibly from *guangololo,* a Lenca word

Gorrión Hummingbird

Gorrión abeja "Bee hummingbird": any of several species

Gorrioncito Small hummingbird

Guacamaya Nonlocal term for macaw

Guácimo See *Caulote*

Guaco Laughing Falcon (onomatopoeic); also the name of a plant that is said to cure snakebite

Gualiqueme *Erythrina* sp. (Papilionaceae), a floodplain tree

Guamíl Fallow agricultural plot in the brush stage

Guanábana *Annona muricata* (Annonaceae)

Guanacaste *Enterolobium cyclocarpum* (Leguminosae)

Guángara See *Guatuza*

Guara Macaw, generally meaning the Scarlet Macaw; the most common Honduran term for the bird

Guara roja Scarlet Macaw

Guardabarrancos "Cliff guardian": Turquoise-browed Motmot

Guatuza Central American agouti, *Dasyprocta punctata*

Guayabero "Guava eater": White-fronted Parrot

Guayabo Guava, *Psidium guajava* (Myrtaceae); *guayaba* is the fruit

Güergüera Dewlap

Güis Golden-fronted Woodpecker (term used in Olancho only by immigrants from southern Honduras)

Hacienda Ranch

Higo *Ficus* sp. (Moraceae)

Higuillo "Little fig": tree, species unknown

Hoja de aire "Air leaf": *Anthurium* sp. (Araceae)

Hoja de piedra "Stone leaf": *Monstera* sp. (Araceae)

Huachíl Melodious Blackbird (onomatopoeic)

Huachín Melodious Blackbird

Huachír Melodious Blackbird

Huerta Dooryard garden

Hueteté White-fronted Parrot (onomatopoeic); also *fueteté*

Indio desnudo "Naked Indian": *Bursera simaruba* (Burseraceae)

Invierno Winter: rainy season

Jagua Genipa americana (Rubiaceae)

Jagüilla White-lipped peccary, *Dicotyles pecari*

Jaraguá Hyparrhenia rufa (Graminae)

Jardín "Garden": in town, what is "on display" to the public (e.g., in front of the house)

Jilguero Slate-colored Solitaire

Jinicuao See *Indio desnudo*

Jobo Spondias sp., probably *S. purpurea* (Anacardiaceae)

Jolote Domestic turkey

Lechuza Barn Owl; spirit in bird form

Lechuza de campanario "Bell-tower owl"; Barn Owl that nests in belltowers

Lechuza de sangre "Blood" owl; Barn Owl

Lechuza mantequera "Candlewax" owl; Barn Owl

León "Lion": puma, *Puma concolor* (in a recent reclassification, *Puma* has replaced *Felis* as its accepted generic name)

Licoy Red-lored Parrot (onomatopoeic)

Limón Lemon, *Citrus limonia* (Rutaceae)

Limón del norte Unidentified *Zanthoxylus* sp. (Rutaceae)

Limpio "Clean": free of agricultural and human pests; cleared of vegetation or undergrowth

Liquidambar Sweetgum, *Liquidambar styraciflua* (Hamamelidaceae)

Llano A plain; any open, grassy sward

Lora Any parrot

Lora de montaña White-crowned Parrot

Loro Any parrot

Loro negro "Black parrot": White-crowned Parrot

Luisito See *Dicho feo*

Madreado Gliricidia sepium (Leguminosae)

Madre de gallina "Chicken's mother": Chachalaca

Maíz Maize, *Zea mays* (Graminae)

Mango Mangifera indica (Anacardiaceae)

Manzana Areal measure equal to 1.75 acres

Mapache Northern raccoon, *Procyon lotor*

Mapachín Northern raccoon

Martín pescador Kingfisher

Mascarita "Little mask": Crested Bobwhite; possibly Ocellated Quail

Medio ambiente The (natural) environment

Mico Central American spider monkey or white-faced capuchin (*Ateles geoffroyi; Cebus capucinus*)

Microcuenca Micro-watershed (drainage basin), often of a creek or river that flows from the *montaña* through the *serranía* to the *valle*

Milpa Maize field

Mono See *Mico*

Montaña "Rain forest" landscape (not "mountain" per se)

Montaña cruda "Raw" forest: same as *pura montaña*

Montaña espesa "Thick" forest: same as *pura montaña*

Montaña virgen Virgin forest

Montañita Small patch of thick forest

Montañuela Small patch of thick forest

Monte Weeds

Monte, el "The countryside": often pejorative term used by city dwellers; could be translated as "the sticks"

Monte alto Tall forest

Monte zumba Lineated or Pale-billed Woodpecker

Morenita Little Blue Heron

Mosquerito "Little fly eater": any small perch-and-sally flycatcher

Mosquero "Fly-eater": generic word for perch-and-sally flycatchers; also refers to an area or situation with many flies

Muérdago Mistletoe

Municipalidad The site of municipal government; the government itself

Municipio Territorial subdivision of department: municipality

Nance *Byrsinoma crassifolia* (Malpiguiaceae)

Naranjero "Orange eater": Golden-olive Woodpecker; White-fronted Parrot

Naranjo Orange tree

Nicho See *Dicho feo*

Nicho feo See *Dicho feo*

Nidito Diminutive of *nido*, "nest"

Niña de Guatemala "Child from Guatemala": also known as *huele de noche;* unidentified ornamental shrub

Nogal Walnut, *Juglans olanchanus* (Juglandaceae)

Norte Cold front

Ñanca See *Guatuza*

Ñura See *Guatuza*

Ocotal Woods of the pine *Pinus oocarpa,* called *ocote* (or other similar pine)

Ocote Pine tree; or stick of dry pine wood used for tinder

Ocotero Green Parakeet

Olingo Mantled howler, *Allouatta palliata*

Orejita "Little ears": screech-owl spp.

Oropéndula Chestnut-headed Oropendola

Pajaral A place filled with birds

Pajarito Little bird

Pájaro azul Eastern Bluebird

Pájaro del norte Bird from the north; bird that comes with a *norte,* or cold front

Pájaro estaca "Stick bird": Northern Potoo

Pájaro león "Lion bird": Squirrel Cuckoo

Pájaro pesquero "Fishing bird": any kingfisher

Pájaro pichete "Lizard bird": Striped Cuckoo

Pajarraco Light-hearted word for "bird"

Paloma Dove or Pigeon

Paloma común "Common dove" or "pigeon" in a generic sense: can refer to Rock Dove and White-winged Dove

Paloma de Castilla Rock Dove, domestic or feral

Paloma de montaña Dove of the *montaña,* especially Short-billed Pigeon

Palomera Dovecote

Parque central "Central park"; Juticalpa's *parque central* is formally known as Parque Flores

Patastera Vine of *Sechium edule* (Cucurbitaceae), the *pataste* (*güisquil* or *chayote*)

Patio Backyard, usually containing a dooryard garden

Patito "Little duck"; can refer to the Masked Duck or Least Grebe

Pato Duck: domestic individuals are almost always Muscovies, rarely Peking

Pato aguja "Needle duck": Anhinga

Pato de monte "Bush duck": Muscovy Duck

Paujín Great Curassow

Pava Crested Guan

Pavilla Highland Guan

Pavo Domestic turkey

Pecho rojo "Red-throated" Parakeet

Pelícano (Brown) Pelican

Perdiz "Partridge": rarely used locally

Perezoso Brown-throated three-toed sloth; Hoffmann's two-toed sloth (*Bradypus variegatus; Choloepus hoffmanni*)

Perico Parakeet (usually long-tailed kind)

Periquito de montaña Barred Parakeet; perhaps Orange-chinned Parakeet

Pespita Sandpiper: often the Spotted Sandpiper; can also refer to waterthrushes

Pía Brown Jay (onomatopoeic)

Picaflor Hummingbird

Picapiedrales "Stone mason": Ferruginous Pygmy-Owl

Picapiedras Ferruginous Pygmy-Owl

Pichiche (Black-bellied) Whistling-Duck (onomatopoeic)

Pichingo Precolumbian clay figurine; *pichingos* or *pichingitos* also means "cartoons"

Pico blanco "White bill": White-crowned Parrot

Pico de oro "Gold bill": Northern Jacana

Pico (de) navaja "Knife bill": Toucan; Keel-billed Toucan

Pico rojo Red-billed Pigeon

Picoy Red-lored Parrot (onomatopoeic)

Pimentero Three-wattled Bellbird

Pimienta gorda Allspice, *Pimenta dioica* (Myrtaceae)

Pimientilla *Hirtella racemosa* (Rosaceae)

Pinabeto, -ales Stands of *Pinus maximinoi*

Pinares Pine woods (term is rarely used locally)

Pino *Pinus* species; *P. oocarpa, P. hartweggii, P. maximinoi, P. caribea, P. ayacahuite, P. patula* ssp. *tecunumanii, P. pseudostrobus* are the Honduran types recognized by most foresters

Piñón *Jatropha curcas* (Euphorbiaceae)

Piñonal Area of *piñón*

Pispa Rusty Sparrow (onomatopoeic)

Pispita Sandpiper or other wader

Pito real Pale-billed or Lineated Woodpecker

Pizote White-nosed coati, *Nasua narica*

Platanar Plantain grove

Platanillo *Heliconia* sp. (Musaceae)

Plátano Plantain, *Musa paradisiaca* (Musaceae)

Polla de agua "Water chicken": American Coot, Common Moorhen, or Purple Gallinule

Polla de monte "Bush chicken": Buffy-crowned Wood-Partridge or Spotted Wood-Quail

Postrera, la Second crop of the growing season

Potrero Pasture

Primera, la First crop of the growing season

Pucuyo Pauraque (onomatopoeic)

Pura montaña "Virgin" or old-growth rain forest

Quebrantahuesos "Bone smasher": Crested Caracara

Quequeo Collared peccary, *Tayassu tajacu*

Quetzal Resplendent Quetzal

Quiebramuela "Molar breaker": unidentified dry forest tree

Racacao Red-throated Caracara (onomatopoeic)

Ratonero "Mouser": any small hawk

Reinita cachetidorada Golden-cheeked Warbler (not a local term)

Rey zope King Vulture

Rínzon Royal Flycatcher (probably onomatopoeic)

Roble Oak

Robledal Oak woods

Ruda *Ruta chalapensis* (Rutaceae), an exotic; believed to bring good luck and banish evil spirits

Sabana "Savanna"; on the micro scale, any open patch of short grass (like a lawn)

Sabanera Ground-dove

Saltarín "Jumper": Blue-black Grassquit

Salvia Sage: *Salvia* sp.

Santa Cruz, (paloma de) "Holy Cross dove": Ruddy Ground-Dove

Semillero "Seed eater:" White-collared Seedeater

Serenqueque Bushy-crested Jay (onomatopoeic)

Serranía Pine forest landscape

Silencio, El "The Silent One": tall humanoid inhabitant of high mountains

Sisimite Anthropoid denizen of deep forests

Soldadito "Little soldier": Crimson-collared Tanager

Subir To go up (to the *montaña*)

Tamarindo Tamarind, *Tamarindus indica* (Cesalpiniaceae)

Tapaculo See *Caulote*

Taragón Motmot; Blue-crowned Motmot

Tempisque *Macrohasseltia macroterantha* (Flacourtiaceae)

Templador Three-wattled Bellbird

Tendones lisos "Straight sinews" or "smooth sinews": see *Guatuza*

Tepescuintle Paca, *Agouti paca*

Tera Crested Caracara

Terrateniente Owner of a large amount of land

Tierra nacional National land: land owned by the state of Honduras

Tigre Jaguar, *Panthera onca*

Tigrillo Margay or ocelot (*Leopardus wiedii; L. pardalis*)

Tijereta Tropical Kingbird, Swallow-tailed Kite

Tijerilla Scissor-tailed or Fork-tailed Flycatcher, Swallow-tailed Kite

Tijúl, tíjul, tijulio Groove-billed Ani (onomatopoeic)

Tilís Collared Aracari (onomatopoeic)

Tilopo Mazama or red brocket deer (*Mazama americana*); also *güisisil*

Tincute Turkey Vulture

Tío Julio Groove-billed Ani (onomatopoeic)

Tocolote Variation of *tecolote,* Mottled Owl

Tordito Bronzed Cowbird

Torreja Masked Tityra

Tortolita Ground-dove

Trepapalos "Tree climber": woodcreeper

Trepatroncos "Trunk climber": woodcreeper

Tres pesos "Three pesos": Short-billed Pigeon (onomatopoeic)

Trompa de chancho "Pig's snout": a type of arboreal wasps' nest

Tubuca Term for *pájaro león,* probably not used in Olancho

Tucán Generic name for toucan; usually refers to Keel-billed Toucan

Tucanillo (verde) Emerald Toucanet

Turca Any terrestrial dove; any dove

Turca chelona Terrestrial rain forest dove

Turca de montaña Terrestrial rain forest dove

Turquita Any of several small terrestrial doves

Urraca Green Jay (not found in central Olancho)

Urrupa Chestnut-headed Oropendola (onomatopoeic)

Valle Plain

Vega Bottomland; gallery forest

Venado White-tailed deer, *Odocoileus virginianus*

Verano Summer: dry season, approximately February-March through May-June

Viuda "Widow": vulture; Blue-gray Tanager; White-tipped Dove

Viudita "Little widow": Blue-gray Tanager

Zacate Any grass (generally tall varieties)

Zacate Alicia Unidentified grass species

Zacate estrella Cynodon nlemfuensis (Graminae)

Zacate gallina Eleusine indica (Graminae)

Zacate Guinea Panicum maximum (Graminae)

Zanate Great-tailed Grackle

Zapotillo An unidentified tree in the Zapotaceae family

Zope Vulture; Black Vulture

Zopilote Black Vulture (also refers to a type of tree)

Zorzal Clay-colored Robin; any similar thrush

Zorzala Female Clay-Colored Robin

Zorzalito Diminutive of *Zorzal*

Bibliography

Acosta, O., and P. del Valle. 1971. *Exaltación de Honduras: Antología.*
Tegucigalpa: Universidad Nacional Autónoma de Honduras.

Aguilar Paz, J. 1970. *Toponimias y regionalismos indígenas de Honduras.*
Tegucigalpa. (Based on a paper given at the V Congreso de Academias de la
Lengua Española in Quito, 1968.)

———. 1981. *El refranero hondureño.* Tegucigalpa: Editorial Guaymuras.

———. 1989 [1933, 1972]. *Tradiciones y leyendas de Honduras.* Tegucigalpa:
Museo del Hombre Hondureño.

American Ornithologists' Union. 1998. *Check-list of North American Birds.* 7th ed.
Washington, D.C.: American Ornithologists' Union.

Anderson, D. 1998. Avian diversity in the Río Plátano Biosphere Reserve,
Honduras: The influence of indigenous agricultural practices. Unpublished
M.S. thesis, Boise State University.

———. 2000. Notes on the breeding, distribution, and taxonomy of the
Ocellated Poorwill (*Nyctiphrynus ocellatus*) in Honduras. *Ornitologia
Neotropical* 11: 233–38.

———, M. Bonta, and P. Thorn. 1998. "New and noteworthy bird records from
Honduras." *Bulletin of the British Ornithologists' Club* 118(3): 178–83.

Antúnez C., Ruben., ed. 1937. *Monografía del Departamento de Yoro.* Tegucigalpa:
Biblioteca de la Sociedad de Geografía e Historia de Honduras.

Archivo Histórico del Municipio de Juticalpa. 22–28 Oct. 1868. "Gobernación
de este Círculo . . ." in Libro de visitas a los pueblos de la municipalidad
por la gobernación del Círculo. (Descriptions of conditions of roads, town
greenbelts ["fajinas"], etc.)

———. 23 Feb. 1874. "Bando de buen gobierno." (14 articles outlining
permitted use of public space.)

Ardón Mejía, M. 1986. *Folklore lúdico infantil hondureño.* Tegucigalpa: Serie
[de] Estudios sobre Cultura Popular Hondureña.

Armstrong, E. A. 1958. *The Folklore of Birds.* (Publisher and place unknown.)

———. 1975. *The Life and Lore of Birds in Nature, Art, Myth and Literature.*
New York: Crown Publishers.

Avedillo, M. 1977. "Comunicación: Passer domesticus (Gorrión común) en
Honduras," *Ceiba* 21: 57–62.

Bengtson, N. 1926. "Notes on the physiography of Honduras," *Geographical
Review* 16: 403–13.

Bonta, M. A. 1994. Inventory of the birds of the Cordillera de Agalta
bioregion. Unpublished manuscript.

———. 1997. Shared Worlds: People and Birds in Central Olancho, Honduras.
Unpublished M.A. thesis, University of Texas, Austin.

——. 1999. "Conteos Comunitarios de Aves en Olancho, Honduras/ Community Bird Counts in Olancho, Honduras." 1999. *Mesoamericana* 4(1): 14–18.

——. 2001. Mapping Enredos of Complex Spaces: A Regional Geography of Olancho, Honduras. Unpublished Ph.D. diss., Louisiana State University, Baton Rouge.

——. 2002. "Jealous Conservationists: *Terratenientes* and Wildlife Conservation in Olancho, Honduras." Pp. 87–95 in M. Steinberg and P. Hudson, eds., *Cultural and Physical Expositions: Geographic Studies in the Southern United States and Latin America*. Geoscience and Man vol. 36. Baton Rouge: Louisiana State University, Geoscience and Man Publications.

Bonta, M. A., and David L. Anderon. 2003. *Birding Honduras: A Checklist and Guide*. Tegucigalpa: Ecoarte and Instituto Hondureno de Turismo.

Bonta, M. A., and F. Urbina. 1999. Aves de Agalta, segunda edición, Lista de pájaros de la Cordillera de Agalta y los valles circundantes. Unpublished.

Brady, J. E., G. Hasemann, and J. H. Fogerty. 1995. "Harvest of skulls and bones." *Archaeology* 48(3): 36–40.

Bullock, S. H., H. A. Mooney, and S. Medina, eds. 1995. *Seasonally Dry Tropical Forests*. Cambridge, U.K.: Cambridge University Press.

Carr, A. "Outline for a Classification of Animal Habitats in Honduras." 1950. *Bulletin of the American Museum of Natural History* 94: 563–94. Reprinted in *Ceiba* 35(2): 117–66 (1994).

Chapman, A. 1992 [1978]. *Masters of Animals: Oral Traditions of the Tolupan Indians, Honduras*. Philadelphia: Gordon and Breach.

Cobo, P. Bernabé. 1956 [1653]. *Obras de P. Bernabé Cobo de la Compañia de Jesús*. Ed. P. Francisco Mateos. Madrid: Ediciones Atlas.

Collar N. J., L. P. Gonzaga, N. Krabbe, A. Madroño Nieto, L. G. Naranjo, T. A. Parker III, and D. C. Wege. 1992. "Honduran emerald *Amazilia luciae*." Pp. 493–95 in *Threatened Birds of the Americas: The ICBP/IUCN Red Data Book* (3rd. ed., pt. 2).

Columbus, Cristopher. 1963 [1492–1502]. *Journals and Other Documents on the Life and Voyages of Christopher Columbus*. Ed. and trans. S. E. Morison. New York: Heritage Press.

Conzemius, E. 1928. *Los indios payas: Estudio geográfico, histórico, etnográfico y lingüístico*. Paris: Société des Americanistes de Paris.

——. 1932. *Ethnographical Survey of the Miskito and Sumu Indians of Honduras and Nicaragua*. U.S. Bureau of American Ethnology Bulletin 106.

Denevan, W. M. 1961. "The upland pine forests of Nicaragua: A study in cultural plant geography." *Univ. Calif. Publ. Geog.* 12(4): 251–320.

Doughty, R. W. 1988. *The Mockingbird*. Austin: University of Texas Press.

Duellman, W. E. 1966. "The Central American herpetofauna: An ecological perspective." *Copeia* 1966 (4): 700–19.

Feld, S. 1996. "Waterfalls of song: An acoustemology of place resounding in

Bosavi, Papua New Guinea. Chap 3, pp. 91–135 in Feld and K. H. Basso, eds., *Senses of Place*. Santa Fe: School of American Research.

Fernández de Oviedo, Gonzalo. 1959 [1535]. *Historia general y natural de las Indias*. 20 vols. Ed. Juan Pérez de Tudela Bueso. Madrid: Atlas.

Figueroa, F. F., ed. 1935. *Monografía del Departamento de Olancho*. Tegucigalpa: Sociedad de Geografía e Historia de Honduras.

Goicoechea y Liendo, J. A. de. 1937 [1807]. "Relación sobre los indios gentiles de Pacura," *Anales de la Sociedad de Geografía e Historia* (Guatemala) 13: 301–15.

Gurney, J. H. 1921. *Early Annals of Ornithology*. London: H. F. and G. Witherby.

von Hagen, V. W. 1945. *Jungle in the Clouds*. New York: Duell, Sloan and Pearce.

Hamblin, N. 1984. *Animal Use by the Cozumel Maya*. Tucson: University of Arizona Press.

Hardy Nelson S., C. 1986. *Plantas comunes de Honduras*. Tegucigalpa: Editorial Universitario.

Helbig, K. M. 1965. *Areas y paisajes del nordeste de Honduras*. Tegucigalpa: Banco Central de Honduras.

Heliodoro Valle, R. 1947. *Semblanza de Honduras*. Tegucigalpa.

Hernández, Francisco. 1957. *Historia natural de Nueva España*, vol. 2. Mexico City: Universidad Nacional de México.

Herrera, Antonio de. 1991 [1601–15]. *Historia general de los hechos de los Castellanos en las Islas y Tierra Firme del Mar Océano*. Ed. Mariano Cuesta Domingo. Madrid: Universidad Complutense de Madrid.

Hobbs, J. 1989. *Bedouin Life in the Egyptian Wilderness*. Austin: University of Texas Press.

Howell, S. N. G., and S. Webb. 1989. "Notes on the Honduran emerald," *Wilson Bulletin* 101(4): 642–43.

———. 1991. "New and noteworthy bird records from Guatemala and Honduras," *Bulletin of the British Ornithologists' Club* 112: 42–49.

———. 1995. *A Guide to the Birds of Mexico and Northern Central America*. Oxford, U.K.: Oxford University Press.

Hunn, E. S. 1977. *Tzeltal Folk Zoology: The Classification of Discontinuities in Nature*. New York: Academic Press.

Hunt, E. 1977. *The Transformation of the Hummingbird: Cultural Roots of a Zinacantecan Mythical Poem*. Ithaca, N.Y.: Cornell University Press.

Ingersoll, E. 1968. *Birds in Legend, Fable and Folklore*. Detroit: Gale Press.

Johannessen, C. 1963. *Savannas of Interior Honduras*. Ibero-Americana 46. Berkeley and Los Angeles: University of California Press.

Komor, H. F. 1930. *La tierra del nuevo hogar*, [including] *Apuntes de viaje por los departamentos de El Paraíso, Olancho y Yoro*. Tegucigalpa: Tipografía Nacional.

Krutch, J. W., and P. S. Eriksson. 1962. *A Treasury of Bird-Lore*. New York: Paul S. Eriksson.

Landa, L. 1970. *Aves regionales de Honduras*. Tegucigalpa: López.

León Pinelo, *Antonio de. 1943 [1656]. El paraíso en el Nuevo Mundo, tomo II*. Lima: Ed. Raúl Porras Barrenechea.

López de Gómara, Francisco. 1966 [1552]. *Historia general de las Indias*. Ed. Pilar Guibelalde. Barcelona: Obras Maestras.

Majnep, S., and Bulmer, R. 1977. *Birds of My Kalem Country*. Auckland, New Zealand: Auckland University Press.

Marcus, M. 1983. "Additions to the avifauna of Honduras," *Auk* 100: 621–29.

———. 1984. "Notes on the great green macaw (*Ara ambigua*) in Honduras," *Ceiba* 25: 151–55.

Martyr d'Anghiera, Peter. 1964 [1524]. *Decadas del Nuevo Mundo, por Pedro Martir de Angleria, primer cronista de Indias*. Mexico City: José Porrua e Hijos.

Membreño, A. 1895. *Hondureñismos: Vocabulario de los provincialismos de Honduras*. Tegucigalpa: Tipografía Nacional.

———. 1994 [1901]. *Toponimias indígenas de Centroamérica (Honduras, El Salvador, Guatemala y Nicaragua)*. Tegucigalpa: Ed. Guaymuras.

Midence, S. 1985a. *Aves silvestres de Honduras*. Tegucigalpa: Asociación Hondureña de Ecología.

———. 1985b. *Conociendo y coloreando 10 de nuestras aves*. Tegucigalpa: Asociación Hondureña de Ecología.

Molina, A. 1974. "Vegetación del Valle de Comayagua," *Ceiba* 18(1–2): 47–69.

Monroe, B. L., Jr. 1963. *Notes on the Avian Genus Arremonops with Description of a New Subspecies from Honduras*. Occasional Papers of the Museum of Zoology 28. Baton Rouge: Louisiana State University.

———. 1968. *A Distributional Survey of the Birds of Honduras*. Ornithological Monograph 7. Washington, D.C.: American Ornithologists' Union.

Muñoz Tábora, J. 1983. *Folklore y educación en Honduras*. Tegucigalpa.

Nelson, R. K. 1983. *Make Prayers to the Raven: A Koyukon View of the Northern Forest*. Chicago: University of Chicago Press.

Newson, L. 1986. *The Cost of Conquest: Indian Decline in Honduras under Spanish Rule*. Boulder, Colo.: Westview Press. Translated as *El costo de la conquista* (1992) by Jorge Federico Travieso. Tegucigalpa: Ed. Guaymuras.

Ortega, P. 1946. *Patrio lares*. 1st ed. Tegucigalpa.

———. 1951. *Patrios lares*. 2nd ed. Tegucigalpa.

Osorio Orellana, A. 1994. *Nuestro pueblo y su folklore, II Libro*. Tegucigalpa.

Pearse, T. 1968. *Birds of the Early Explorers in the Northern Pacific*. Comox, British Columbia: Theed Pearse.

Pedraza, Cristobal de. 1898 [1544]. "Onduras e Igueras: Relación de la Provincia de Honduras y Higueras [sic] por el obispo D. Cristobal de Pedraza, Obispo de Honduras." Pp. 385–434 in *Relaciones de Yucatán;* vol. ii in *Colección de documentos inéditos relativos al descubrimiento, conquista y organización de las antiguas posesiones españoles de ultramar, segunda serie*.

Perry, J. 1990. *The Pines of Mexico and Central America*. Portland, Ore.: Timber Press.

Phillipps, W. J. 1963. *The Book of the Huia*. Christchurch, New Zealand: Whitcombe and Tombs Limited.

Portig, W. H. 1965. "Central American rainfall." *Geographical Review* 65(1): 68–90.

Ramos, K., and M. Valenzuela. 1996. *Literatura oral de la Zona Sur,* vol. 3: *Por cuentas, aquí en Nacaome.* Tegucigalpa: Secretaría de Cultura y las Artes.

———. 1997a. *Literatura oral de la Zona Sur,* vol. 4: *Por cuentas, aquí en Sabanagrande.* Tegucigalpa: Secretaría de Cultura y las Artes.

———. 1997b. *Literatura oral de la Zona Sur,* vol. 5: *Por cuentas, aquí en Texiguat.* Tegucigalpa: Secretaría de Cultura y las Artes.

Rappole, J. H. 1996. Golden-cheeked Warbler Winter Habitat Delineation. Final report to the National Biological Service. Lafayette, La.: National Biological Service, Southern Science Center.

———. 1999. "Winter ecology of the endangered Golden-cheeked Warbler." *Condor* 101(4): 762–70.

Reid, F. 1997. *A Field Guide to the Mammals of Central America and Southeast Mexico.* Oxford, U.K.: Oxford University Press.

Ridgely, R., and J. Gwynne, Jr. 1989. *A Guide to the Birds of Panama, with Costa Rica, Nicaragua and Honduras.* Princeton, N.J.: Princeton University Press.

Rowland, B. 1978. *Birds with Human Souls: A Guide to Bird Symbolism.* Knoxville: University of Tennessee Press.

Rubí Zapata, V. 1986. *Mi Juticalpa y yo: Retazos de dos biografías en un agradable revoltijo.* Juticalpa, Honduras.

Sahagún, Fray Bernardino de. 1946 [1579]. *Historia general de las cosas de la Nueva España.* Mexico City: Ed. Nueva España.

———. 1950–69 [1579]. *Florentine Codex: General History of the Things of New Spain.* 12 vols./books. Ed. and trans. C. E. Dibble and A. J. O. Anderson. Monographs of the School of American Research and the Museum of New Mexico. Santa Fe: School of American Research; Salt Lake City: University of Utah.

Sarmiento, J. A. 1990. *Historia de Olancho.* Tegucigalpa: Ed. Guaymuras.

Savage, J. M. 1966. "The origins and history of the Central American herpetofauna." *Copeia* 1966(4): 719–66.

Schorger, A. W. 1955. *The Passenger Pigeon: Its Natural History and Extinction.* Madison: University of Wisconsin Press.

———. 1966. *The Wild Turkey: Its History and Domestication.* Norman: University of Oklahoma Press.

Skutch, A. 1983. *Birds of Tropical America.* Austin: University of Texas Press.

Snow, D. 1982. *The Cotingas, Bellbirds, Umbrellabirds and Other Species.* Ithaca, N.Y.: Cornell University Press.

Sosa, A. 1999. *Aves del manglar.* Tegucigalpa: Línea Gráfica.

Squier, E. G. 1855. *Notes on Central America.* New York: Harper and Brothers.

Standley, P. 1930. "The woody plants of Siguatepeque, Honduras," *Journal of the Arnold Arboretum* 11: 15–46.

Stotz, D., J. W. Fitzpatrick, T. Parker III, and D. Moskovits. 1996. *Neotropical Birds: Ecology and Conservation*. Chicago: University of Chicago Press.

Stuart, L. C. 1966. "The environment of the Central American cold-blooded vertebrate fauna." *Copeia* 1966(4): 684–99.

Thompson, D. 1995. Observations of Golden-cheeked Warblers Wintering in Guatemala and Honduras. Austin: U.S. Fish and Wildlife Service.

Turcios, F. 1990 [1911]. *Tierra maternal: Olancho*. Tegucigalpa: Ed. Universitaria.

Walker, M. C. 1908. *Bird Legend and Life*. New York: Baker and Taylor.

Wells, W. V. 1856. "Adventures in the gold fields of Central America." *Harper's New Monthly Magazine* 12: 315–36.

———. 1857. *Explorations and Adventures in Honduras, Comprising Sketches of Travel in the Gold Regions of Olancho, and a Revision of the History of General resources of Central America*. New York: Harper and Brothers.

Wilson, L. D., and J. R. Meyer. 1985. *The Snakes of Honduras* (2nd ed.). Milwaukee: Milwaukee Public Museum.

Ximenez, Fray Francisco. 1967 [1722]. *Historia natural del Reino de Guatemala*. Sociedad de Geografía e Historia de Guatemala, publicación especial no. 14. Guatemala City: Ed. José de Pineda Ibarra.

Yuncker, T. G. 1939. "Notes on a semi-arid region in the Aguan River Valley, Republic of Honduras," *Torreya* 39(5): 133–39.

———. 1940. "Flora of the Aguan Valley and the coastal regions near La Ceiba Honduras," *Botanical Series, Field Museum of Natural History* 9(4) (Publication 466): 243–346.

———. 1945. "The vegetation of Honduras: A brief review." Pp. 55–56 in *Plants and Plant Science in Latin America,* ed. F. Verdoorn. Waltham, Mass.: Chronica Botanica.

Index

acacia, 63, 76, 111
achiote. *See* annatto
Aechmea bracteata, 77
Africans, 27–28, 39
Agalta, Cordillera de, 2 fig. 1, 31, 32, 107, 125, 128, 158. *See also* Babilona, Montaña de; Sierra de Agalta
Agalta, Pico de, 10 fig. 2, plate 14
Agalta, Sierra de, 10 fig. 2, 18, 33, 42–43, 86, 125; Black-and-white Owl in, 116; in count workshop, 152–53; Red-throated Caracara in, 109; plate 6, plate 11, plate 16. *See also* Agalta, Cordillera de; Babilonia, Montaña de; Sierra de Agalta National Park
Agalta, Valle de, 2 fig. 1, 10 fig. 2, 32, 33 fig. 3, 44, 79–81, 133, plate 6, plate 16; as habitat for Honduran Emerald, 70, 74–77, 79; in count workshop, 152–53; Red-throated Caracara in, 108, 109–10, 112, 113; Scarlet Macaw's disappearance from, 91; Three-wattled Bellbird in, 128. *See also* La Venta; San Esteban
agave, 30–31, 38, 111
agouti, Central American, 43, 48, 85, 134, 139, 157
agribusiness. *See* export agriculture
agronomist, 44, 68, 81
Agua Blanca, Montaña de, 10 fig. 2
Agua Buena, Cerro (above El Boquerón), 10 fig. 2, 38, 39, 42–44, 48, 131–32, 143, plate 9, plate 26, plate 27; Resplendent Quetzal on, 130; Three-wattled Bellbird on, 128

aguacatillo, 130
Aguán, Río, 2 fig. 1, 31
Aguán, Valle de, 2 fig. 1, 70, 74, 75, 128n. 2
águila pesquera. *See* Osprey
Aguila, Cerro del, 139
Aguila, Quebrada del, 139
Aguilar Paz, Jesús, 19n. 3, 55, 94, 95, 116, 140–41
águilas. *See* eagles
águilas pescadoras.*See* Osprey
aguiluche. *See* Eagle, Ornate Hawk-; Hawk, Common Black-
ajoque. *See* Heron, Green
AK-47s, 97, 158
alcaraván. *See* Thick-knee, Double-striped
alcoholism, 97
allspice, 3, 127
alma de perro. *See* Roadrunner, Lesser
altitude. *See* elevation
altitudinal migration, 72–73, 129–32, 140; of Band-tailed Pigeon, 71; of Collared Trogon, 131; of Highland Guan, 140; of Masked Tityra, 67; of Resplendent Quetzal, 22–23, 72, 129–31, 132; of Short-billed Pigeon, 37; of toucans, 131; of tres pesos, 72; of thrushes, 58; of Three-wattled Bellbird, 128; of Violaceous Trogon, 131; of White-crowned Parrot, 72, 81
Amacuapa, Valle de, 10 fig. 2
Amazilia luciae. *See* Emerald, Honduran
American Ornithologists' Union, 8
Anderson, David L. 10n. 9

conservation planning, 151, 153–54
conservation projects, 123, 125,
    146–60
conservationists, and conservation,
    29, 44, 75, 122, 123, 142, 143;
    Francisco Urbina, as archetype,
    105–106; landscape reading, 155;
    and hydroelectric projects,
    135n. 6; and local people, 46,
    135–36; and Ornate Hawk-Eagle,
    100; salaries of, 126; and Scarlet
    Macaw, 89; solutions for rain
    forests, 126, 135–36, 145;
    terratenientes as, 69–87
contraband trade, 33
Conzemius, Eduard, 28–29
cooperatives, farming, 35
Coot, American, 80, 82
Copán department, 2 fig. 1
Copán Ruins, 2 fig. 1, 90
core zone (nucleus), 131, 135, 151
corn. See maize
corridors, biotic, 43–44, 75, 79
corte, 133
Cortés, department, 2 fig. 1
Cosecha, La. See coffee, shaded
Costa Rica, 145; Red-throated
    Caracaras in, 109n. 2
Cotinga, Blue/Lovely, 22–23
Cotingidae, 127n. 1
cotton, 76
count workshops, 8, 152–53
countryside, 29
Cowbird, Bronzed, 15
Coyocutena, 58–59
coyol palm, 41, 99, plate 4, plate 10
coyote, 111
crabs, freshwater, 46, 47. See also
    Hawk, Common Black-
crayfish, 46, 47
credit, 76, 105
criollos, 112, 112
Cristobal, 93
Crossbill, Red, 16

Cruz, Cerrito de la (Juticalpa), 58
cryptofauna, 144–45
cryptozoology, 91n. 2
cucaracheros. See wrens
Cuckoo, Squirrel, 93, 95, 103
Cuckoo, Striped, 38, 72n. 2, 94, 95,
    102–103
cuclillo rayado, 94
cultural landscape, 5, 68, 103–104
Curassow, Great, 8, 139, 140
Cusuco, Parque Nacional, 131
cusucos. See armadillo, nine-banded
cute. See buzzard
cuyamel, 47

dances, inspired by birds, 56, 137–38
danto. See tapir, Baird's
dawn, birds at, 12, 77, 140
death, birds associated with: Barn
    Owl, 115; Black Vulture, 54, 66;
    Laughing Falcon, 71, 137
debt, Honduran national, 125, 149
deer, red brocket, 139
deer, white-tailed, 44, 77, 111;
    hunting of, 31, 44–45, 47, 97,
    111–12, 139, 142; and Great
    Horned Owl, 115
deforestation, 4, 125, 135; frontier of,
    2 fig. 1, 31, 32, 35, 106, 124, 125, 131,
    150–51; of Montaña de Babilonia,
    126, plate 14
degradation, 106, 131
Denevan, W. M. 118n. 9
descombro, 133, 135
destruction, environmental,
    51–53, 89
development, sustainable. See
    sustainable development
dewlap, 48
Diablo, Cerro del, 128
dicho (feo), 93, 99, 99n 8. See also
    Flycatcher, Social
Dickcissel, 82, 84
diseases, avian, 91, 144

Osorio Orellana, Antonio, 95
Osprey, 79, 137
Otoro, Valle de, 2 fig. 1
ovenbirds (Furnariidae), 96, 159
Oviedo, Gonzalo Fernández de. *See*
    Fernández de Oviedo, Gonzalo
Owl, Barn, 54, 66, 67, 84, 115, 116, 117
Own, Black-and-white, 116
Owl, Ferruginous Pygmy-, 67, 72, 116
Owl, Great Horned, 14, 66, 96, 115,
    118, 119
Owl, Mottled, 84, 115
Owl, Spectacled, 116
Owl, Stygian, 101n. 9
Owl, Vermiculated Screech-, 116–17
owls, 27, 108, 115–16, 117–18, 136, 144
ownership, over birds, 62, 71, 80–81

paca, 157; hunting of, 43, 134, 139
Pacific Coast. *See* South Coast
Pacura, 110
Padilla, Eliberto, 116–17
Padilla, Visitación, 19n. 3
pajaral, 7, 88–89, 96, 103, 104–106, 155
pajarito. *See* bird, local words for
pájaro. *See* bird, local words for
pájaro azul. *See* Bluebird, Eastern
pájaro búho, 117
pájaro cafetero (párajo campana).
    See Bellbird, Three-wattled
pájaro estaca, 96
pájaro león, 95. *See also* Cuckoo,
    Squirrel
pájaro pichete, 95
pájaro pesquero. *See* kingfishers
pajarraco. *See* bird, local words for
pajuíl. *See* Curassow, Great
palms, 135, 150
paloma chinga. *See* Tinamou, Little
palomas de Castilla. *See* Dove, Rock
palomas de montaña. *See* Pigeon,
    Band-tailed
palomas franjoles, 94
palomas guamileras/comunes, 94

palomas torcazas. *See* doves
palomas zoritas. *See* doves
Panama, 145, 109n. 2, 128, 130
Panama Canal, 109n. 2
Panuaya (village), 12
papagayos. *See* parrots
Parakeet, Barred, 93
Parakeet, Green, 16, 93, 119
Parakeet, Olive-throated, 93
parakeets, 26
pardales. *See* sparrows, Old World
Parque Central of Juticalpa, 51, 53
Parque Nacional Sierra de Agalta. *See*
    Sierra de Agalta National Park
Parrot, Mealy, 63
Parrot, Red-lored, 63, 64, 93
Parrot, White-crowned, 15, 26, 72,
    81, 85, 93–94, 140, plate 12
Parrot, White-fronted, 41, 93
Parrot, Yellow-naped, 25–26, 27
parrots, 25, 27, 45, 46, 51 61, 65, 96,
    100, 101, 140. *See also* Psittacids
Partridge, Buffy-crowned Wood-, 141
partridges, 25, 140
partridges, wood-, 139
passionfruit, 99
pastoralism. *See* pastures
pasture, and scrub, 67, 95
pastures, 31, 33 fig. 3, 42, 43, 44,
    45, 51, 67, 73, 76, 81, 82, 83, 95,
    101, 118, 122, 133
Pataste, Río, 10 fig. 2
patastera, 62
patios (backyards), 52, 53, 58–67,
    plate 28, plate 29
patito, 84
pato aguja. *See* Anhinga
pato de monte. *See* Duck, Muscovy
patos. *See* ducks
patrimonio, La Picucha as, 129
Patuca rain forest, 114
Patuca, Río, 2 fig. 1, 10 fig. 2
paujíl. *See* Curassow, Great
paujín, 139

sorghum, 76
South America, 101; quetzals in, 130n 5; Red-throated Caracara in, 108
South Coast (Honduras), 2 fig. 1, 71, 80, 117
space, urban, 53, 57
Sparrow, Chipping, 16
Sparrow, Green-backed, 75, 103
Sparrow, House, 53
Sparrow, White-eared Ground, 42–44
sparrows, 27, 67, 96, 102, 119
sparrows, Old World, 26. See also gorrión
spatial marginalization. See marginalization
spirits, birds as: Barn Owl/Lechuza, 115; Great Horned Owl/Estiquirín, 115, 117
Spoonbill, Roseate, 80, 82
sport, bird-killing for, 36, 46; waterfowl, 80
squash, 30
squirrels, 40, 46, 68
Standley, Paul, 75n. 7
state-owned land, 121
status symbols, birds as, 90
steppe, 150
Stilt, Black-necked, in Valle de Agalta, 80
stories, 41, 46–47
Stork, Wood, 19, 77, 80, 82
stuffed birds, 67
Sula, Valle de, 2 fig. 1
Sumu (Sumo). See Tawahka
Sungrebe, 102, 105
Susmay, Montaña de, 10 fig. 2
Susmay, Río, 10 fig. 2
sustainable conservation. See conservation projects
sustainable development, 35
swallows, 36, 54, 61, 67, 77, 82, 84, 102, 104

sweetgum: resin, 34; plate 24
swidden. See fire-fallow agriculture
symbols, birds as: Golden-cheeked Warbler, 121; Resplendent Quetzal, 130; Three-wattled Bellbird, 129

Taguzgalpa, 30, 32–33
talcacao, 108n. 1
Talgua, Río, 10 fig. 2
Talgua Caves, 40
tamarind, 52, 99
Tanager, Blue-gray, 19, 37, 54, 60–61, 63, 101
Tanager, Crimson-collared, 101
Tanager, Hepatic, 120
Tanager, Yellow-winged, 60
tanagers, 37, 96, 99, 100, 102, 104
tapaculo tree. See guácimo
tapestries, feather. See feather tapestries
Tapiquile, 10 fig. 2, 12
tapir, Baird's, 43, 140, 144
tapuca palm, 134
taragón. See Motmot, Blue-crowned
Tawahka, 2 fig. 1, 29, 124, 125
teachers, 129, 152, 153; and profession, 61, 68, 81
tecolote. See Owl, Mottled
Tegucigalpa, 2 fig. 1, 29, 30, 70, 118, 125, 130, 148
Tela, 2 fig. 1
television, effects of, 29, 46, 57
Telica, Río, 10 fig. 2; 78 fig. 4, 85, 86
templador, 127
tendones lisos, 48
Tenochtitlán, 23
Tepescuintle Cave, 40
tepescuintle, 134. See also Paca
tera. See Caracara, Crested
terns, in Valle de Agalta, 80
terrain, hunters' knowledge of, 139

ISBN 1-58544-249-6